MEMORIES
and VISIONS of
PARADISE

MEMORIES
and VISIONS *of*
PARADISE

*Exploring the Universal Myth
of a Lost Golden Age*

RICHARD HEINBERG

Foreword by Roger Williams Wescott

JEREMY P. TARCHER, INC.
Los Angeles

Copyright acknowledgments appear on page 283.

Library of Congress Cataloging in Publication Data

Heinberg, Richard.
    Memories and visions of paradise: exploring the universal myth of a lost
    golden age / Richard Heinberg.
        p. cm.
    Includes bibliographical references and index.
        ISBN 0–87477–515–9
        ISBN 0–87477–526–4 (pbk).
        1. Paradise—comparative studies. I. Title.
    BL540.H45 1989   88–31537
    291.2'4—dc19   CIP

Jeremy P. Tarcher, Inc.
9110 Sunset Blvd.
Los Angeles, CA 90069

Distributed by St. Martin's Press, New York

Design by Deborah Daly and Richard Heinberg

Manufactured in the United States of America
10 9 8 7 6 5 4 3 2 1

This book is lovingly dedicated to my friends
Michael and Nancy Exeter.

Contents

Somewhere down in the underworld we were created by the Great Spirit, the Creator. We were created first one, then two, then three. We were created equal, of oneness, living in a spiritual way, where life is everlasting. We were happy and at peace with our fellow men. All things were plentiful, provided by our Mother Earth upon which we were placed. We did not need to plant or work to get food. Illness and troubles were unknown.

HOPI ELDER DAN KATCHONGVA

The most ancient human beings lived with no evil desires, without guilt or crime, and therefore without penalties or compulsions. Nor was there any need of rewards, since by the prompting of their own nature they followed righteous ways. Since nothing contrary to morals was desired, nothing was forbidden through fear.

ROMAN POET TACITUS
(first century A.D.)

[In the First Age] there was but one religion, and all men were saintly: therefore they were not required to perform religious ceremonies. There were no gods in the First Age, and there were no demons. The First Age was without disease; there was no lessening with the years; there was no hatred, or vanity, or evil thought whatsoever; no sorrow, no fear. In those times, men lived as long as they chose to live, and were without any fear of death.

THE MAHABHARATA OF INDIA

In the Age of Perfect Virtue they were upright and correct, without knowing that to be so was righteousness; they loved one another, without knowing that to do so was benevolence; they were honest and leal-hearted without knowing that it was good faith; in their simple movements they employed the services of one another without thinking that they were conferring or receiving any gift. Therefore their actions left no trace and there was no record of their affairs.

CHINESE SAGE CHUANG TZU
(fourth century B.C.)

And GOD said, Let us make man in our image, after our likeness: and let them have dominion over the fish of the sea, and over the fowl of the air, and over the cattle, and over all the earth, and over every creeping thing that creepeth upon the earth. So GOD created man in his own image, in the image of GOD created he him; male and female created he them. . . .

And the LORD God planted a garden eastward in Eden; and there he put the man whom he had formed. . . .

And the LORD God took the man, and put him into the Garden of Eden to dress it and to keep it.

GENESIS 1:26, 27; 2:8, 15

William Blake, *Adam Naming the Beasts* (1810).

Acknowledgments

I'm delighted to at last have the opportunity to publicly thank some of the people who helped in the creation of this book.

First, I would like to thank Marilyn Ferguson and Jeremy Tarcher, who saw that there was a book to be written and made it possible for me to write it; and the entire staff at Jeremy P. Tarcher, Inc., who applied their various publishing skills with genuine warmth and enthusiasm.

I'm indebted also to Susan Rogers, who tirelessly scoured the libraries and bookstores of Portland, Oregon, for me, and sent innumerable books and articles that I would never otherwise have been able to find; and to Roger Migchelbrink, who accompanied me on many trips to libraries in Colorado, and sleuthed out obscure but relevant passages from the world's religious literature.

I cannot adequately express the depth of my gratitude for the generosity and tolerance of the 150 residents of the Sunrise Ranch community, who supported me during the two otherwise unproductive years I spent preparing the manuscript. It is their willingness to bring Paradise into earthly form on a daily basis through the quality of their living that makes this book more than merely a theoretical exercise.

Finally, I would like to thank my editor, Dan Joy, who came to share the vision that inspired this book, and who gently and persistently cultivated all that was harmonious to the vision and patiently weeded out ideas and language that failed to adequately embody it. In the process of working together for months or years, dissecting thoughts and pruning paragraphs, authors and their editors get to know the insides of each other's minds like the floor plans of their own kitchens. In some cases, I'm sure the experience is harrowing for both parties; in this instance, the entire process has been an unalloyed pleasure.

Foreword

I'S BEEN SAID OF THE MUSIC OF MOZART that it might have been written before the Fall. The same could be said of Richard Heinberg's *Memories and Visions of Paradise*.

Heinberg is an explorer in the realms of myth and prophecy. These realms are strange, in that the world depicted in both myth and prophecy is so different from the world we know as to make us, at first, incredulous of both. But an explorer is more than a traveler, who may simply stare briefly and disbelievingly at exotic landscapes, and then, with a sigh of relief, return to his familiar haunts. An explorer must linger in unfamiliar surroundings and have enough courage to brave the disorientation that inevitably results from his sojourn. Then, once he is reoriented, he must have the openness of heart and mind to see significance in what he has encountered and the generosity of spirit to transmit that significance to others less adventurous than he. All this Heinberg has done.

He is doing far more, however, than introducing the myth-shy to bizarre tales and farfetched predictions. He is telling them—and us—that there is a hidden component in our reluctance to believe old stories and accept depictions of things to come. This hidden component, he says, is that, far from being alien to us, the shadowy realms of past and future are not fictions at all. On the contrary, the mythic domain is the long-term actuality of our collective ancestry, while the prophetic dream is a concrete possibility for those willing to actualize it. We are like adopted children who, on discovering that our real parentage is other than we had assumed, refuse to acknowledge either that parentage or the altered prospects that may flow from it.

The great intellectual task that Heinberg poses for us is what Jungian psychoanalysts call *anamnesis*, or the recovery of buried memory, both individual and collective. As the Greek origin of the word suggests, anamnesis is by no means a modern proposal. Plato insisted that all thought is recollection. And devotees of the Orphic Mysteries sought to offset Lethe, the traditional River of Forgetfulness, with a Lake of Remembrance, in which their initiates would bathe to regain recall of the primal cosmos and their place in it. In the nineteenth century, Friedrich Nietzsche, whose career as a philosopher began with an intensive study of classical philology, took a keen interest in these ideas and advocated the development of what he called *mnemotechnics*—a systematic method of remembering what might otherwise suffer oblivion.

One of the most adventurous of the thinkers who fell heir to the analytic vision was the Austrian-American physician Wilhelm Reich, who declared that "the dream of Paradise . . . is rational and necessary."[1] Reich, whose therapeutic goal was the restoration of energetic creativity to people who felt deeply dispirited, became convinced that the great political movements of his time, both revolutionary and reactionary, were desperate but misguided efforts to restore a lost prehistoric social order.

Although Richard Heinberg's exposition takes the form of prose, the vision it embodies is poetic. To use a term borrowed from the *Paradise* epics of poet John Milton, Heinberg shows us what it was like, and what it would again be like, to live "emparadised." But the richest verse expression of this vision that I know comes from Milton's admirer and successor William Wordsworth. It is his ode *Intimations of Immortality from Recollections of Early Childhood* (in which we may construe his "childhood" as that of humanity at large, and the pronoun "I" as referring to our entire species):

> There was a time when meadow, grove, and stream,
> The earth, and every common sight,
> To me did seem
> Apparelled in celestial light,
> The glory and the freshness of a dream.

It is not now as it hath been of yore;—
Turn wheresoe'er I may,
By night or day,
The things which I have seen I now can see no more . . .

The Pansy at my feet
Doth the same tale repeat:
Whither is fled the visionary gleam?
Where is it now, the glory and the dream? . . .

Our birth is but a sleep and a forgetting:
The Soul that rises with us, our life's Star,
Hath had elsewhere its setting,
And cometh from afar:
Not in entire forgetfulness,
And not in utter nakedness,
But trailing clouds of glory do we come
From God, who is our home . . .

O joy! that in our embers
Is something that doth live,
That nature yet remembers
What was so fugitive! . . .

Hence in a season of calm weather
Though inland far we be,
Our souls have sight of that immortal sea
Which brought us hither,
Can in a moment travel thither,
And see the children sport upon the shore,
And hear the mighty waters rolling evermore . . .

Thanks to the human heart by which we live,
Thanks to its tenderness, its joys, and fears,
To me the meanest flower that blows can give
Thoughts that do often lie too deep for tears.

More recent, if indirect, support for the Heinberg thesis comes from British biologist Rupert Sheldrake's theory of formative causation.[2] According to Sheldrake, both physical "law" and human behavior are mutable, being in large part determined by patterns laid down

Paul Gauguin, *Doù venons-nous? Que sommes-nous? Où allons-nous?*
(Where do we come from? What are we? Where are we going?) (1898).

in earlier times. The fact that so much of our religious iconography and
so many of our artworks, verbal and nonverbal alike, depict a world
radically different from any known to history may indicate, in terms of
formative causation, that our paradisal dreams are in fact group memories. Perhaps we resonate to the concept of Paradise because we once
dwelt in Paradise and have never wholly abandoned the subliminal
hope of returning to that state.

The conventional wisdom of our age has it that all talk of Paradise
is either hyperbole or fantasy. Describing a vacation spot as Paradise is
regarded as exaggeration for effect. Analogously, having a vision of
Paradise is regarded as "mere imagination." But what is imagination?
Literally, it's imaging—that is, forming or perceiving images. And
although some of our images are formed deliberately, most of them
simply come to us; where they come from, we don't know.

Most imagination, in other words, is not invention ex nihilo but the reappearance in individual minds of ancient and collective images. Most envisioning is memory revivified: Paradise is not so much created as re-created.

If, on the other hand, those enriching works of art and science that we commonly regard as personal creations are in fact resurrections of vanished humanity, a reciprocal observation seems equally valid: that acting as a vehicle for this immortal consciousness is itself among the highest forms of creativity to which individuals can aspire. By reminding us of Paradise and helping us to re-envision it, Richard Heinberg has shown himself to be a most compassionate and creative explorer of the human spirit.

ROGER WILLIAMS WESCOTT
Professor of Anthropology
Drew University

April 1989

Whether it happened so or not I do not know; but if you think about it you can see that it is true.

BLACK ELK

Introduction

EARLY ALL HUMAN ENDEAVORS—from the search for better jobs and more fulfilling relationships to the founding of nations and the pursuit of technological and social progress—can be seen as expressions of a primal longing for an ultimate state of happiness and fulfillment. This longing, which fires the passions of each generation, can be traced back through the earliest expressions of the human imagination in literature and folklore to the primordial memory of an original Paradise where human beings lived in innocent and miraculous harmony with Nature and Cosmos. The paradisal image still beckons us with a power and insistence that are truly archetypal, yet its source and meaning are nevertheless mysterious. Like a forgotten hypnotic suggestion, it compels our behavior but itself remains obscure.

In 1979 a series of events conspired to catapult me into a decade-long quest for the meaning of this universal myth of Paradise. At the time, I had just spent five years working with a group of friends in developing a small, spiritually based commune in Ontario. I had a modest educational background in art, music, and Buddhist sacred texts and was a voracious reader of books and articles about the frontiers of scientific research. Through a friend, Mrs. Grace Van Duzen, I heard that the controversial cosmologist/historian Immanuel Velikovsky was in need of a research assistant. Since I admired Velikovsky's works for their scholarship and originality, I asked Grace, who knew the elderly scientist, to recommend me to him. After a few letters and phone calls I moved to the Velikovskys' home in Princeton,

New Jersey. Five days later Dr. Velikovsky, who was eighty-four, died. At his family's request I stayed and helped edit two of his manuscripts, later published as *Mankind in Amnesia* (1981) and *Stargazers and Gravediggers* (1983).

Velikovsky had pioneered a new way of reading ancient mythology. He had collected widespread traditions of flood, fire, and other catastrophes and had compared those traditions with the evidence of geology and astronomy. He concluded that the myths were not merely childish fantasies—as many previous scholars had assumed—but were memories of historical events. This idea was a revelation to some of his readers, an outrage to others. Scientific discoveries since the publication of *Worlds in Collision* in 1950 have tended to confirm many of Velikovsky's proposals, but in academic circles the mention of his name still evokes mixed responses.

As I gained increasing familiarity with the myths of ancient catastrophes that Velikovsky had used as source material, I began to come across older traditions of a time of peace and abundance. I soon discovered that the image of a vanished Paradise and the quest for its restoration are staple themes in world folklore. Nearly all ancient peoples had traditions of a primordial era when humanity lived a simple yet magical existence in attunement with Nature. The ancients said that this original Golden Age came to an end because of some tragic mistake or failure that forced a separation between Heaven and Earth. Further, they said that the rupture between the two worlds precipitated a descent into the separateness, fear, and greed that characterize human nature as we know it today. They said that it was only after this change in the human mode of being—the Fall—that the Earth was subjected to horrendous global catastrophes whose geologic, climatic, and psychological impact erased nearly every trace of the former "golden" condition.

The words *Paradise* and *Fall* inevitably call to mind the Hebraic story of Adam and Eve in the Garden of Eden—the version of the ancient Paradise narrative that is best known to Westerners, and that millions of people still take quite literally. I was determined to pursue the origin and meaning of the Eden story, but I was equally fascinated by the dozens of similar myths to be found among peoples as diverse as the Native Americans, the ancient Greeks and Hindus, the tribal peoples of Africa, and the Aborigines of Australia. Here, it seemed to me, was an idea larger than any single religion could contain.

I felt compelled to ask, as Velikovsky certainly would have done, whether there might be some historical truth at the core of the Paradise myth. *Was there really a Golden Age?* I began to apply an inter-disciplinary method, correlating the findings of archaeology, anthro-pology, and psychology with the archaic traditions of our ancestors. The results of that investigation—summarized in the later chapters of this book—provided insight into the meaning of the myth, but they also challenged most of my assumptions about history, psychology, and religion. I soon began to see that the Paradise tradition can indeed be viewed as history, but only by acknowledging that it is also a profound metaphor.

The metaphorical meaning of the myth, I discovered, flows from the sacred worldview of the ancients. Their approach to life was thoroughly spiritual in character but lacked any sense of sectarianism or dogmatism. They seemed to have an understanding of the universal order and meaning of existence that guided them in their relations with Heaven and Nature. The Paradise myth, in its descriptions of miraculous landscapes and wondrous powers lost because of a disas-trous change in human character, embodied that worldview and at the same time told how and why it had gradually been eclipsed. As I came to see through the eyes of the primordial mythmakers, my own view of life and human culture was transformed. I began regarding modern religions as remnants of a formerly universal spiritual tradition, and the history of civilization as the record of humanity's progressive loss of its original sense of sacred purpose.

Increasingly, I began to suspect that the mythic world picture has a special meaning for us in the present generation. Though we in the modern industrial world tend to pride ourselves on our achievements, at the same time we are deeply uneasy. Every civilization has had its unique problems to contend with, but ours seems especially burdened. Indeed, the ultimate effects of pollution, war, and overpopulation are potentially so severe as to have required the coining of a new term—*omnicide*. Could it be that our current dilemmas, rather than being the necessary accompaniments to the process of human evolu-tion, are instead symptoms of some universal cultural neurosis? Could it be that we have lost touch with an inner dimension of being so vital and nourishing that our estrangement from it has left a hole in our hearts—a hole we try in vain to fill through personal achievement and material acquisition? And could it be that the ancients, in their stories of a vanished Eden, were seeking to give us important information about the nature of that loss and how it can be redressed—information that we need at the present stage of history if we are to return to a sane and stable mode of existence?

Now, after these years of research and writing, I think I understand more fully why the Paradise myth has drawn me so irresistibly, and why it has fascinated multitudes for generations. Having surveyed the relevant mythological literature, as well as the related findings of anthropology and archaeology, I feel compelled toward the view that our cultural memories of a Golden Age of harmony are the residue of a once-universal understanding of the spiritual dimension of human consciousness, and are at the same time memories of how contact with that dimension has been almost completely severed. And I cannot but note the fortuity of the fact that the comparative study of mythology has come of age, and is leading us back toward the sacred worldview, just as our modern industrial society approaches what can only be called a spiritual crisis.

The leading-edge thinkers of our era are proclaiming the need for a new basis for living and a new set of assumptions about Earth and humankind. Psychoanalyst Carl Jung encapsulated this situation when he said that humanity needs a new myth, a new foundation of meaning to anchor the superstructure of our complex civilization.

That new myth does seem to be emerging, expressed in various ways by thinkers in divergent disciplines. Biologist James Lovelock, for example, suggests in his Gaia hypothesis that the Earth is a living entity capable of regulating its own internal systems. George Wald, winner of the 1967 Nobel Prize for Physiology or Medicine, argues that consciousness, rather than being a recent evolutionary development, must be inherent in the very structure of the Cosmos. Our century's most insightful economist, E. F. Schumacher, showed us that while "wealth, education, research, and many other things are needed for any civilisation . . . what is most needed today is a revision of the ends which these means are meant to serve"[1]—ends that must proceed from nonmaterial ideals and values such as truth, temperance, and beauty. And medical and psychological researchers are discovering that our emotional states directly affect our physical health. Their experiments suggest that the expression of the finer qualities of the human spirit is not just a laudable ideal, but the necessary basis for a healthful approach to living.[2]

Respect for the Earth as a living entity, acknowledgment of purpose and consciousness in the Cosmos, recognition of universal spiritual values, and acceptance of responsibility for the expression of noble character are attitudes and ideas often summed up in a word that defines the new myth we are straining toward about as well as any single word can: *holism.* Holism is the belief that it is wholes (organisms and ecologies, for example) that determine the design, function, and health of their parts, rather than the other way around.

Many of our foremost thinkers are drawn toward a holistic worldview, approaching it from every category and department into which human thought has fragmented itself. But the further this trend toward holism proceeds, the more vivid is the impression that someone has been here before. As our philosophies advance toward recognition of cosmic order and respect for Nature's inherent design, we are recapitulating in many ways the ancient spiritual worldview. We seem about to come full circle, in a path leading away from specialization and toward integration, away from technological excess and toward respect for natural process, and away from materialism and toward a renewed sense of the sacred.

Perhaps none of this should surprise us. If our new myth is to have the depth of resonance required in order for it to ring clear through the mass of the collective unconscious, it needs to sound from the ultimate Source of human identity, meaning, and purpose. And that Source— whether we call it Brahma, God, or the universal ground of Being—is no modern invention.

Indigenous peoples, such as the Native Americans and Australian Aborigines, have never assumed, as we do, that Nature exists for human benefit. Instead, they have believed for millennia that we humans have a profound responsibility to the Earth as channels for the revelation of Heaven. They view the essential purpose of life in spiritual rather than material terms, and they see the Universe itself as aware and benevolent. We may congratulate ourselves by thinking that intellectual and spiritual leaders in the modern world are entertaining similar thoughts at a higher turn of the evolutionary spiral, but we can afford little arrogance in comparing our way of life with that of the tribal peoples. They were masters of holism long before we got around to coining the term.

The idea that we can somehow bring back a lost Paradise may seem the most quixotic of enterprises at this late date. We live in a cynical world and have all but lost the ability to envision a past that is anything other than barbaric or a future that is anything more than survivable. Many have come to accept the loss of innocence as necessary and irreversible, and to regard any recollection or dream of a truly fulfilling existence as no more than an exercise in sentimentalism, romanticism, or nostalgia. The Paradise myth, in contrast, offers a vision of an age of miracles and wonders, of magical simplicity, of peace and joy. It tells us that it is possible to live in trust. Do we still have the courage to entertain such a vision? On our answer to this question may hang the reality of our future. "Without vision," goes the Proverb, "the people perish."

ટર્

Given the mind-boggling breadth and variety of the material that fairly begged to be included in this volume, I have tried to make our journey through myth, prophecy, history, anthropology, and psychology as logical and straightforward as possible.

Part One of the book (chapters 1 through 5) is composed of a sequential survey of the mythic view of world history. It is a guided tour through Creation, Paradise, and Fall. These chapters will, I hope, be of interest to all scholars and lovers of myth.

Part Two is an exploration of the paradisal vision as it has re-emerged through historical human cultures. As we will see in chapter 6, prophecies of a coming day of purification and of the ultimate return of Paradise are ubiquitous, transcending cultural boundaries. Moreover, as we will find in chapter 7, memories and dreams of a past or future Eden have shaped our own civilization's literature and social ideals to an astonishing degree.

Part Three is an investigation of humanity's attempts to discover the meaning of the paradisal image. In chapter 8 we will explore the anthropological and archaeological evidence bearing on the question of whether there really was a Golden Age many millennia ago, and in chapter 9 we will see how the Paradise myth may metaphorically describe alternate states of consciousness.

Part Four presents some speculative implications that naturally arise from our approach to the Paradise myth. As we will see, there is reason to think that if we are willing to confront and change many of our present assumptions and values and much of our social conditioning, the miraculous world of Paradise may actually be attainable, both for ourselves individually and for humankind as a whole.

PART ONE

Memory

Hieronymus Bosch, *The Garden of Earthly Delights* (ca. 1500). Left panel.

CHAPTER 1

The Mysteries of Myth

 NCE UPON A TIME *all human beings lived in friendship and peace, not only among themselves but with all other living things as well. The people of that original Age of Innocence were wise, shining beings who could fly through the air at will, and who were in continual communion with cosmic forces and intelligences. But a tragic disruption brought the First Age to an end, and humanity found itself estranged from both Heaven and Nature. Ever since then we have lived in a fragmented way, never really understanding ourselves or our place in the Universe. But occasionally we look back, with longing and regret, and dream of a return to the Paradise we once knew.*

Paradise may be the most popular and intensely meaningful idea ever to have gripped the human imagination. We find it everywhere. "In more or less complex forms, the paradisiac myth occurs here and there all over the world,"[1] wrote the great modern authority on comparative religions Mircea Eliade. The Hebraic Garden of Eden, the Greek Golden Age, the Australian Aborigines' Dreamtime, and the Chinese Taoist Age of Perfect Virtue are but local variants of the universally recalled Time of Beginnings, whose memory has colored all of subsequent history.

The impact of the paradisal image on the collective human consciousness is as deep as it is broad. In no tradition is it a recent or peripheral theme; rather, it is at the very core of the perennial spiritual impulse, reemerging in every generation's literature, art, and social ideals. Indeed, if one were seeking a motif on which to base an outline summary of human culture, one might well begin with our collective memories of a lost Golden Age and our longings for its return. The great enterprises of history—the Crusades, the millenarian revolts of the Middle Ages, the search for the Grail, the discovery and colonization of the New World, utopian movements in literature and politics, Marxism, and the cult of progress—all are in some way rooted in the soil of the original mythic Garden. The more familiar we are with the essence of the story, the more frequently we recognize its reflection in the nostalgic reveries and fervent aspirations of every culture in every era.

While the image of Paradise is in some respects timeless, its most familiar and potent expressions are to be found in oral traditions and ancient religious scriptures—that is, in *myths*. For the West, Hebraic Eden and the Greek Golden Age have served as prototypes for all subsequent visions of Paradise in art and literature. The situation is similar elsewhere. In every tradition, the image of Paradise is derived from a myth that dates back to the beginnings of human culture. The nature of Paradise is bound up with the nature of myth. Therefore, in order for us to arrive at any new insights about the universal longing for Paradise, it would seem helpful to first have a basic understanding of the nature and meaning of myth in general. But this is no simple matter: the question of the meaning of myth has plagued scholars for millennia, and continues to do so.

Are myths distorted memories of historical events? Or are they allegories for moral or psychological insights? These are the two primary lines of inquiry that scholars have explored in their search for the origin of the bewildering panoply of the world's mythology. And we can reframe both of these questions in terms of the universal story of Paradise: Was there a real Golden Age? If not, what psychological truth were the ancients seeking to convey through their ubiquitous stories of a lost world of happiness and abundance?

Since the interpretation of this Story of stories cannot be undertaken without some general understanding of the nature of mythology, we will begin by briefly examining in this chapter the principal theories, beliefs, and speculations that have exercised scholars of myth through the centuries. Then, having explored the context of our subject, we will proceed throughout the remainder of Part One with a survey of the mythical accounts of Creation, Paradise, and Fall from around the world, in all their variety and color.

Interpreting the Ancients

In most conversation, the word *myth* is interchangeable with *lie*. We speak of exposing myths, dispelling them, and laying them to rest. This equation of myth with fiction is not particularly new; indeed, it can be traced back at least as far as the sixth century B.C., when the earliest Greek philosophers undertook a critical evaluation of Homeric mythology. It is in the writings of Xenophanes, a Greek philosopher of the sixth century B.C., that we find the first expression of disbelief in the traditional pantheon. In particular, Xenophanes protested Homer's descriptions of gods in anthropomorphic terms: "If cattle and horses had hands, or were able to draw with their hands and do the works that men can do, horses would draw the forms of gods like horses, and cattle like cattle."[2]

Xenophanes was a literate man, and for early literate peoples myths were no longer part of a living religious experience; rather—for reasons that are obscure—they had become matters of interpretation and debate. The early Greeks thus faced a problem: their culture was suffused with rituals and stories of great antiquity, but the meaning behind those traditions had largely evaporated. How to make sense of them?

It was a question to which curious and ingenious minds enthusiastically applied themselves. Among the early Greeks we can already discern the beginnings of the two primary interpretive schools that have dominated the study of myth down to the present. Theagenes, a writer of the fifth century B.C., created the *allegorical school* of interpretation by suggesting that all the Homeric gods represent either human faculties or natural elements. It is to Theagenes that we owe the idea, for example, that since Hera was the goddess of the air, the tales of her tempestuous relations with her husband, Zeus, are to be understood as metaphoric descriptions of actual atmospheric disturbances such as thunderstorms and hurricanes. According to Theagenes and his followers in later centuries, myths are always signs or symbols of something else; to take them literally is to miss their point altogether.

Two centuries later, at the beginning of the third century B.C., a Greek writer named Euhemerus initiated the *historical school* of interpretation. In his widely read collection of philosophical excursions, *Sacred Writings*, he argued that myths are exaggerated accounts of events actually witnessed by early peoples, and that the Homeric gods were historical kings. Zeus, Apollo, and the rest of the pantheon were real human beings who had been deified out of gratitude or flattery, their exploits in war and peace forged into sacred traditions to be handed down faithfully from generation to generation. When we read a myth, according to Euhemerus, we are actually reading distorted history. So influential was Euhemerus' book that it was the first Greek text to be translated into Latin, and scholastic discussion of the Greek pantheon through the Middle Ages and into the Renaissance continued to be dominated by *euhemerism*—the treatment of myth as garbled history.

Dissecting Myth and Religion

The debate between metaphoricists and historicists continues to the present, and we shall consider it in more depth shortly. But this is not the only issue in the ancient and ongoing quest for the meaning of myth. Mythology is inseparable from religion, and so Western civilization's changing attitudes toward the mysterious and universal sense of the sacred have also deeply affected both popular and scholarly ideas about the nature of myth.

During the Middle Ages, the church declared that all traditions other than its own were by definition pagan and idolatrous, and—with the exception of Greek and Roman myths, which were granted purely historical interest—should be given no attention whatever by God-fearing people. Consequently, the study of Celtic, Germanic, Zoroastrian, Islamic, and other non-Christian mythologies was suppressed. Later, however, as the church's stranglehold on free inquiry loosened and as explorers returned with news of the customs and folklore of native peoples in the Americas, Africa, and the Pacific islands, philosophers began to question the church's parochial views of religion and culture—cautiously and quietly at first, but with gradually increasing vigor.

By the mid-nineteenth century, so much new data was arriving from ethnologists and anthropologists in the field that theorists, in their attempts to deal with the glut of information, clamored for a simple, all-embracing organizational scheme—preferably, one completely independent of ecclesiastical influence. The ideal basis for such a scheme seemed to be supplied by the increasingly popular idea of evolution. Even before the publication of Darwin's *Origin of Species*, theorists began applying the evolutionary principle (the law of the development of the simple to the complex, the low to the high—and, by implication, the inferior to the superior) everywhere and to everything. While astronomers theorized about the evolution of the Universe, historians and scholars pursued the evolution of language, culture, and mythology.

In the evolutionist view, tribal peoples were holdovers from an early, prerational stage of human development. This conclusion led several generations of anthropologists to adopt attitudes toward indigenous cultures and their religions that were nearly as condescending as those of the earlier Christian theologians. Meanwhile, Western scientists were expressing increasing antagonism toward the religious roots of their own culture as well. The church had kept a lid on scientific inquiry for centuries; now scientists were free to question and theorize, and they were determined to turn the tables on the theologians by treating religion and myth as nothing more than peculiar psychological aberrations afflicting archaic humanity.

These two influences together—the evolutionist insistence on arranging all human cultures on a value-laden theoretical ladder, and the general distrust among scientists of anything exuding the remotest scent of religion—led nineteenth-century mythologists to construct what now appear as narrow, rationalist schemes to explain the seemingly irrational obsessions of the ancients. Thus, philologist Max Müller saw mythology as a "disease of language" in which primitive peoples, unable to clearly distinguish metaphors from factual statements, came to refer to natural objects as living things suffused with a spirit. Anthropologist Lucien Levy-Bruhl tried to account for contemporary cultural traditions by tracing their origin to "pre-logical" modes of thought. And folklorist Sir James Frazer, whose encyclopedic study *The Golden Bough* dominated comparative mythology for decades, held that a skeptical attitude toward *all* religion was a necessary foundation for the scientific approach to the study of *any* religion.

Nor did this antireligious and antiprimitivist tide ebb with the turn of the century. Twentieth-century anthropology can be said to have begun with Émile Durkheim and his functionalist, sociological approach to myth and culture. Durkheim emphasized the significance of the *Conscience Collective*—the collective way of thought of a community—which is qualitatively different from individual thought. For Durkheim and the functionalists, the sense of the sacred was the sense of society itself; mythology primarily served a social function. Thus, it is useless to speculate about the philosophical meaning of a given culture's creation myth, for example; we should instead examine the myth's effect on the customs and attitudes of people. The social function of the myth *is* its meaning.

Meanwhile, early psychologists, led by Sigmund Freud, studied anthropological data in order to validate their theories of the personality and its aberrations. Freud viewed myths as primitive humanity's disguised expressions of unconscious sexual and aggressive compulsions. In his *Totem and Taboo* (1912), he traced the institutions, beliefs, and fears of both modern and primitive cultures to a hypothesized drama in the family life of Stone Age peoples—the murder of the tribal father by his sons for the purpose of possessing their mother. This drama is epitomized in the Greek myth of Oedipus. For Freud and his followers, all mythic motifs were Oedipal and sexual in origin and were filled with symbols capable of being decoded only by the analyst already familiar with dream interpretation. In chapter 9 we will take a more thorough look at the Freudian approach to myth, with specific reference to the image of Paradise.

Few early-twentieth-century anthropologists escaped the influence of Durkheim or Freud, who both sought to identify religion with illusion and to explain myth by reference to physical, social, or psychological phenomena. Durkheim had discovered that mythology can serve practical social functions, and Freud had shown that myths are expressions of the collective unconscious. Yet, as the new century wore on it became clear that something significant was missing from their theories. Like entomologists studying butterflies, they had collected, dissected, classified, and compared the myths of the world, but in the process they had ignored or eliminated the vivifying principle in the object of their study—a principle that would be defined by the next generation of mythologists as *the sense of the sacred*.

The Return of the Sacred

In the last few decades, many psychologists, anthropologists, and historians of religion have abandoned the reductive approaches of Durkheim and Freud. Among both scholars and the general public there is a growing—though by no means as yet universal—appreciation that the myths of ancient and indigenous peoples were not just social tools or collective psychological aberrations, but instead were ways of conveying universal truths. Myths, in this emerging view, are doors to a realm of experience that was, and is, both real and profoundly meaningful.

This radical new approach to myth owes much to the work of psychoanalyst Carl Jung. Like Freud, his early mentor, Jung saw myths as pathways to and from the collective unconscious. But while Freud tended to view the unconscious with suspicion and even horror and to despise religion in all its forms, Jung saw the unconscious as an essentially beneficent realm and considered the religious experience as fundamentally therapeutic. He saw myths as "original revelations of the preconscious psyche, involuntary statements about unconscious psychic . . . processes." To Jung, "a tribe's mythology is its living religion, whose loss is always and everywhere, even among the civilized, a moral catastrophe."[3]

During the study of his own dreams and fantasies, which he allowed free expression, Jung noted strange images that seemed to relate to passages in neglected medieval Hermetic and alchemical texts, which he proceeded to study in depth. From these experiences he developed his theory of the archetypes, which are instinctive, universal patterns in the collective psyche—the Hero, the Wise Old Man, the Great Mother, and so on—which are expressed similarly in the dream imagery and behavior of people everywhere. For Jung, the characters and actions of myth are simply expressions of universal archetypes. "The collective unconscious," he wrote, "contains the whole spiritual heritage of mankind's evolution born anew in the brain structure of every individual."[4] During his long career, Jung contributed several important studies of archaic and oriental traditions[5] and exerted a considerable influence on the work of many important scholars—notably Joseph Campbell, whose books and articles have perhaps done more to popularize the study of mythology than those of any other contemporary author.

Developments in religious studies in the twentieth century have also played a part in the evolution of the contemporary attitude toward myth. As we have seen, the tendency in the late nineteenth century was to explain religion in social or psychological terms. In 1917, however, psychologist Rudolf Otto published *The Idea of the Holy*, in which he emphasized the fundamental reality and irreducibility of the religious experience in all its manifestations.

Then, in the 1930s and 1940s, French philosopher René Guénon pointed to what he called the Primordial Tradition of universal truths that lies at the core of every living religion. All traditions, according to Guénon, are paths for the practical realization of innate spiritual principles in the lives of human beings. Turning nineteenth-century cultural evolutionism on its head, Guénon protested in the strongest terms the loss of true spirituality in the modern world. "The material prosperity of the West is incontrovertible," he wrote, "but it is hardly a cause for envy. Indeed, one can go further; sooner or later this excessive material development threatens to destroy the West if it does not recover itself in time and if it does not consider seriously a 'return to the source.'"[6]

The Rumanian-American historian of religion Mircea Eliade applied this new attitude toward religion directly to the study of mythology. Eliade refused to reduce myths to economic, social, cultural, psychological, or political meanings; instead, he emphasized the primacy of the experience of *the sacred* in all traditions. Moreover, he placed tribal religions and the scriptural religions of East and West side by side (rather than arranging them in an evolutionary sequence, as had become customary) in order to reveal and clarify their common motifs.

Like Jung, Eliade saw mythic themes as unconscious archetypes. Going further, he identified the two core themes of world myth as the nostalgia for a Paradise that has been lost because of a primordial tragedy (the Fall), and the initiatory scenario whereby the original golden world is partially restored. Both primitive and scriptural religions, according to Eliade, betray

the *Nostalgia for Paradise*, the desire to recover the state of freedom and beatitude before "the Fall," the will to restore

communication between Earth and Heaven; in a word, to abolish all the changes made in the very structure of the Cosmos and
in the human mode of being by that primordial disruption.[7]

Eliade's easy encompassment of a wide range of religious data, his
ability to perceive universal patterns, and his use of nontheological
terms in an elegant and lucid literary style all contributed to his
profound influence on the modern study of myth.

The Mythic Worldview

Through the work of Jung, Otto, Guénon, Campbell, and Eliade
runs a current of respect for the sense of the sacred as expressed in all of
the world's religions and mythologies. Through their writings we gain
some sense of the worldview of the ancients, in which rocks, trees,
rivers, and clouds were living parts of a living whole; in which the
Cosmos was alive and conscious, partaking of the same intelligent
force by which we ourselves are animated; and in which human beings
were the link between Heaven and Earth—between the inner dimension of spirit and the outer world of form. Through them we are
reacquainted with the context of ancient thought, in which every
event was meaningful and every individual knew that his or her life
was the embodiment of principle and purpose. In the archaic vision of
reality, even the most mundane activities had an overarching significance and were performed not as personal, private acts but as part of a
cosmic drama.

For the ancients, the respect for the sacred derived from an awareness of the creative processes of Nature, and it implied a hesitancy to
arbitrarily intrude on those processes. To the sanctified consciousness,
time and space were themselves sacred, and every atom of creation was
part of one joyful chorus. In the Creation-Time, according to the
myths of the native Australians, Africans, and Americans, human
beings had a specific responsibility in the whole of Nature, which was
to provide a living bridge between levels of being.

To say that a thing or an act is sacred is to imply that it has
relevance in a universal plane of values and ideals, and that it is
therefore a point of contact between two worlds. To the ancients all
was sacred, because everything had significance in both a mundane

and also a cosmic context; matter itself was sacred substance. The role of humankind—established in the paradisal age of the first ancestors—was to *realize* that sacredness by coordinating traffic between Heaven and Earth.

Ancient peoples had an acute sense of responsibility not just to family or tribe, but to the whole of life. Its welfare was the reason for their existence. The Hopi Indians of the American Southwest, for example, knew the spirit of the Earth as *Maasauu*. They said that their purpose was to be apprentices to Maasauu, to be stewards of the Earth. According to their myths, in the early days Maasauu left this plane of existence, having given the Hopi instructions to carry out ceremonies to keep the Earth in balance and to keep the Plan of Life intact. The Hopi still see their ceremonies as essential to the nourishment of all living things on the planet. There is a ceremony for each kind of plant or animal, and the full cycle of ceremonies may continue for weeks.

It is perhaps understandable why this universal insistence on the sacredness of life was overlooked by nineteenth-century mythologists, who were simultaneously rebelling against their own religious heritage and exploring the powerful new philosophies of evolutionism and positivism. Now, however, scholars are beginning to admit that the religious concepts of the ancients and of tribal peoples, rather than being mere stages in an evolutionary pattern of beliefs, were already complete, sophisticated, functional, and self-consistent cosmological systems.

Yet, to characterize tribal religions as belief systems—even as complex and compelling ones—does not adequately convey their real depth. For tribal peoples, the sacred dimension was not just an object of speculation; it was experienced reality. For them, deity was not a concept but an immanent power and intelligence emanating from a nonphysical but thoroughly real Source. A native of Orinoco in Latin America once told a missionary, "Your God keeps himself shut up in a house, as if he were old and infirm; ours is in the forest, in the fields, and on the mountains of Sipapu, whence the rains come." The explorer Humboldt, after quoting the Indian's remark, added that the natives of the region had difficulty understanding the Europeans' churches and religious art: "On the banks of the Orinoco there exists no idol."[8]

It is difficult to overstate the significance of this increasing

At first water was every-where.

 Above the water in the mist was the Manito (the God-Creator).

 He caused to be land, clouds, waters, and the wide skies.

 He caused to be the Sun, the Moon, and the stars.

 Winds blew hard, clearing the deep water and making it run off.

 Light shone and an island appeared.

 Then he created the first beings.

 Afterward, he created the man-being, ancestor of man.

 He gave to man the first mother of men.

 He gave fishes, turtles, beasts and birds.

 At first all beings were friends together.

 But an evil Manito created monsters.

 Then, secretly, the magician snake brought discord and grief.

 Wickedness, crime, and unhappiness thus came to the world.

Excerpts from the Walam Olum, the Creation story
of the Lenape Indians

acknowledgment, on the part of psychologists and anthropologists, of the reality of the sacred dimension. As long as researchers denied its importance and based their explanations entirely in earthly terms, we were effectively denied the possibility of fully understanding or bene-fiting from myth. Worse, by discounting the sense of the sacred we disassociated ourselves from a universal, timeless dimension of signifi-cance whose point of access lies deep within the human psyche, where the individual and the collective, the ancient and the modern, merge indistinguishably. With the return of the sacred, a world opens before us that is at once pristine and primordial.

Myth: History or Metaphor?

But if many modern scholars hold myths to be the very antithesis of lies, this is not to say that myths are now commonly equated with historical fact. The authorities mentioned above—Jung and Campbell, especially—tended to see myths not as a collective memory of real characters and events, but as allegories for inner processes of spiritual transformation—that is, as stories that are *symbolically* but never *factually* "true."

Many tribal peoples, such as the Pawnee of the North American plains, drew a sharp distinction between symbolically "true" and "false" stories. A narrative may consist entirely of factual elements, and yet be a "false" story if it has been taken out of context to make a point that is self-serving or merely entertaining. Another story may be entirely fictional, yet remind us of situations we have all encountered and, by drawing us into the action of the narrative, may tell us something about ourselves and the workings of the world that we may not yet have seen. That is a "true" story.

To take advantage of true stories requires that we be awake to more than one level of discourse. When we read a Native American myth of the creation of the world from a bit of mud dredged up by a muskrat, or an African Bushman myth about Mantis stealing fire from Ostrich, we are inclined to smile at the simple imagery and may close our minds to its meaning. But the ancients and the tribal peoples shared a keen sense of symbol, and only by cultivating a similar sensibility in ourselves can we hope to understand their myths.

The French ethnologist Marcel Griaule has told of how he came to discover this necessity. He was listening to Dogon wise man Ogo-temmeli relate a myth about a celestial granary, on each step of which many large animals were supposedly perched. Griaule calculated the dimensions of the steps and asked, "How could all these animals find room on a step one cubit wide and one cubit deep?" Ogotemmeli carefully explained, "All of this has to be said in words, but everything on the step is a symbol—symbolic antelopes, symbolic vultures, symbolic hyenas. . . . Any number of symbols could find room on a one-cubit step." And, as Griaule reports, "for the word 'symbol' he used a compound expression, the literal meaning of which is 'word of this lower world.' "[9]

Myths, then, serve to connect two realities—the visible and the invisible, Earth and Heaven—and this process of bringing worlds into relation is accomplished through metaphor, symbol, and allegory. The ancients' symbolic treatments of universal human longings, fears, and aspirations serve as guides to our present experience by making the contents of the personal and collective unconscious accessible. This metaphoric approach to myth has gained popular attention in recent years through the works of post-Jungian psychologists. Robert Johnson's books *He, She,* and *We* and Jean Shinoda Bolen's *Goddesses in Everywoman* have educated a generation of readers in the use of myths as touchstones in the process of self-discovery.[10]

But while the mainstream of modern myth studies—represented by the works of Jung and Campbell—flows along the channel of Thea-genes' allegorism, there is also a modern euhemerist current. This school of thought holds that, at least in some cases, myths may contain *more than* metaphoric content—that they originated as descriptions of real events and are therefore not just "true" stories in an allegorical sense but *factual* ones in a historical sense. The modern euhemerist school is represented notably by Immanuel Velikovsky, who argued that worldwide legends of ancient Earth-wrenching catastrophes must have had their bases in actual cosmic debacles witnessed by our distant ancestors.

It would seem at first that myth and history have little in common. After all, myths are tales of the origins of things and take place in the miraculous Age of the Gods, while history is concerned with events taking place in ordinary human time. And yet, when we examine myth and history closely the dividing line between the two becomes ever more faint and ambiguous. History itself, as a discipline, originated in myth: when Herodotus, who is generally acknowledged as the first historian in the modern sense, wrote his *Investigations* as factual narratives of wars between the Greeks and the Persians, he took pains to trace the origins of the conflict back to the gods and Titans of Olympus.

Moreover, anthropologists and archaeologists have uncovered many instances in which myths do unquestionably conceal elements of historical fact. For instance, the Klamath Indians of the Pacific Northwest tell the story of an ancient battle between a magical bird and a magical turtle. When the turtle lost, Mount Mazama, on which he had stood during the battle, collapsed on top of him. His blood formed a lake, and his back protruded from the lake as an island. Today, Mount Mazama, which may once have risen as high as 10,000 feet, is known as Crater Lake, and geologists say that the Klamath must have mythologized a volcanic eruption that actually happened more than 6,500 years ago.[11] Similarly, prehistoric animals of Australia that have been extinct for 10,000 to 15,000 years are remembered in Aboriginal myth, together with contemporaneous changes in climate and landscape.[12]

To be sure, when collective memory preserves an impression of an event, it tends to do so in an "archetypal" manner, disregarding specifics that do not correspond with a preexistent universal pattern. There are innumerable instances in modern times in which we can actually observe the metamorphosis of a historical figure into a mythical hero (as, for example, in some popular biographies of Washington, Lincoln, and Lenin). And yet the factual core of the mythologized narrative unquestionably persists, whether in the biography of a heroic political leader, in a historic Russian folktale of the Napoleonic invasion, or in a Greek epic narrative of the Trojan Wars. History exists in myth as surely as "myth" persists in history.

The historical interpretation of myth presents archaeologists and anthropologists with a unique challenge: just how literally should any traditional narrative be taken? It is a challenge that most researchers would simply prefer to avoid. Ever since the eighteenth century, historians have been disputing the literal interpretation of the Bible, and most students of folklore seem to have fallen prey to the seldom-stated fear—common throughout academia—that the historical validation of *any* myth could open the door to a return to Bible-based science. The intensity of this fear can be sensed in anthropologist Robert Lowie's declaration that he could not "attach to oral traditions any historical value whatsoever under any conditions whatsoever,"[13] and in anthropologist Edmund Leach's determination to regard the prophets and kings of the Old Testament as purely "mythical" characters with absolutely no basis in fact.

Yet, it is obviously possible for a story to be factual and at the same time "true" in an allegorical sense: a historical event can be used to illustrate a universal truth. Through their fusion of memory and moral, myths of this sort tend to be particularly powerful, and they are epitomized in stories of the lives of the founders of world religions. Extreme metaphoricists may argue that Moses, Jesus, Buddha, and Lao Tzu never really existed, while literalists may insist on the factual integrity of even the most minute details of their traditional biographies. The truth, however, probably lies somewhere between these two positions.

As we shall see in chapters 8 and 9, the allegorical and the historical approaches are equally necessary tools in our exploration of the Paradise myth.

The Problem of Mythic Unity

Whether we interpret myths as allegories or as historical memories, we are confronted with what is emerging as the great problem of myth—the worldwide similarity of mythic themes. During the past century, as ethnologists have recorded and compared the folklore of hundreds of cultures from every part of the world, they have repeatedly noted the fact that myths everywhere tend to follow common patterns. Joseph Campbell has written that the myths of the world "resemble each other as dialects of a single language."[14] And in a recent survey of creation myths from around the world, Raymond Van Over asks, "Why such similarity of mythic ideas and images throughout these distant cultures? . . . The scholarly argument has raged for decades and it continues to this day. No definitive answer seems to have developed, but theories abound."[15]

It is possible, of course, to exaggerate the extent of this unity. It would be not only an oversimplification but a gross distortion to imply that there is no variety or nuance among the myths of the world's cultures. On one level the variety is astounding. It encompasses both the cyclic view of time of the Hindus, and the linear historical concepts of the Hebrews; the arboreal imagery of the early agriculturalists, and the animal gods of the primitive hunters; the dualism of the Iranian Avesta, and the unitive theology of the Hindu Upanishads. And yet beneath even the most divergent traditions one quickly discovers underlying thematic similarities. The Hindus and Hebrews, the hunters and the agriculturalists all looked back to an original Paradise, all remembered a worldwide Flood, and all believed in a nonphysical Otherworld.

As Campbell and Eliade have shown, there is really only one story, translated in the traditions and circumstances of myriad peoples. It is the myth of a lost idyllic Time of Beginnings, and of a hero's journey to restore the world to its pristine condition of paradisal splendor. As we shall see in the following chapters, the parallels among various cultures' descriptions of this primordial Time, and of its loss, are striking.

Hence the problem: *Why would ancient peoples in geographically remote places, under unique circumstances, have arrived at such similar beliefs?* There are really only a few possible answers to the question. Either the fundamental themes of myth were distributed among the world's peoples long ago through a process of borrowing and diffusion, perhaps before those peoples had migrated to their present locations, or similar motifs somehow occurred independently to people already living far apart. If the themes originated independently and spontaneously, they must have done so either because of a universal similarity in human psychology, or because all humanity participated in real and probably global historical events that impressed themselves on the memory of every culture.

We will return to the problem of mythic unity in chapter 3, where we will consider specific examples of the Paradise myth from various cultures. We will not, however, attempt to solve the problem once and for all; rather, we will suggest that all of the above explanations may be partly valid and will offer a likely scenario that could account for the facts as we have them.

But now, having considered some of the primary issues in the modern study of mythology, we are ready to explore the myths themselves—the universal stories of how the world came to be the way it is. These we shall survey according to the sequence of events they describe: Creation, Paradise, and Fall.

These things are really the thoughts of all men in all ages and lands, they are not original with me.

WALT WHITMAN

CHAPTER · 2

In the Beginning

I N EVERY MYTHOLOGY, Creation is the first act in a grand cosmic drama. That drama unfolds by stages through a Golden Age of peace and plenty, a Fall or period of degeneration, and a catastrophe that brings the sacred Age of the Gods to an end and initiates the present, profane age of the world. While the centerpiece in our investigation is the original Paradise, we cannot really hope to understand this core phase of the great mythic sequence without considering the whole pattern of which it is a part. And so we commence our survey of the Paradise myth where we must—*in the beginning*—with the universal story of Creation.

The spiritual life of all ancient and tribal peoples revolved around the maintenance of sacred rhythms and balances through rituals designed to recapitulate the Creation. Creation was the ultimate sacred act, to be commemorated and symbolically repeated on significant occasions in the life of the individual and in the collective life of the tribe. The creative process was at once a cosmic, historical phenomenon and a pattern of design and control in everyday life, the practical means for harmonizing Heaven and Nature. The Creation story was therefore of both universal and immediate significance: it described the nature of absolute reality in a way that was both transcendent (true for all times and places) and immanent (true here and now).

The original Creation marked the beginning of the Age of the Gods. Eliade has written, "It would be impossible to overstress the tendency—observable in every society, however highly developed—to

21

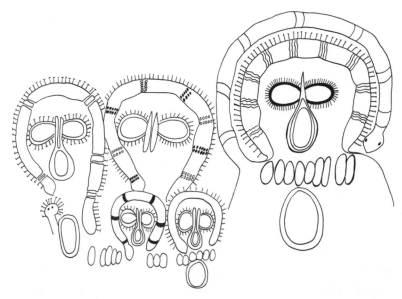

Wandjina figures. Rock painting from central Australia. Wandjinas were ancestral Creator-Beings of the Alcheringa, or Dreamtime, who left their likenesses imprinted on cave walls before returning to the spirit world.

bring back that time, mythical time, the Great Time."[1] That Great Time was the model for all times, so that accessions of new chiefs or kings, initiation rites, weddings, games, planting, hunting, and, especially, new year celebrations were all occasions for the symbolic reenactment of what had occurred *in the beginning*. The Aborigines of central Australia practiced rituals of circumcision and fashioned "X-ray" bark paintings in precisely the ways their Creator-Ancestors had taught them in the Dreamtime. The Yurok Indians of northern California performed world-renewing dances that the Immortals had revealed to them when the world was young. And according to Joseph Epes Brown, a modern authority on Native American religions, the Pima and Papago tribes of the American Southwest saw the act of basketmaking as

> the ritual recapitulation of the total process of creation. The completed basket is the universe in an image; and in the manufacturing process the woman actually plays the part of the Creator. Similarly, in establishing the dynamic interrelationship between the vertical warp and the horizontal weft, the Navajo

blanket weaver participates in acts that imitate the creation of the universe itself.[2]

The ancient Hindu sages stated the matter with quintessential brevity: "Thus the gods did; thus men do."[3]

The nostalgia for origins is, as Eliade says, a desire "to recover the active presence of the gods" and "to live in the world as it came from the Creator's hands, fresh, pure, and strong."[4] In every culture, we find the same longing to reenter the sacred time when the gods were immediately *present*, creating and organizing the world.

There are thousands of Creation myths among the world's peoples, but, as Eliade and Campbell pointed out, they are all really only one story told in different ways. While some cultures emphasize the role of Father God and relate the myth from a heavenly perspective, others portray a feminine principle of Creation, the Earth Mother. But even in describing the process from different viewpoints, the ancients formulated variations on one or another of only a handful of themes: the Creation from Nothing, in which a solitary Creator-God brings forth Heaven and Earth by means of a thought or word; the Cosmic Egg myth, in which the Universe unfolds from the interaction of the primordial masculine and feminine principles; the Earth Diver story, in which a representative of the upper, spiritual realm plunges into unformed chaos and dredges up bits of mud that grow to form the entire world; and the Emergence myth, in which the First People come forth into the daylight of physical being from various levels of underworld.

We will first explore how each of these stories of the Great Time of Creation exemplifies the universal creative process, and we will then consider myths of the origin of humankind in the primordial Paradise.

Fiat ex Nihilo

In the myth of Creation from Nothing, an all-powerful deity, dwelling alone in the void of space, causes first Heaven and then Earth to appear. The method of creation is deliberate and orderly, proceeding from a thought or word. The best-known account of this type is the Hebraic Creation story from the Book of Genesis:

In the beginning God created the heaven and the earth. And the earth was without form, and void; and darkness was upon the face of the deep. And the Spirit of God moved upon the face of the waters. And God said, Let there be light: and there was light. And God saw the light, that it was good: and God divided the light from the darkness. And God called the light Day, and the darkness he called Night.

As anthropologists Andrew Lang, Wilhelm Schmidt, and Wilhelm Koppers have shown, the idea of a single original Creator is universal and primordial. Yet, it would be simplistic to ignore the differences between, for example, the Hebrew Yahweh and the Hindu Brahma: the former is usually regarded as personal and wholly *other*, while the latter is viewed as immanent in every detail of the created universe, like the Tao of Lao Tzu:

> There exists something which is prior to all beginnings and endings,
> Which, unmoved and unmanifest, itself neither begins nor ends.
> All-pervasive and inexhaustible, it is the perpetual source of
>   everything else. . . .
> If I am forced to describe it, I speak of it as "Ultimate Reality."[5]

But while this creative principle may be described somewhat differently in various cultures, its singularity and absoluteness are nonetheless universally acknowledged.

The Hebrews' Yahweh exists alone before the Creation of Heaven and Earth; so does the Egyptian god Khepri, who asserts that "when I had come into being, being (itself) came into being . . . before heaven came into being, before earth came into being. . . ."[6]

In many accounts, the first act of Creation consists of the summoning of light, as in this myth from the Maoris of New Zealand:

> Io dwelt within the breathing-space of immensity.
> The Universe was in darkness, with water everywhere.
> There was no glimmer of dawn, no clearness, no light.
> And he began by saying these words—
>   "Darkness become a light-possessing darkness."
> And at once light appeared.
> (He) then repeated those self-same words in this manner.
>   "Light, become a darkness-possessing light."

Brahma, the Creator, facing the four directions.

As in Genesis, Creation occurs by sound or word. This is a theme found also among the Egyptians, the Celts, and the Mayas. The Maori priest refers to the words of Io as

> *The ancient and original sayings.*
> *The ancient and original words.*
> *The ancient and original cosmological wisdom (wananga).*
> *Which caused growth from the void,*
> *The limitless space-filling void.*[7]

In a Hawaiian myth, the Great God Kane exists alone in the deep intense night. He first brings about light, then the heavens, then the Earth and the ocean, then Sun, Moon, and stars.[8]

The Hopi Indians of Arizona tell how Taiowa, the Creator, began by making a subordinate to carry out the rest of the process of Creation:

The first world was Tokpela [Endless Space].

But first, they say, there was only the Creator, Taiowa. All else was endless space. There was no beginning and no end, no time, no shape, no life. Just an immeasurable void that had its beginning and end, time, shape, and life in the mind of Taiowa, the Creator.

Then he, the infinite, conceived the finite. First he created Sótuknang to make it manifest, saying to him, "I have created you, the first power and instrument as a person, to carry out my plan for life in endless space. I am your Uncle. You are my Nephew. Go now and lay out these universes in proper order so they may work harmoniously with one another according to my plan."

Sótuknang did as he was commanded. From endless space he gathered that which was to be manifest as solid substance, and molded it into forms.[9]

The created Universe is produced from no-*thing*; that is, it has no physical antecedent. It is preceded instead by pure Being, undifferentiated consciousness.

The Cosmic Egg

In the Cosmic Egg myth, Creation occurs by the relation of balanced masculine and feminine (active and receptive) principles, interacting from a state of primordial union described metaphorically as an egg. The unity of the two sexual principles is an image of perfection and also of potency, life, and imminent birth. For the Chinese, the symbol of the cosmic egg—the T'ai Chi Tu, or Diagram of the Supreme Ultimate—was a reminder of the profound necessity of bringing the yang (active) and yin (receptive) forces of Nature into balance in every action, and in every aspect of human society, in order to release the power of Creation:

The ancient Japanese, whose cosmology was influenced by the Taoist philosophy of China, said that

of old, Heaven and Earth were not yet separated, and the In and Yo [the masculine and feminine principles] not yet divided. They formed a chaotic mass like an egg, which was of obscurely defined limits. . . . The purer and clearer part was thinly diffused and formed Heaven, while the heavier and grosser element settled down and became Earth. The finer element easily became a united body, but the consolidation of the heavy and gross element was accomplished with difficulty. Heaven was therefore formed first, and Earth established subsequently. Thereafter Divine Beings were produced between them.[10]

Many myths that characterize the primal reality as chaos or water include the symbolism of an egg as the immediate source of all life, the womb of Creation. In the Greek Orphic tradition, Time (Cronos) creates the silver egg of the Cosmos, from which bursts Phanes-Dionysus, who embodies both sexes and contains the seeds of all the gods. A Mande creation myth from Africa describes twins of opposite sex conceived in the "Egg of God," which is also the "Egg of the World." The Hindu text *The Laws of Manu* states:

He [that is the self-existent] desiring to produce beings of many kinds from his own body, first with a thought created the waters and placed his seed in them. That [seed] became a golden egg, in brilliancy equal to the sun; in the [egg] he himself was born as Brahman, the progenitor of the whole world. . . . The divine one resided in that egg during a whole year, then he himself by his thought [alone] divided it into two halves; and out of those two halves he formed heaven and earth, between them the middle sphere, the eight points of the horizon, and the eternal abode of the waters.[11]

In the Cosmic Egg myth, the masculine and the feminine, Heaven and Earth, spirit and form are in purposeful balance, engaged in divine creative interplay.

The Earth Diver

Earth Diver myths tell the creation story from the perspective of a representative from the upper world who dives into the primordial chaos to bring forth the first seed of order. The Earth Diver myth tells of how a divine being (usually an animal) descends into the water to bring up bits of mud, which grow to form the whole Earth or even the entire Universe. Earth Diver myths are common among the northern North American tribes, whose cosmologies feature an original upper world inhabited by the immortal Elders and an unformed chaos of water below.

The symbolism in Earth Diver myths is often whimsical: the Diver is often pictured as a muskrat, a duck, or a turtle. Yet the underlying meaning of the myths is nonetheless profound. Water is the unformed reality out of which matter appears, and the descent into the abyss is analogous to baptism, in that it is at once a cleansing and a creative act. "In the beginning there was nothing but water," says a Huron myth.

Similarly, the Hindu *Vishnu Purana* tells of an original chaos of waters:

> He, the Lord, concluding that within the waters lay the earth, and being desirous to raise it up. . . . He, the supporter of spiritual and material being, plunged into the ocean.[12]

The Maidu tribe of California, in their Creation myth, tell of Earth Diver, Turtle, and two other cosmic beings, Father-of-the-Secret-Society and Earth-Initiate, who is a mysterious presence from above:

> In the beginning there was no sun, no moon, no stars. All was dark, and everywhere there was only water. A raft came floating on the water. It came from the north, and in it were two persons, Turtle and Father-of-the-Secret-Society. The stream flowed very rapidly. Then from the sky a rope of feathers was let down, and down it came Earth-Initiate. When he reached the end of the rope, he tied it to the bow of the raft, and stepped in. His face was covered and was never seen, but his body shone like the sun. He

sat down, and for a long time said nothing. At last the Turtle said, "Where do you come from?" and Earth-Initiate answered, "I come from above." Then Turtle said, "Brother, can you not make for me some good dry land, so that I may sometimes come up out of the water?" . . . Earth-Initiate replied, "You want to have some dry land: well, how am I going to get any earth to make it out of?" Turtle answered, "If you will tie a rock about my left arm, I'll dive for some." Earth-Initiate did as Turtle asked, and then, reaching around, took the end of a rope from somewhere, and tied it to the Turtle. . . .

Turtle was gone a long time. He was gone six years; and when he came up, he was covered with green slime, he had been down so long. When he reached the top of the water, the only earth he had was a very little under his nails; the rest had all washed away. Earth-Initiate took with his right hand a stone knife from under his left armpit, and carefully scraped the earth out from under Turtle's nails. He put the earth in the palm of his hand, and rolled it about till it was round; it was as large as a small pebble. He laid it on the stern of the raft. By and by he went to look at it: it had not grown at all. The third time he went to look at it, it had grown so that it could be spanned by the arms. The fourth time he looked, it was as big as the world, the raft was aground, and all around were mountains as far as he could see.[13]

Later in the myth, Earth-Initiate—who, rather than Turtle, is the real Creator-figure of the story—makes the first human beings:

By and by there came to be a good many people. Earth-Initiate had wanted to have everything comfortable and easy for people, so that none of them should have to work. All fruits were easy to obtain, no one was ever to get sick and die. As the people grew numerous, Earth-Initiate did not come as often as formerly. . . . He went away. He left in the night, and went up above.[14]

Here already we see, as we shall again in so many other instances, the universal pattern of Paradise followed by the separation of the divine from the human.

The Emergence

The Emergence myth centers around the symbolism of Mother Earth, from which human beings emerge through various stages or levels of underworld. Emergence myths are found among the Hopi, Navajo, Pueblo, and Pawnee Native Americans, and certain groups in the South Pacific islands. In the Emergence myth the Earth is the fertile source of being, containing within herself the essences and potencies of all life. The lower world is described not as a hell, but as a previous mode of existence, a womblike Paradise. Neither is the underworld considered to be a literal subterranean cavern, but rather a place "where at death we will all return," another plane of existence "under"—that is, *underlying*—the perceptible physical world. Sun or Corn is often the agent of transformation and quickening, leading the First People up into the light. "Before the World was we were all within the Earth," begins a Pawnee myth; "Mother corn caused movement. She gave life."[15]

In part, the Emergence myth is a metaphor for the journey from a spiritual plane of existence into manifestation in the material world. But the myth also epitomizes the role of the feminine in Creation: it is a symbol and a memory of the primordial Mother, the Earth herself, as she originally was—fresh, new, fertile, the source of all form, the receptacle of all seeds, the nurturer of all life. The tale is told from the perspective of the Creation, emerging from the womb of Earth Mother.

Not only are there but a few basic themes expressed through all of the hundreds of the world's apparently independent mythologies, but even these few themes tend to flow together as tributaries in the description of the one universal creative process. As we gain familiarity with the mythic archetypes of Creation, we see ever more clearly how all proceed from a single source. While a particular myth might expand especially on one episode in the great Story, we are nearly always able to recognize other episodes and elements latent in its seemingly unimportant details. It is when we see the Story as one whole that all of the elements and episodes make sense.

Lucas Cranach the elder, *The Garden of Eden* (1530).

In the beginning there is One—a preexisting Intelligence, alone and limitless. The One, in which the polarities of existence are united in perfect harmony, exerts a conscious act of will and becomes Two—masculine and feminine, active and receptive, Heaven and Earth. The Two work as equal partners in initiating the cyclic cosmic pulsations from which all life emanates.

The reciprocal—one could say sexual—interplay of the Two generates a multiplicity of divine beings, whose further activity, based in the same creative principles, results in the appearance of a manifest Universe of infinite scope and detail. The divine beings plunge into the watery abyss of chaos and return with the first seeds of physical form. Attaching themselves to these nuclei of substance, they continue to gather material about themselves and gradually emerge from the inner, invisible realms of eternity into the visible, tangible world of space and time.

Through this grand process, the One Intelligence differentiates itself into a myriad of self-conscious beings incarnate in material form. And thus there is generated a Universe of limitless diversity, of which each minute part is grounded in a single ultimate Reality.

The Origin of Human Beings

Myths of the origin of human beings are generally of two types: creation from clay or dust, and descent from Heaven. Occasionally, a single myth will incorporate both themes, for they are neither mutually exclusive nor contradictory. Just as the Earth-Diver and Creation-from-Nothing myths describe Creation from the perspective of the Creator while the Emergence myth describes the same process from the view of that which has been created, the descent-from-Heaven myth recounts human origins from the standpoint of the divine while the creation-from-clay story describes the process from an earthly perspective.

The creation from clay is familiar from the Genesis account (2:7), in which the Lord formed man "out of the dust of the ground, and breathed into his nostrils the breath of life; and man became a living soul." But there are many variations on the theme. Among many South American Indian tribes, the first man is shaped from clay or wood not by the Supreme Being but by a culture hero. The Miwok of California say that man was created by a committee of animals, each desiring to shape a lump of clay in its own image. The Crow Indians of the northern plains say that the Great One came down from Sky-land to the Earth-land to fashion human beings from clay, and had to repeat the process three times before he succeeded. And, according to the Maoris of New Zealand, the Creator, Tane, used his own blood to moisten the clay.

Among nearly all of the variants on the creation-from-clay story, the *breath of life* is a common feature. For example, according to a Hawaiian myth, Kane and Ku breathed into the nostrils and Lono into the mouth of a clay image, which thereupon became a living being. In an Australian Creation story, Bunjil, the All-Father of the southeastern tribes, is said to have made two clay images, male and female, which he shaped onto pieces of bark. He looked at them, was pleased, and danced around them for joy. Finally he lay down on them and blew into their mouths, noses, and navels, after which they stirred and arose. Likewise, the natives of the Kei islands of Indonesia say that their ancestors were fashioned out of clay by the Creator, Dooadlera, who breathed life into the earthen figures.

In many languages, the words for "spirit" and "breath" are identical. Creation-from-clay myths imply that the breath within us—the essence of our being, our life—is a divine gift, a spark of deity. "I am Osiris," declares the God of ancient Egypt. "I enter in and reappear through you, I decay in you, I grow in you."[16] The fundamental message of the Hindu Upanishads, similarly, is that Atman (the individual's innermost Self) is identical with Brahman (the ultimate Cause of All-That-Is). *Tat tvam asi*—"That thou art"—perhaps the most famous phrase in Sanskrit, is a proclamation of this underlying oneness of God and man, a oneness that ultimately extends to all creation:

> *You are everything . . .*
> *O self of all beings!*
> *From the Creator (Brahmâ) to the blade of grass*
> *all is your body, visible and invisible,*
> *divided by space and time. . . .*
> *O Transcendent Self! We bow to you as the Cause of*

causes, the principal shape beyond compare, beyond Nature
(pradhâna) and Intellect. . . .
We bow to you, the birthless, the indestructible,
You are the ever-present within all things,
as the intrinsic principle of all.
We bow to you, resplendent Indweller (Vâsudeva)!
the seed of all that is![17]

While the story of the animation of clay by an all-powerful Creator describes the union of spirit and matter from creation's standpoint
(matter receiving the breath of spirit), the story of the descent of spirit
beings to Earth, sometimes described as their taking on coats of flesh,
describes the same process from the heavenly view of the Creator.
According to the Molama clan of the Zulu, their remotest ancestors
were a man and woman who came down from the sky and alighted on
a certain hill. A similar idea is met with among the Wakuluwe, who
live between lakes Nyasa and Tanganyika; they say that the first
human couple came down from Heaven and produced their offspring
from parts of their bodies.

The examples one could cite are almost endless: according to a
myth of the Caribs of Venezuela, "At first the earth was very soft. . . .
The first man, named Louquo, came down from the sky and, after
living on the earth and producing many children, he returned to his
sky home. When his descendants die they too ascend to the heavens,
and there become stars."[18] In Orinoco and Guiana, Latin America, we
find a similar tradition:

> Long ago, when Warau lived in the happy hunting-grounds
> above the sky, Okonorote, a young hunter, shot an arrow which
> missed its mark and was lost; searching for it, he found a hole
> through which it had fallen; and looking down, he beheld the
> earth beneath, with game-filled forests and savannahs. By means
> of a cotton rope he visited the lands below, and upon his return
> his reports were such as to induce the whole Warau tribe to
> follow him thither; but one unlucky [woman], too stout to
> squeeze through, was stuck in the hole, and the Warau were thus
> prevented from ever returning to the sky-world.[19]

The Omaha Indians of the North American plains also believed in
the heavenly or spiritual preexistence of human beings prior to their

appearance on Earth in physical form. "At the beginning," they say, "all things were in the mind of Wakonda."

> All creatures, including man, were spirits. They moved about in space between earth and the stars (the heavens). They were seeking a place where they could come into bodily existence. . . . Then they descended to the earth. They saw that it was covered with water. They floated through the air to the north, the east, the south and the west, and found no dry land. . . . Suddenly from the midst of the water uprose a great rock. It burst into flames and the waters floated into the air in clouds. The hosts of the spirits descended and became flesh and blood. They fed on the seeds of the grasses and the fruits of the trees, and the land vibrated with their expressions of joy and gratitude to Wakonda, the maker of all things.[20]

The Malagasy of Madagascar agree that at first, human beings and all creatures lived in the sky with God. Among the natives of Oceania, people were often spoken of as having descended from gods who came down to live on Earth.

In eastern Indonesia, it is said that the original ancestors came down from the sky, which was formerly nearer to the Earth, by means of a tree or a vine. The idea of a heavenly origin appears also on the island of Nias, to the west. The Toba Batak of Sumatra say that humankind is descended from a divine maiden who came down to Earth and the heavenly hero who followed her. In the southern Celebes, the Bugi of Macassar say that their people descended from the son of the Heaven-deity and his six wives, much as the ancient Greeks said that humankind descended from the god Zeus and his wives. Among the Ifugao in Luzon, we also find the belief in a direct descent from deities. The Ifugao of Kiangan say that the first son of Wigan, called Kabigat, went from the sky-region, Hudog, to the Earth World. Myths according a divine origin to humankind are found also in the Carolines, where it is said that Ligobund descended from the sky to the Earth and there gave birth to three children, who became the ancestors of humanity. And Hawaiian mythology recognizes a prehuman period when spirits alone peopled first the sea and then the land.

Both the story of the breath of life and the tradition of the divine ancestors describe an original connection between humankind and the spiritual world. And both imply an original intent on the part of the Creator-ancestors. The understanding that humankind was created—or came down from Heaven—to fulfill a unique role in the world is extremely widespread. Joseph Epes Brown notes that, according to most Native American traditions,

> although humans were created last of all the creatures, they are also the "axis," and thus in a sense the first. For if each animal reflects particular aspects of the Great Spirit, human beings, on the contrary, may include within themselves all the aspects. A human being is thus a totality, bearing the Universe within himself or herself and through the intellect having the potential capacity to live in continual awareness of this reality.[21]

Humankind is made in the image and likeness of God, in order to serve as the Creator's means of expression on Earth. The Creator dwells within the heart of each human being. This primal awareness of a sacred link between the essence of humanity and a greater spiritual Being is reflected in the following Navajo song. The word *hozhoni* expresses the relation between macrocosm and microcosm, between the spirit of the Earth and humankind:

Hozhoni, hozhoni, hozhoni
Hozhoni, hozhoni, hozhoni
The Earth, its life am I, hozhoni, hozhoni
The Earth, its feet are my feet, hozhoni, hozhoni
The Earth, its legs are my legs, hozhoni, hozhoni
The Earth, its body is my body, hozhoni, hozhoni
The Earth, its thoughts are my thoughts, hozhoni, hozhoni
The Earth, its speech is my speech, hozhoni, hozhoni
The Earth, its down-feathers are my down-feathers, hozhoni, hozhoni
The sky, its life am I, hozhoni, hozhoni—
The mountians, their life am I—
Rain-mountain, its life am I—
Changing-woman, her life am I—
The Sun, its life am I—
Talking God, his life am I—
House God, his life am I—
White corn, its life am I—

Yellow corn, its life am I—
The corn beetle, its life am I—
Hozhoni, hozhoni, hozhoni
Hozhoni, hozhoni, hozhoni[22]

The Lakota (Sioux) medicine man Black Elk expressed the same thought with his characteristic eloquence:

> Peace . . . comes within the souls of men when they realize their relationship, their oneness, with the Universe and all its powers, and when they realize that at the center of the Universe dwells *Wakan-Tanka*, and that this center is really everywhere, it is within each of us.[23]

According to the universal creation story, this sense of oneness among humankind, Deity, Nature, and Cosmos was at first complete. In the days when the world was fresh and new, full of power and vitality, human beings lived in a magical Paradise of ease and plenty, in perfect harmony both with God and with the animals. It was a time that all people in all nations would remember with envy and regret.

And the Lord God planted a garden eastward in Eden; and there he put the man whom he had formed. And out of the ground made the Lord God to grow every tree that is pleasant to the sight, and good for food; the tree of life also in the midst of the garden, and the tree of the knowledge of good and evil. . . . And the Lord God took the man and put him into the garden of Eden to dress it and to keep it.

GENESIS 2:8, 9, 15

CHAPTER · 3

In Search of Eden

HE IDEA THAT THE FIRST HUMAN BEINGS were happy, innocent, and wise is so widespread that we could begin a geographical survey of Paradise myths in virtually any inhabited place, with any ethnic group. Nevertheless, it seems inevitable that we should commence our search with what is by far the best-known example: the story of lost Eden. As we compare the Hebraic narrative with Paradise myths from other cultures, we will keep in mind the question raised at the end of chapter 1: *Did the myth originate in one region, spreading from there to other peoples and places by a process of borrowing and diffusion, or did it appear in many parts of the world spontaneously and independently?*

The Genesis account of Adam, Eve, the Garden, and the serpent has inspired generations of theologians and scholars; its imagery is part of the very sinew of Western civilization. It carries with it the resonance of millions of retellings. Yet, its exposition at the beginning of the Hebraic canon is so laconic as to require only a few sentences to recount. Eden was a place full of fruit-bearing trees, gold, and precious stones. It was the source of the Earth's sweet waters; the river flowing through it divided into four streams that flowed out to the four quarters of the world. God placed the first human beings there in the Garden of Eden to tend and keep it.

The Genesis text appears to be the conflation of two accounts. In the first (Genesis 1:26, 27), man and woman are created together. In the second (Genesis 2:7, 18-23), God makes Adam alone, then relieves the man's solitude by forming the beasts and birds, and finally

An early Christian Garden of Paradise. A cedar tree, surrounded by flying birds, is flanked by a wild goat, rosebushes, lilies, and ivy. Central frieze of a mosaic, end of fifth century A.D. Bitola, Museum of Heraclea.

the first woman, Eve. Afterward, the original couple lives naked and unashamed, in harmony with each other and with the animals.

For the moment, we need not concern ourselves with the meaning of the story. Instead, let us consider the Eden text simply as a literary document. *Who wrote it? Where did it come from? And when did it originate?*

There are two principal schools of thought regarding these questions. Fundamentalist commentators treat the Eden story as a factual and divinely inspired account recorded by Moses some 3500 years ago, describing events that occurred 25 centuries previously. According to this still-common belief, all similar narratives from other cultural traditions must either be early borrowings from the original Mosaic version or garbled memories preserved by the scattered descendants of Noah's sons. In short, the story of Adam and Eve as preserved in Genesis is seen as literal truth, pure and simple.

On the other hand, most modern students of biblical criticism tend to see the Eden story as a composite of texts written or compiled by Israelite priests between the ninth and fourth centuries B.C., stories that in turn had probably been derived from or inspired by earlier Mesopotamian myths. Modern literary, historical, and textual critics seek to establish the original texts of the biblical documents and to reach conclusions about their structure, date, and authorship on the basis both of internal evidence (vocabulary, style, and genre) and of comparison with other texts and related archaeological evidence. While, as we shall see, this approach has yet to yield a final answer to the question of the Eden story's origins, it does provide a point of entry—as good as any—to the Paradise trail.

Sumeria and Dilmun

According to linguists, the Hebrews probably borrowed the word *eden* from the Sumerians, who occupied the Tigris-Euphrates valley from about the fifth to the third millennium B.C. To the Sumerians, *eden* meant "fertile plain." But the word may have an even older source. In 1943, Assyriologist Benno Landsberger theorized that the Sumerian names corresponding with "Eden" and "Adam" were borrowed from a still more ancient preliterate Mesopotamian cultural group known as the Al-Ubaid. The Ubaidi seem to have founded the oldest southern Mesopotamian cities, Eridu and Uruk, around 5000 B.C. according to most authorities.

Since the Ubaidi themselves do not seem to have had a written language, we will probably never know whether they were indeed the ultimate source of the biblical Eden narrative. But even the idea that the elements of the Genesis story derive from fragments of early Mesopotamian literary epics—as is accepted by most Bible scholars—is not easily proven. The closest parallel to the Eden story discernible in Sumerian texts is a series of inscriptions describing a land to the east called Dilmun. While the biblical Eden and the Sumerian Dilmun share an easterly location and are places of peace and abundance, scholars have—often to their disappointment—found more dissimilarities than likenesses between the two mythical Paradises.

The Sumerians, who for many decades were credited with the invention of civilization, were a culture surrounded by mystery. While other ancient peoples in the region can be traced either to

Indo-Iranian or Semitic stock, the Sumerians were a group unto themselves. Their documents were written in what linguists call a "language isolate," meaning that it has no apparent relation to any other known tongue. When the Sumerians appeared on the delta of the Tigris and Euphrates rivers around 4000 B.C., they brought with them agriculture, writing, metallurgy, trade, temples, priests, laws, and a mythological literature that told of how the god Enki and his wife were placed in the magical land of Dilmun to institute "a sinless age of complete happiness":

> That place was pure, that place was clean.
> In Dilmun the raven croaked not.
> The kite shrieked not kite-like.
> The lion mangled not.
> The wolf ravaged not the lambs. . . .
> None caused the doves to fly away.

The Sumerians had migrated to Mesopotamia. Therefore, it is possible that the myth of Dilmun is an idealized description of their former home. In some passages Dilmun is described as having existed in the distant past:

> Once upon a time, there was no snake, there was no scorpion,
> There was no hyena, there was no lion,
> There was no wild dog, no wolf,
> There was no fear, no terror,
> Man had no rival.
> Once upon a time . . .
> The whole universe, the people in unison
> To Enlil in one tongue gave praise.

In other passages Dilmun is described as a "land of the living," reserved for gods or for those who, like Ziusudra (the Sumerian mythic equivalent of Noah), have been given "life like a god."

On still other occasions, however, Dilmun is described as a country with which Sumeria had contemporary trade relations. Many archaeologists now believe that Dilmun was located on the islands of Bahrain and Failaka or the eastern coast of Saudi Arabia, which were hubs of international trade during the time when Sumeria still dominated the region.[1] Yet the characterization of Dilmun as an international trade center hardly explains why it was so often referred to in magical and paradisal terms.

The Babylonians, successors to the Sumerians, also located their "land of the living" in Dilmun. Here was the "abode of the immortals," where Utnapishtim (the Babylonian Noah figure) and his wife were allowed to live after the Flood.

In short, researchers have arrived at no agreement as to the location or even the nature of Dilmun. The general parallels between the Eden and Dilmun texts (with both describing a land of peace and immortality) are hardly convincing evidence of their common origin. The Dilmun story shares neither *dramatis personae* nor plot with the Eden narrative; in it there is no serpent, no forbidden fruit, and no primordial couple. Much closer parallels to the Eden story can be found in myths from farther afield. In ancient Persia or Iran, for example, we find the tradition of a universal ancestor reminiscent of the biblical Adam.

The Iranian Garden

The word *paradise* itself comes from the Avestan (Old Iranian) word *Pairi-daeza*, meaning a walled or enclosed garden. The prototype of all such gardens was that of Yima, the first man. According to folklorist Albert Carnoy, "The story of Yima is the most interesting and the only extensive myth of the Iranians, and it is certain that the legend dates back to Aryan, or at least to Indo-Iranian, times."[2]

It is said of Yima that "he was the most glorious of all mankind . . . and so powerful that he gave men and beasts immortality."[3] Eventually, Yima became the Persians' king of the dead, in whom good souls would take refuge during the final apocalyptic battle between the powers of good and evil.

Yima's Garden was situated on a mythical mountain, the source of the Water of Life, where there grew magical trees, including a Tree of Life. Yima's Age was a time of perfection:

In the reign of Yima the valiant there was neither heat nor cold, neither old age nor death, nor disease. . . . Father and son walked together, each looking but fifteen years of age, or so did they appear.[4]

In the Avesta, the sacred book of Zoroastrianism, the Garden of Yima is also called Airyana Vaejo, which is described as a perfect country with a mild climate. But the Age of Yima was brought to an end by the appearance of Angra Mainyu (Ahriman), the embodiment of evil, who caused a catastrophic winter to descend on the land. The original Garden was lost in snow and ice.

The Iranians' Yima tradition parallels the Hebrew Eden story in several details. Both speak of a Tree of Life, a River of Life, a singular original man (Adam/Yima), a Garden, and a Fall. Yet, culturally the ancient Iranians had more in common with the Indic peoples than with the Sumerians, Babylonians, or Hebrews. Scholars agree that Yima was the Iranian equivalent of the Hindu Yama, the first mortal being and preparer of the kingdom of the departed. But no direct connection can be traced between Yima and the Adam of Genesis.

The Age of Rê

R. T. Rundle Clark, in his *Myth and Symbol in Ancient Egypt*, tells us that Egyptian mythology is fundamentally different from other Middle Eastern literature:

> Most early Egyptian myths are quite short episodes and can be told in one or two sentences. They are not long involved relations like those which have been recovered from the contemporary Sumerians of Mesopotamia.[5]

Yet, like the Sumerians, Hebrews, and Iranians, the Egyptians had a Paradise myth of their own.

For the Egyptians, all life was predicated on the reenactment of the events of the First Time (Tep Zepi), which, according to Rundle Clark, constituted "a golden age of absolute perfection—'before rage or clamour or strife or uproar had come about.' No death, disease, or disaster occurred in this blissful epoch, sometimes known as the time of Rê (the god of the Sun)."[6] Lenormant says that

> among the Egyptians the terrestrial reign of the god Ra, who inaugurated the existence of the world and of human life, was a Golden Age, to which they continually looked back with regret

The Sun-god Rê

and envy: to assert the superiority of anything above all that imagination could set forth, it was sufficient to affirm that "its like had never been seen since the days of the god Ra."[7]

One early Egyptian text says of the primeval gods that

order was established in their time and truth . . . came forth from heaven in their days. It united itself with those who were on earth. The land was in abundance; bodies were full; there was no year of hunger in the Two Lands. Walls did not fall; thorns did not pierce in the time of the Primeval Gods.[8]

Another text says that "there was no unrighteousness in the land, no crocodile seized, no snake bit in the time of the First Gods."[9] Rundle Clark emphasizes that the partial restoration of this Golden Age was the chief object of ritual in the Egyptian religion.

But Egyptian mythology mentions few details that might relate it to the biblical Paradise story. Therefore, while the influence of Egyp-

An Egyptian celestial tree, planted in the "waters of the depths," from which a goddess distributes the food and drink of immortality. Detail from a painting of the thirteenth century B.C.

tian religious and mythological motifs can be traced in Greek philosophy and early Gnostic literature, no one has pointed to the Tep Zepi of the Egyptians as a prototype for the Eden of the Hebrews.

The Golden Race

Next to the biblical Eden narrative, the Paradise story that has had the greatest impact on the Western world is the Greek legend of the Golden Age. The term "Golden Age" is a translation of Ovid's Latin phrase *aetas aurea*, which in turn referred to the time of the "golden race" described by the Greek poet Hesiod in his moralizing epic, *Works and Days*. Writing probably in the eighth century B.C., Hesiod lamented the degenerate condition of his contemporary society, which venal and rapacious barons ruled by force, extracting bribes and tribute from the rural populace. Though profoundly pessimistic of the future—"Zeus will destroy this generation of mortals"—Hesiod idealized the remotest past in a passage that was to spawn scores of elaborations by later generations of Greek and Roman philosophers and poets, and thousands of analyses and interpretations by still later generations of European and American scholars:

> First of all the deathless gods having homes on Olympus made a golden race of mortal men. These lived in the time of Cronus when he was king in heaven. Like gods they lived with hearts free from sorrow and remote from toil and grief; nor was miserable age their lot, but always unwearied in feet and hands they made merry in feasting, beyond the reach of all evils. And when they died, it was as though they were given over to sleep. And all good things were theirs. For the fruitful earth spontaneously bore them abundant fruit without stint. And they lived in ease and peace upon their lands with many good things, rich in flocks and beloved of the blessed gods.[10]

According to Hesiod, the Golden Age was followed by the Ages of Silver, Brass, Heroes, and Iron, of which the last is the present, most decadent age. Since his writings are among the earliest surviving literary sources of Greek mythology, we may never know whether this Boeotian farmer invented the story of the Ages of Man or whether, as seems more likely, he was merely setting down for posterity an already ancient belief. In either case, the idea of the original blessedness of human beings and their subsequent degeneration seems to have been generally accepted as historical fact by most Greeks and Romans.

Unlike the mythologies of most other ancient cultures, that of Greece was recorded and commented upon by many authors whose names have been preserved for us. We may never know who wrote the passages about the *yugas* in the *Mahabharata*, but concerning the Greek tradition of the Golden Age we have statements from some of the most famous authors of antiquity.

Western philosophy owes an incalculable debt to Plato, in whose works we find the paradisal current running clear and strong. In the *Laws*, Plato writes that "we must do all we can to imitate the life which is said to have existed in the days of Cronus; and in so far as the immortal element dwells in us, to that we must hearken, both in private and public life."[11] In *The Statesman*, Plato offers his account of human history. In outline, it consists of a time of Paradise, during which the world is under the governance of God; the separation of the world from God; the entry of evil into the world, followed by decay and destruction; and finally the present age, in which humans, though fundamentally miserable, are able to civilize themselves after a fashion through the gifts of Prometheus.

The third-century B.C. Neoplatonist Porphyry said that the Greek philosopher Dicaearchus, of the late fourth century B.C., spoke of

> men of the earliest age, who were akin to the gods and were by nature the best men and lived the best life, so that they are regarded as a golden race in comparison with the men of the present time . . . of these primeval men he says that they took the life of no animal. . . . Dicaearchus tells us of what sort the life of that Age of Cronus was: if it is to be taken as having really existed and not as an idle tale, when the too mythical parts of the story are eliminated it may by the use of reason be reduced to a natural sense. For all things then presumably grew spontaneously, since the men of that time themselves produced nothing, having invented neither agriculture nor any other art. It was for this reason that they lived a life of leisure, without care or toil, and also—if the doctrine of the most eminent medical men is to be accepted—without disease. . . . And there were no wars or feuds between them; for there existed among them no objects of competition of such value as to give anyone a motive to seek to obtain them by those means. Thus it was that their whole life was one of leisure, of freedom from care about the satisfaction of their needs, of health and peace and friendship. Consequently this manner of life of theirs naturally came to be longed for by men of later times who, because of the greatness of their desires, had become subject to many evils. . . . All this, says Dicaearchus, is not asserted merely by us, but by those who have thoroughly investigated the history of early times.[12]

The classical Roman authors Ovid, Cratinus, Pausanias, Tibullus, Virgil, and Seneca expanded freely on Hesiod's story of the original golden race, always emphasizing those qualities that characterize the benefits of the simple, primitive life—freedom, self-sufficiency, and lack of dependence on technology and complex social organization. Ovid's *Metamorphoses* was for centuries standard fare in all European schools, and his description of the Golden Age in *Book I* became the definitive form of the myth for the Middle Ages and the Renaissance:

> The first age was golden. In it faith and righteousness were cherished by men of their own free will without judges or laws. Penalties and fears there were none, nor were threatening words inscribed on unchanging bronze; nor did the suppliant crowd fear the words of its judge, but they were safe without protectors. Not yet did the pine cut from its mountain tops descend into the flowing waters to visit foreign lands, nor did deep trenches gird the town, nor were there straight trumpets, nor horns of twisted brass, nor helmets, nor swords. Without the use of soldiers the peoples in safety enjoyed their sweet repose. Earth herself, unburdened and untouched by the hoe and unwounded by the ploughshare, gave all things freely. . . . Spring was eternal . . . untilled the earth bore its fruits and the unploughed field grew hoary with heavy ears of wheat.[13]

Elsewhere, Ovid speaks of the peaceful amity of Nature herself, before the degeneration of humankind. "That ancient age," he writes,

> to which we have given the name of Golden, was blessed with the fruit of trees and the herbs which the soil brings forth, and it did not pollute its mouth with gore. Then the birds in safety winged their way through the air and the hare fearlessly wandered through the fields, nor was the fish caught through its witlessness. There were no snares, and none feared treachery, but all was full of peace.[14]

As we have seen, the Western world has a heritage of at least five apparently independent traditions of an original Paradise: the Hebraic Garden of Eden, the Sumerian Dilmun, the Iranian Garden of Yima, the Egyptian Tep Zepi, and the Greek Golden Age. There does not appear to be a traceable connection between any of them. Two of these traditions, the Hebraic and the Greek, continue to shape Western values and ideals. In Part Two, we will explore the influence of these two traditions, particularly on the development of European and American literature and social theory.

But it is not Western civilization alone that has been shaped by the Paradise myth; the great civilizations of the Orient have, too.

Paradises of the East

The ancient bards of India described the First Age, the Krita Yuga, in terms similar to those used by Hesiod in his story of the golden race. The Hindus remember four *yugas* or ages: following the Krita were the Treta, the Dvapara, and the Kali. Like the Greeks, the Indians believed that the sequence of the ages follows a process of moral degeneration, and said that we are now living in the last, most deca-dent and materialistic *yuga*. According to the epic historical poem, the *Mahabharata:*

> The Krita Yuga [Perfect Age] was so named because there was but one religion, and all men were saintly: therefore they were not required to perform religious ceremonies. Holiness never grew less, and the people did not decrease. There were no gods in the Krita Yuga, and there were no demons.... Men neither bought nor sold; there were no poor and no rich; there was no need to labour, because all that men required was obtained by the power of will; the chief virtue was the abandonment of all worldly desires. The Krita Yuga was without disease; there was no lessening with the years; there was no hatred, or vanity, or evil thought whatsoever; no sorrow, no fear. All mankind could ob-tain to supreme blessedness.[15]

There is a similar passage in the *Vaya Purana:*

> In the Krita age human beings appropriated food which was produced from the essence of the earth.... They were character-ized neither by righteousness nor unrighteousness; they were marked by no distinctions.... They were produced each with authority over himself.... They suffered no impediments, no susceptibilities to the pairs of opposites (like pleasure and pain, cold and heat), and no fatigue. They frequented the mountains and seas, and did not dwell in houses. They never sorrowed, were

full of the quality of goodness, and supremely happy; they moved about at will and lived in continual delight. . . . Produced from the essence of the earth, the things which those people desired sprang up from the earth everywhere and always, when thought of. That perfection of theirs both produced strength and beauty and annihilated disease. With bodies which needed no decoration, they enjoyed perpetual youth. . . . Then truth, contentment, patience, satisfaction, happiness and self-command prevailed. . . . There existed among them no such things as gain or loss, friendship or enmity, liking or dislike.[16]

In China, we again find the Paradise myth flavored somewhat according to local cultural sensibilities, but nevertheless characterizing humankind's earliest condition as one of ease, plenty, and freedom. Taoist philosophy, profoundly and often sardonically primitivist, has permeated Chinese thought for at least the last two and a half millennia. According to the earliest Taoist sages, Lao Tzu and Chuang Tzu, it is Nature herself who is wise, and the intelligent man knows better than to impose on her creative rhythms. "Profound intelligence," according to Lao Tzu, "is that penetrating and pervading power to restore all things to their original harmony."[17]

In all the canonical Taoist writings, there is the implicit understanding that in the earliest age "the whole creation enjoyed a state of happiness. . . , all things grew without labour; and a universal fertility prevailed."[18] According to Lao Tzu, "In primitive times, intelligent men had an intuitively penetrating grasp of reality which could not be stated in words."[19] The identification of intelligence with Nature's way, together with a concern for the restoration of all things to their original harmony, are hallmark themes that reemerge in Confucianism and Zen Buddhism, and that represent the core of Chinese wisdom.

The Paradise traditions of India and China share certain similarities with that of ancient Greece. Could there have been a direct influence of one upon the others? If so, that influence would have had to come early, probably around the time of the earliest development of agriculture, when great migrations were occurring throughout Europe, Asia, and the Americas. Because this was so long ago, however, there is really no definitive answer to the question.

Primitivism among the Primitives

Civilized peoples have always maintained myths glorifying the happy life of the distant past when human beings lived in harmony among themselves, with the animals, and, indeed, with all of Nature and Cosmos. But such memories are not restricted to civilized cultures. When we look to the traditions of Australian, Native American, and African tribes, many of which retained a simple gatherer-hunter existence well into the modern era, we again find Paradise myths with similar themes: a former oneness with Nature, a former abundance of food, a former simple and supremely satisfying way of life. Eliade comments that

> the savages regarded themselves, neither more nor less than if they had been Western Christians, as beings in a "fallen" condition, by contrast with a fabulously happy situation in the past. Their actual condition was not their original one: it had been brought about by a catastrophe that had occurred *in illo tempore* [in those times]. Before that disaster, man had enjoyed a life which was not dissimilar from that of Adam before he sinned.[20]

In North America, for example, there is a Cheyenne myth that tells of a paradisal age when human beings were naked and innocent amid fields of plenty. This age was followed by a time of flood, war, and famine, which ensued from the gift of knowledge.[21] West Coast lore is in great part composed of tales of the First People, who were manlike in form and conduct but who existed prior to the creation of humankind as presently constituted. The present order began with the catastrophic close of the age of the First People. According to the Hopi, the people, birds, and animals of that First Age "all suckled at the breast of their Mother Earth, who gave them her milk of grass, seeds, fruit, and corn, and they all felt as one, people and the animals."[22]

Similar stories of a community of First People appear throughout South and Central America. "In a time long past, so long past that even the grandmothers of our grandmothers were not yet born," say the Caribs of Surinam,

> the world was quite other than what it is today: the trees were forever in fruit; the animals lived in perfect harmony, and the

little agouti played fearlessly with the beard of the jaguar; the serpents had no venom; the rivers flowed evenly, without drought or flood; and even the waters of cascades glided gently down from the high rocks.[23]

In Orinoco and Guiana, the natives say that

in the beginning of this world the birds and beasts were created by Makonaima—the great spirit whom no man had seen. They, at that time, were all endowed with the gift of speech. Sigu, the son of Makonaima, was placed to rule over them. All lived in harmony together and submitted to his gentle dominion.[24]

The South American Indians of Gran Chaco and Amazonia say that in the earliest times, there was a place where work was unknown; the fields produced abundant food untended. When the people there grew old, they did not die but instead were rejuvenated. But today, they say, the people no longer remember the way to this "Happy Place."[25]

The native Australians also have a Paradise tradition, which they preserve in their memories of the "Dreamtime" that they believe occurred in the indeterminably distant past. The Dreamtime is not just the era of the primordial Creator-ancestors; it is also a transcendent, magical dimension of existence accessible in the present through altered states of consciousness. Eliade writes that

the Australians consider that their mythical ancestors lived during a golden age, in an earthly Paradise in which game abounded and the notions of good and evil were practically unknown. It is this paradisal world that the Australians attempt to reactualize during certain festivals, when laws and prohibitions are suspended.[26]

The Aborigines believe implicitly and unquestioningly in the superiority of their Dreamtime ancestors, who had many miraculous powers that they themselves have lost.

The tribes of central and southern Africa preserved myths of an original time when the celestial God and human beings were friends, before the separation of Heaven and Earth. It was an age that was typified in the saying of the Ngombe tribe of Zaire: "In the beginning there were no men on earth. The people lived in the sky with Akongo

and they were happy."[27] Ethnologist Paul Schebesta recorded the
following tradition from the Bambuti Pygmies of central Africa:

> After God had created the world and men, he dwelt among
> them. He called them his children. They gave him the name of
> father. . . . He showed himself a good father to men for he so
> placed them in this world that they could live without much
> effort and were above all free from care and fear. Neither ele-
> ments nor animals were inimical to man and foodstuffs grew
> ready to his hand. In short, the world was a paradise as long as
> God dwelt among men. He was not visible to them but he was in
> their midst and spoke to them.[28]

Summarizing African myths about the First Age, folklorist Herman
Baumann wrote:

> In the view of the natives, everything that happened in the
> primal age was different from today: people lived forever and
> never died; they understood the language of animals and lived at
> peace with them; they knew no labor and had food in plenitude,
> the effortless gathering of which guaranteed them a life without
> care; there was no sexuality and no reproduction—in brief, they
> knew nothing of all those fundamental factors and attitudes
> which move people today.[29]

It was only when the people set themselves against the other creatures
that God was driven away and the original harmony of Nature was
destroyed.

Baumann remarks that while the African Paradise tradition is
remarkably similar to that of the ancient Hebrews, there is no possibility that it was merely borrowed from missionaries. Anthropologist
Wilhelm Koppers agrees: "We are probably nearer the mark if we
assume that the Bible version as well as the others derive from an
older, common source."[30]

Our search has taken us from Mesopotamia to Iran, Egypt, India,
China, Australia, North and South America, and Africa. Everywhere,

we have encountered essentially the same myth—the story of a primordial era when humanity and Nature enjoyed a condition of peace, happiness, and abundance. As for our quest for a geographical point of origin for the myth, we must conclude that if a single cultural source did exist, the diffusion from that source must have occurred so long ago that the process of borrowing is now impossible to trace. The myths can just as easily be interpreted as having originated independently in many locations.

In our geographical survey of Paradise myths, we have considered only the broadest outline of the story; we have as yet hardly touched upon the specific images that are reiterated in all its countless versions. It is largely to these characteristic details, which we shall consider next, that the myth owes its profound and universal appeal.

The Nature of Visionary Fancy or Imagination, is very little known, & the Eternal nature & permanence of its ever Existent Images is considered as less permanent than the things of Vegetative and Generative Nature; yet the Oak dies as well as the Lettuce, but its Eternal Image & Individuality never dies but returns by its seed; just so the Imaginative Image returns by the seed of Contemplative Thought.

WILLIAM BLAKE

Myth is the history of the soul.

WILLIAM IRWIN THOMPSON

CHAPTER · 4

Images of Paradise:
Common Themes

N MANY PACIFIC ISLANDS, one encounters myths that parallel the Eden story of Genesis in astonishing detail. While contact with missionaries has undoubtedly tainted the local folklore, much of the similarity in traditions antedates the first missionary contacts, as the following passages from Sir James Frazer's *Folklore in the Old Testament* suggest:

> A very generally received tradition in Tahiti was that the first human pair was made by Taaroa, the chief god. They say that after he had formed the world he created man out of red earth, which was also the food of mankind until bread-fruit was produced. Further, some say that one day Taaroa called for the man by name, and when he came he made him fall asleep. As he slept, the Creator took out one of his bones . . . and made of it a woman, whom he gave to the man to be his wife, and the pair became the progenitors of mankind.

Frazer notes that the missionary who recorded the myth assumed it to have been "a mere recital of the Mosaic account of creation, which they had heard from some European." But the Tahitians insisted otherwise. And Frazer comments that the same tradition, which dates to the time of the earliest missions to the island, has been recorded not just in Tahiti but in other parts of Polynesia as well.[1]

Thus, it is more than merely the general idea of an original age of happiness that appears in culture after culture throughout the world. Specific and unmistakable themes characterize the Paradise myth wherever we find it. As Wilhelm Koppers once wrote, "numerous as are the variations in the details of the story, there are certain fundamental elements that always recur."[2]

In this chapter we will explore these characteristic features of the Paradise myth—the landscape of magical rivers, trees, and mountains; the traditional placement of the paradisal age at the beginning of a series of world ages; the miraculous abilities, pristine character, and immortality of the First People; the presence on Earth of the God or Goddess; and also the presence of a wondrous bridge connecting Heaven and Earth.

In pondering these images, we enter a world steeped in nostalgia and longing. Here—in word pictures that seem inevitably to reappear in story after story, from pole to pole and continent to continent—is the universal, primordial description of humanity's happy and innocent beginnings.

The Magical Landscape

Upon entering the mythical world of Paradise, we notice first its unique and remarkable landscape: in narrative after narrative we find a description of four sacred rivers, along with a magical tree and/or a cosmic mountain.

The four sacred rivers—which, as we have seen, feature prominently in the biblical story of the Garden of Eden—appear also in the Navajo story of the Age of the Beginnings, when First Man and First Woman lived in a paradisal land later destroyed by a catastrophe. "In its centre," says the myth, "was a spring from which four streams flowed, one to each of the cardinal points."[3]

Kwen-lun, the Paradise mountain of the Chinese, likewise had a central fount from which flowed "in opposite directions the four great rivers of the world."[4] The Scandinavian *Edda* tells of four streams flowing from the spring Hvergelmir in the land of the gods; and the Siberian Kalmucks remember four rivers flowing from the central primordial Sea of Life toward the four points of the compass. The Hindu tradition repeats the image as well: according to the *Vishnu Purana*, the Paradise of Brahma is the site from which four magical streams flow in the four directions.

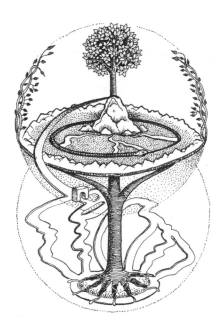

The cosmic tree of the Norse, Yggdrasil, links the three planes of existence—Asgard, Midgard, and Utgard.

The idea of a miraculous tree capable of conferring immortality is another theme we meet repeatedly in the Paradise stories of nearly all cultures. The Avesta of the ancient Iranians tells of how Ahura Mazda, the God of Light, planted the heavenly *haoma* tree on the mythical Mount Haraiti,[5] declaring, "Whoever eats of it becomes immortal."[6] In the Eden narrative in Genesis there are two trees, the Tree of Life and the Tree of the Knowledge of Good and Evil. The Babylonians told of a Tree of Life and a Tree of Truth, both located at the eastern entry to Heaven.

In Genesis, the Tree of the Knowledge of Good and Evil is at the center of the Garden; other traditions speak of a "world tree," which is the *axis mundi,* or pole of the world. The Altaic peoples of central Asia told of a giant fir growing from the Earth's navel, the branches of which rose to Heaven. The Scandinavians called the cosmic tree *Yggdrasil*—the Pillar of Heaven. And in India and China, as well as among many North American tribes, we hear of a cosmic axis variously described as a tree, pole, or pillar.

Tree of Life and Knowledge, bronze, India. On the central stem, the lotus-Sun-wheel is surmounted by a five-headed serpent. Two monkey-headed figures cling to the stem, which at its base is flanked by two bulls. Vigayanagar period, 1336–1546.

Innumerable peoples also speak of a cosmic mountain at the center of Paradise. In some traditions—the Egyptian, Iranian, and Eskimo, for example—the mountain replaces the central tree. In others, such as the Chinese, Hindu, and Siberian, the mountain is the site on which the tree is said to grow. Sumerian texts seem to connect the lost Paradise with a cosmic mountain—one text speaks of "the mountain of Dilmun, the place where the sun rises."[7] The legends of India located the origin of humankind at Mount Meru, the home of the gods and the place where Heaven and Earth meet. As mentioned earlier, the ancient Chinese called the cosmic mountain Kwen-lun, describing it as "a stupendous heaven-sustaining mountain"[8] on whose summit lay a celestial homeland. The Finns say that the First Man appeared, radiating light, on a cosmic mountain; this was the site of the original Paradise, the source of the four world-sustaining rivers and the place of perpetual spring. The pyramids of Egypt, Babylonia, and

Tree of Life: Design from a Goldi shaman's costume, Amur River, Siberia, late nineteenth century.

Mexico have been interpreted by Mircea Eliade as representations of the cosmic mountain, whose image is reflected also in the Greeks' Mount Olympus, the home of the gods.

World Ages

If the magical landscape fixes Paradise in space, its position in time is defined by its placement at the beginning of a series of world ages. We have already noted the Greek and Hindu conceptions of the ages or *yugas* of the world, respectively; there are also close parallels among other cultures. The Iranians, for example, knew four cosmic ages that, in a lost Mazdaean book, the *Sudkar-nask*, are referred to as the ages of gold, silver, steel, and "mixed with iron." In the Iranian conception, as

The Tree of the Universe. From a rubbing of a relief in the Chamber of the
Offerings, by Won Yong, China, 168 A.D.

in the Greek and Hindu, each age is a step in the world's deterioration,
a process that is leading to a final apocalyptic cleansing.[9]

The Mayans counted their world ages as consecutive Suns—
Water Sun, Earthquake Sun, Hurricane Sun, and Fire Sun—according
to the nature of the catastrophe that closed the epoch. The Hopi also
spoke of four worlds—Tokpela, Tokpa, Kuskurza, and Túwaquchi—
the first of which is described in paradisal terms. Following their
creation in the Tokpela world,

> the first people went their directions, were happy, and began to
> multiply. With the pristine wisdom granted them, they under-
> stood that the earth was a living entity like themselves. She was
> their mother; they were made from her flesh. . . . In their wisdom
> they also knew their father in two aspects. He was the Sun, the
> solar god of their universe. . . . Yet his was but the face through
> which looked Taiowa, their creator. . . . These universal entities
> were their real parents, their human parents being but the instru-
> ments through which their power was made manifest. . . . The

Two caprids feeding on the Tree of Life. Frieze from Gordium, Phrygia, sixth century B.C.

first people, then, understood the mystery of their parenthood. In their pristine wisdom they also understood their own structure and functions—the nature of man himself. . . . The first people knew no sickness. Not until evil entered the world did persons get sick in the body or head.[10]

Eventually some of the people forgot or ignored the Great Spirit's laws, and the Tokpela world was destroyed. The same fate met the second and third worlds as well.

In the Lakota (Sioux) system of ages, the world is protected by a great metaphoric buffalo, who stands at the western gate of the Universe and holds back the waters that periodically inundate the Earth. Every year the buffalo loses a hair on one of its legs; every age it loses a leg. When the buffalo has lost all its legs, the world is flooded and renewed.[11]

The landscape of Paradise and the ages of the world provide a setting in space and time for the unfoldment of a story. And just as that story's setting is a place and time of ultimate peace and beauty, its heroes and heroines—the mythical ancestors, the citizens of the Golden Age—are the best and wisest of people.

Assyrian relief: two royal personages worshiping the sacred tree. Above the tree is a representation of the winged sky-god.

The Age of Miracles and Wonders

According to virtually all accounts, human beings in the paradisal age were possessed of qualities and abilities that can only be called miraculous. They were wise, all-knowing, and able to communicate easily not only with one another but also with all other living things; moreover, they could fly through the air, and they shone with visible light.

In contrast to the contemporary view of early humans as dull and brutish, the myths speak of them as sages. In Jewish folklore, Adam is described as being so wise and so beautiful to behold that the creatures of the Earth mistook him for the Creator and, together with the angels of Heaven, bowed down and chanted, "Holy, holy, holy." It is also said that God revealed the whole of the future to Adam, as well as the geography of the entire Earth.[12] In these respects, Adam resembled Adapa, the Babylonian First Man, who "was equipped with vast intelligence. . . . His plane of wisdom was the plane of heaven."[13]

The ancient Mayans similarly described the four First People as wise and all-knowing. According to the *Popul Vuh*, the Mayan book of lore and customs, the people of the first age were so perceptive that when "they lifted up their eyes . . . their gaze embraced all; they knew all things; nothing in heaven or earth was concealed from them." These created ones rendered thanks, saying,

> "Truly, thou gavest us every motion and accomplishment! We have received existence, we have received a mouth, a face; we speak, we understand, we think, we walk; we perceive and we know equally well what is far and what is near; we see all things, great and small, in heaven and upon the earth. Thanks be to you who created us, O Maker, O Former!" But the Makers were not pleased to hear this.[14]

In the Mayan legend, the Makers were afraid that these miraculous First People would be "as gods"; therefore, the Heart of the Sky breathed a cloud on the eyes of the four original men, obscuring their vision.

Many traditions say that the first human beings spoke a single language. In Genesis, as in the myths of the Chins and the Twyan of Indochina, all people could understand one another's speech until the collapse of a tower or ladder built in an attempt to reach Heaven. The Mayans likewise say that the First People "had but a single language."[15] Some traditions go further, suggesting that in Paradise humanity was telepathic; the Hopi, for example, say that the First People "felt as one and understood one another without talking."[16]

This one language seems to have extended to the animal kingdom as well. Whether it is said that animals could speak as humans or that human beings could understand the animal languages, the result in either case was a state of trust and friendship between man and beast. Jewish legends say that "in all respects, the animal world had a different relation to Adam from their relation to his descendents. Not only did they know the language of man, but they respected the image of God, and they feared the first human couple, all of which changed into the opposite after the fall of man."[17]

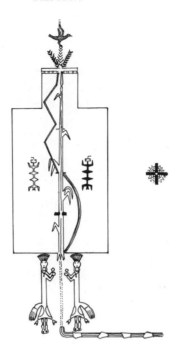

Navajo sandpainting: The Tree of Life, with the "pollen-path" or "blessing-way" running up the center. On the left side of the plant, the masculine zig-zag of lightning; on the right, the feminine curve of the rainbow; above, the bird of happiness, representing the freedom of flight.

The Greek storyteller Aesop wrote wistfully that "during the time of the golden race the . . . animals had articulate speech and knew the use of words. And they held meetings in the middle of the forests; and the stones spoke, and the needles of the pine tree . . . and the sparrow spoke wise words to the farmer."[18]

This ability of human beings and animals to understand one another resulted in a condition in which, according to the fifth-century B.C. Greek philosopher Empedocles, "All were gentle and obedient to men, both animals and birds, and they glowed with kindly affection towards one another."[19]

In African folklore, as in the myths of the ancient Greeks, the harmony of humanity with the animals is reflected in the vegetarian diet of the First People. That our earliest ancestors shunned the killing of animals for food is also implied in the Bible: God tells Adam and Eve, "Behold, I have given you every herb bearing seed, which is upon the face of all the earth, and every tree, in the which is the fruit of a tree yielding seed; to you it shall be for meat" (Genesis 1:29). It is not until after the Deluge that God tells Noah, "Every moving thing that liveth shall be meat for you; even as the green herb have I given you all things." But because human beings are now permitted to kill and eat the animals, "The fear of you and the dread of you shall be upon every beast of the earth, and upon every fowl of the air, upon all that moveth upon the earth, and upon all the fishes of the sea" (Genesis 9:2-3).

Many traditions say that the First People had the capacity of flight, or had access to Heaven by means of a rope, tree, mountain, vine, or ladder. The Navajo, for example, called the first people the "Air-Spirit People":

> They are people unlike the five-fingered earth-surface people who come into the world today, live on the ground for a while, die at a ripe old age, and then leave the world. They are people who travel in the air and fly swiftly like the wind.[20]

Similarly, according to the Jorai cosmogony of the indigenous Indochinese peoples, the original human beings lived with their God, Oi Adei, and enjoyed a deathless existence in which they could fly like birds.[21] The Indian epic *Mahabharata* notes that in the *Krita Yuga* human beings "ascended to the sky and returned to earth at will."[22] In some myths, ascent into the sky was made possible via fire or smoke, a rainbow, a sunbeam, clouds, a fabulous bird, or a chain of arrows. The Koryaks of central Asia tell of the mythical era of Great Raven, when all people could go up to Heaven easily; now it is only the shamans who can do this. The ancient Egyptians used a bird to symbolize the human spirit released from bondage to the material world, and in all cultures and eras flight and wings are symbolic of the freedom of the paradisal condition.

Another miraculous quality of the first human beings was their luminosity. According to legend, their flesh was not as dense as ours and gave off visible light. The apocryphal *Books of Adam and Eve*—of which a number of versions survive, most dating from around 200 B.C.—say that one of the first effects noticed by the original couple upon their expulsion from the Garden was the change in the substance of their bodies: "When Adam looked at his flesh, that was altered, he wept bitterly, he and Eve, over what they had done."[23]

The Siberian peoples likewise believed that human beings living before the Fall were luminous. When the First People ate of the forbidden fruit, the world around them became dark. According to the ancient Iranians, the First Man was white and brilliant; only later was he overcome by the powers of darkness. The Kalmucks of central Asia agree that during the time of Paradise the First People gave off light. In those days there was neither Sun nor Moon; however, these were unnecessary, since human beings lit their surroundings by their natural radiance. But when they ate of the forbidden fruit their light was extinguished altogether, all Nature became dark, and God created the Sun and Moon to relieve the gloom. The Tibetans say that in the early days of the world the gods inhabited the world and glowed like stars. Later, when they ate of a substance oozing from the Earth, their powers began to diminish. Their lives grew short, and gradually they declined into selfishness, greed, and violence, so that the beings who had originally been gods became human, subject to desire, suffering, and death.

Saintliness of Character

Again according to all accounts, the miraculous abilities of the First People flowed from a sanctified state of consciousness. The mythical ancestors were saintly without pretense of holiness, innocent without being foolish or naive. According to the Mahabharata,

> the holy men of old, partaking of Brahma's nature, were not frustrated in the results at which they aimed; they were religious and truth-speaking. . . . And they died when they desired, suffered few annoyances, were free from disease, accomplished all their objects, endured no oppression. Self-subdued and free from envy, they beheld the gods and the mighty prophets.[24]

The Greeks and Romans also emphasized the saintliness of the first human beings. In his Annals, the first-century Roman historian Tacitus wrote that

> the most ancient human beings lived with no evil desires, without guilt or crime, and therefore without penalties or compul-

sions. Nor was there any need of rewards, since by the prompting of their own nature they followed righteous ways. Since nothing contrary to morals was desired, nothing was forbidden through fear.[25]

The ancient Chinese said that in the first age there was no need for laws or moral codes, for these relate to the "Way of Man," while the people of the Golden Age followed instead the "Way of Heaven (T'ien)." Their actions were spontaneous and effortless, like those of Nature herself. The Taoist sage Chuang Tzu wrote:

> The True Man of ancient times did not rebel against want, did not grow proud in plenty, and did not plan his affairs. Being like this, he could commit an error and not regret it, could meet with success and not make a show. Being like this, he could climb the high places and not be frightened, could enter the water and not get wet, could enter the fire and not get burned.[26]

When the Golden Age ended, people began to think of themselves as self-sufficient, as isolated from the divine and separate both from the Way of Heaven and from one another. Then the great sages of old relinquished their kingship and gave human beings the dubious privilege of governing themselves. It was then that people's innate miraculous powers began to atrophy, and they began to live by their animal senses and to seek out "many inventions."

Communion with Deity: The Divine Parents

Originally, according to myths of every continent, all humanity was perpetually in the divine presence and continually in harmony with divine will. The Africans' insistence that at first God lived on Earth with the people, and the Australians' memory of the Dreamtime, when the Creator-Heroes walked the land, echo the biblical image of Adam and Eve strolling naked and unashamed in the Garden with God.

Universal tradition affirms the existence of a great spiritual Being, which some cultures identified with the life and consciousness of the Earth itself—Maasauu of the Hopi, Geb of the Egyptians, Gaia of the

Maat, the goddess of truth. Bas-relief from the tomb of Sethos I. Nineteenth
Dynasty. Archaeological Museum, Florence.

Greeks. Other cultures saw the deity as an omnipotent sky-god—
Ahura Mazda of the Zoroastrians, Yahweh of the Hebrews, and Zeus of
the Greeks. Still others spoke of the universal creative Principle—the
Tao of the Chinese, Wakan of the Lakota, Manitou of the Algonquin.
This entity or principle is greater than any human, just as a human is
greater than a cell in his or her own body. From this Great One, within
whose enfolding presence we live and move, we derive our very being.

Many early peoples maintained that in the Golden Age this Being
was embodied in the person of a World-King (the Greek Cronos, the
Chinese Huang-ti, the Egyptian Rê) or a Divine Ancestress (the
Babylonian Ishtar, the Egyptian Isis, the Hindu Great Mother). Often
male and female deities were pictured together as a divine couple (Isis
and Osiris in Egypt, Tammuz and Ishtar in Babylonia, and Shiva and
Parvati in India). The couple lived in the celestial garden or city atop
the cosmic mountain and presided with exemplary love and wisdom
over the affairs of human beings.

In early historical times the Chinese, Japanese, Mesopotamians, Egyptians, Mayans, and innumerable other peoples regarded their monarchs as the direct descendants of the World-Parents who ruled in the original Paradise. As was documented by anthropologist A. M. Hocart,[27] the first kings and queens were, without exception, priests and priestesses. In China, the emperor was viewed as the human link between Heaven and Earth; it was he who established celestial order in human affairs. Likewise, the Egyptian pharaohs—who in some cases were women—were considered to be incarnations of *Maat*. This term, while often translated as "truth," carried a meaning for the Egyptians that modern Westerners might equate with "self-evident rightness." Maat—sometimes personified as a goddess—was the word used to describe the character of the original Creation, the quality of the Golden Age.

In many traditions the creative interplay of Heaven and Earth was symbolically represented in the *hieros gamos*, or divine marriage. The Hindu husband to this day may say to his bride, quoting the Upanishad, "I am Heaven; thou art Earth" (*dyaur aham, pritivi tvam*). Through the marriage of the World-King and the Queen of Heaven, the relations between woman and man, Nature and Cosmos, were continually revitalized, as the primal power of love was released through the collective consciousness of humanity and into the Earth. The divine couple was an active representation and embodiment of the creative process, and all the world shared in the currents of life expressed through their union.

Immortality

Few things in Nature seem more axiomatic than the inevitability of death. It is remarkable, therefore, that one of the most consistently encountered themes in Paradise myths is that of the original immortality of human beings. The myths tell us that death is in some sense not *natural* at all, but rather the result of sin or sorcery. They say that death, rather than being a necessary part of the order of Nature, originated from a mistake or misdeed on the part of ancestors in the First Age. Had it not been for that primordial crime or blunder, we would all be immortal.

For examples of this belief, we can turn to the myths and folklore of nearly every culture. The Iranians' Age of Yima was, as we have seen, a time when "men never looked on death," and "father and son walked together, each looking but fifteen years of age." Likewise, the Egyptians said that neither death nor disease was known during the Time of Rê. The natives of Vanuatu (New Hebrides) believe that at the beginning of time people did not die, but instead cast their skins like snakes and so renewed their youth. Nearly all the tribes of south and central Africa say that people were immortal until they offended God and forced him to retreat to the sky-world.

In myths where immortality is not explicitly indicated, something close to it is implied. For the Greeks, the Golden Age was a time when there was no disease or old age; likewise, according to the Hindus, the *Krita Yuga* was a time "without disease; there was no lessening with the years. . . . In those times, men lived as long as they chose to live, and were without any fear of [the god of Death]."[28] The Kalmucks of central Asia said that in the beginning human beings, if not immortal, could at least live through a world epoch of 80,000 years; gradually, their longevity decreased, so that at present their average life-span is only 60 years. The Bible and ancient Babylonian king lists both record human beings' decreasing longevity after the Fall.

If ancient peoples considered death unnatural, they tended to hold similar ideas about its biological antipode, birth. Perhaps this was in response to a practical problem: If there was no death during the First Age, what would have kept the population from increasing uncontrollably? But for whatever reason—whether it was invention based on logical necessity, or memory of some condition that had once actually prevailed—the ancients often connected the origin of death with the introduction of reproduction and sex in their present form.

Among the African tribes, for instance, there is the idea that the reproduction of the human species is necessitated by death. Before death appeared, human beings reproduced differently, if at all.[29] According to several of the Jewish *midrashim* (commentaries on the Old Testament, composed between the fourth and twelfth centuries), Adam was at first androgynous—a man on the left side, a woman on the right. Later, God split him into two halves.[30] The early Christian Gnostics not only held that the First Man was an androgyne, but also taught that the reunion of male and female principles is the essence of

Giovanni di Paolo, *Expulsion from Paradise* (ca. 1445).

mystical fulfillment. Plato also described humankind's primeval ancestor as a hermaphroditic, spherical being: in the *Symposium*, the myth
of the divine androgyne blends imperceptibly into the myth of the
Cosmic Egg.

Heavenly and Earthly Paradises

In many cultures the description of the original Golden Age is
exactly paralleled by a story of the Otherworld to which souls journey
after death. Frequently, the same word is used to refer to both—as is
the case in English, where the word *paradise* can refer either to Eden or
to Heaven. In the abode of spirits we find a palace or garden strewn
with jewels and crystal. We may encounter, according to Vedic and
Iranian myth, a holy mountain, and trees with precious fruits. There
are no storms in the heavenly Paradise, and the people there neither
hunger nor thirst. Nor do they age: all look perpetually youthful. The
Midrash Konen of the Jews even tells us that the Tree of Life grows in
Gan 'Eden, the world beyond death.

The existence and nature of the otherworldly Paradise constitutes
one of the great themes of world myth and folklore. The Aborigines of
central Australia call the Otherworld the Dowie; it is not somewhere
distant in space, but is all about us and can be contacted at any time,
given the proper conditions. The Polynesians knew the Otherworld as
Pulotu, a magical realm in the midst of which grew an immense tree
whose leaves supplied all wants. Following physical death, according
to tradition, a stream floated the spirit away to Pulotu:

> All floated away together, well- and ill-favoured, young and old,
> sound and sick, chiefs and commoners; they must look neither to
> the right nor left, nor attempt to reach either side, nor must they
> look back. Little more than half alive, they floated on until they
> reached Pulotu, where they bathed in the waters of Vaiola, when
> all became lively, bright and vigorous, every infirmity vanishing,
> and even the aged becoming young again. Everything went on in
> Pulotu much as in the world of life, except that here their bodies
> were singularly volatile, so that they were able to ascend at night,
> becoming luminous sparks, or vapours, revisiting their former

homes, but retiring again in early dawn to the bush or to Pulotu.[31]

The original Paradise on Earth was a materialization of the Paradise that now exists only beyond the portals of death. Likewise, the Greeks' otherworldly Elysium was considered to be the spiritualized counterpart of the condition that had once prevailed in the physical world. In his account of the end of the Golden Age, Hesiod tells us that Zeus, upon his overthrow of Cronos, banished the latter to the Islands of the Blessed (the Otherworld) to rule over the heroes. African myths convey essentially the same message: Paradise is not gone; rather, it is transposed to a place or dimension that is only accessible *post mortem*.

The Rainbow Bridge

According to universal tradition, the original earthly Paradise and the still-existent otherworldly Paradise were at first united, or in any case were in close proximity and communication. The means of connection is described variously in different cultures—most vividly, perhaps, as a rainbow. In the traditions of Japan, Australia, and Mesopotamia, the rainbow was seen as a reminder of a bridge that once existed between Heaven and Earth and was accessible to all people. The seven colors of the rainbow were the seven heavens of Hindu, Mesopotamian, and Judaic religion. Among the central Asians, shamanic drums were decorated with rainbows symbolizing the shaman's journey to the Otherworld. Similarly, the seven levels of the Babylonian ziggurat (stepped pyramid) were painted with the seven colors of the rainbow, and the priest, in climbing its stories, symbolically mounted to the cosmic world of the gods.[32]

The primordial world-bridge is elsewhere remembered as a ladder or a rope. According to pre-Buddhist Tibetan traditions, called Bon, there originally existed a rope that bound Earth to Heaven and that was used by the gods to come down to meet human beings. The first king of Tibet was said to have come down from Heaven by a rope, and the first Tibetan kings did not die but mounted again into Heaven. After the Fall and the coming of death, the link between Heaven and

Earth was broken. Once the rope was cut, only spirits could ascend to Heaven; their bodies remained on Earth. In many Tibetan magical practices, especially those of Bon, people try even today to climb to Heaven by means of a magic rope and believe that at death the pious are drawn to Heaven by an invisible cord.[33] The "magic rope," which appears in the myths of innumerable cultures, may be akin to the biblical "silver cord." According to Ecclesiastes 12:6, this ethereal link between the spiritual and physical bodies is loosed only at death.

Since the original ancestors were all capable of traveling between Heaven and Earth at will, the principal sign of spiritual authority for saints, prophets, and shamans throughout history has been their ability to emulate the First People by visiting the Otherworld. The stories of Moses' ascent of Mount Sinai to speak with Jehovah, Jesus' transfiguration on "a high mountain," and Buddha's enlightenment beneath the Bodhi tree all exemplify the widespread theme of the Anointed One's visit to Heaven.

Ancient and primitive peoples were vitally concerned, then, not merely with the existence of the Otherworld, but also with the relation between that dimension and our own, with the means of connection between the two worlds, and with the implications of these relations and connections for the processes of birth and death. Universally, they believed that the loss of immortality came about because of a rupture in communication between Heaven and Earth. As a result of this separation, we are today ordinarily aware of only one plane of existence, the physical world of the senses. Of the nature of the Otherworld, we have only the sporadic, secondhand reports of mystics and shamans. If the paradisal state is to be recovered, Heaven and Earth must be brought back into union.

Lost Continents

The image of Paradise as existing on a lost island or continent is perhaps not as widespread as the other mythic themes we have considered in this chapter, but it is nevertheless common enough—and intriguing enough—to warrant our attention.

In the *Timaeus* and *Critias*, Plato conveys what he describes as an ancient tradition concerning a lost paradisal island empire—Atlantis. Plato quotes Solon, "the wisest of the Seven Sages," who says, on the authority of certain Egyptian priests, that shiftings of the celestial bodies produce catastrophes on Earth at recurrent intervals, either through flood or fire. There usually remains a small remnant of human beings who gradually relearn the arts of civilization. In Plato's description of the civilization that preceded the most recent destruction, we hear the characteristic tones and cadence—though perhaps only an echo—of Hesiod's earlier song of the original golden race:

> For many generations, as long as the divine nature lasted in them, they were obedient to the laws, and well-affected towards the gods, who were their kinsmen; for they possessed honorable and in every way great spirits, uniting gentleness with wisdom in the various chances of life. . . . They despised everything but virtue, little esteeming their present state of life, and bearing lightly the burden of gold and other property they possessed; neither were they intoxicated by luxury, nor did wealth deprive them of their self-control and thereby cause their downfall. On the contrary, in their soberness of mind, they saw clearly that all these good things are increased by mutual good will combined with virtue, whereas to honor and strive after these goods destroys not only the goods themselves, but also virtue with them.[34]

But the people of Atlantis degenerated. The divine strain in their ancestry became more and more diluted, and their human nature got the upper hand. They gradually grew avaricious and became imperialists of the most ambitious sort. The wealth and luxury of the Atlanteans were their undoing: the gods sent a cataclysmic flood, and in a single day and night the island kingdom sank beneath the waves.

There are several European traditions of a lost island to the west—among them, the Welsh Avalon, the Portuguese Antilia, and St. Brendan's Island (which was common to sagas of many languages and appeared on maps until the eighteenth century). But we also find the idea of a paradisal homeland, destroyed by cataclysms, in the myths of cultures geographically far removed from Europe and the Mediterranean countries. The Mayans and the Hopi both maintained well-preserved traditions of an original paradisal home on a sunken island or continent. When Hernán Cortés landed in Mexico, the

Aztec king Montezuma informed him that the natives' ancestors had come from a distant place called Aztlan (which means "surrounded by waters"), where there was a high mountain and a garden inhabited by the gods. The book of the prophet Chilam Balam (one of the few surviving Mayan texts) tells of the first people of the Yucatán, known as Ah-Canule ("People of the Serpent"), arriving in boats from the east. The *Popul Vuh* also describes their journey:

> Then they came; they pulled up stakes there and left the East. . . . Each of the tribes kept getting up to see the star which was herald of the sun (Venus). The sign of the dawn they carried in their hearts when they came from the East, and with the same hope they left there, from that great distance, according to what their songs now say.[35]

The Hopi spoke of their original home as Muia, an island in the Pacific that their ancestors had left following some catastrophe of Nature. The Pacific islanders themselves also have stories of a lost paradisal island home. While the Samoans speak of their homeland as Mu, most Polynesian peoples remember a place called Hava-Iki, which, again, was lost in a cataclysm. According to the creation myths of Hawaii (which was named after Hava-Iki), Kane, the Creator, gave Kumuhonua, the first man, a beautiful garden in which to live. The garden, called Kalana-i-hauola, was situated in the land of Kahiki-honua-kele ("the land that moved off"). Kane fashioned a wife for Kumuhonua out of his right side; she was called Ke-ola-Ku-honua, or Lalo-hana. In their paradisal garden there grew a sacred tree, the apples of which caused death if eaten by strangers.

In another tradition, the gods Kane and Kanaloa are described as living in human bodies in an earthly Paradise located on one of the twelve mythic islands believed to lie off the Hawaiian group. These islands are often mentioned in ancient chants and stories, dating from before the last Paao migration from Tahiti. Today they are called the "lost islands" or "islands hidden by the gods." They are considered sacred and must not be pointed at.

In still another ancient story, the hidden land of Kane is called Paliuli. Again, it is the original Paradise, where the first two human beings were made and where they first lived. According to the natives, Paliuli is now deep under the seas. Paradise is lost beneath the waves.

In this chapter we have noted the characteristic features frequently attributed to the original Paradise, or Golden Age. We must emphasize that not every myth contains every one of these elements. However, there is a theme—one that we have as yet only touched upon—that *can* safely be called universal: in no tradition does the Golden Age last forever. According to all peoples, Paradise came to a tragic end. And it is this calamity, whose implications have tormented the human race throughout its history, that we shall consider next.

God did not make death, and he does not delight in the death of the living; the generative forces of the world are wholesome and there is no destructive poison in them.

THE WISDOM OF SOLOMON, 1:13, 14

CHAPTER 5

The Saddest Story

W HAT IS EVIL? Is evil suffering, or the cause of suffering? In either case, evil may be said to be inherent in Nature—in predation, decay, disease, and famine. Yet people in every culture and in every age have held to the belief that in the human world there exists another kind of evil that is profoundly *unnatural*. We may look to Nature for the source of human tendencies toward waste, warfare, greed, and the restless urges to possess, dominate, and kill, but no clear analogy suggests itself. Nature's evils tend to exist in balance, predation and famine mitigating overpopulation, whereas the human version of evil apparently knows no bounds. From the earliest times, human beings have believed that there is a quality in themselves that sets them apart from the animals—a quality that manifests itself as a sense of alienation and insufficiency and as an abnormal capacity for destructiveness and cruelty.

Ancient peoples insisted that evil in this latter sense has not always existed, and that it had a specific cause. In their myths, the evil that is unique to humanity is described as having resulted from the Fall—the tragic event that brought the Golden Age to an end. They said that human nature is not *natural* at all, because it has been distorted by some fundamental mistake or failure that has been perpetuated from generation to generation.

Every religion begins with the recognition that human consciousness has been separated from the divine Source, that a former sense of oneness with the ground of Being has been lost, and that only by a

81

process of purification and transcendence can we be reconnected with the sacred dimension. Whether it is the Judeo-Christian guilt for the sin of Adam and Eve in the Garden, the Taoist nostalgia for the era before the Way of Heaven was corrupted by the ways of men, or the Africans' sorrow for humanity's betrayal of the animals, everywhere in religion and myth there is an acknowledgment that we have departed from an original condition of wise innocence and can return to it only through the resolution of some profound inner discord.

What caused the Fall? Why and how was the Age of Innocence brought to an end? These questions have perplexed theologians and philosophers for millennia, and we cannot hope to answer them with finality in a few pages, though we must at least pose and consider them. The myths themselves do not present a straightforward, unified explanation; rather, in describing what seems to be a shift in the fundamental polarity of human consciousness, they employ a variety of images that seem to be metaphors for some subjective, spiritual event.

In this chapter we will investigate the cause of the Fall— which is described variously as disobedience, as the eating of a forbidden fruit, and as spiritual amnesia—and its effects on both the human mode of being and on the very structure of the world.

Change of Character

According to nearly every tradition, the Fall occurred because of a debasement of the quality of character expressed by human beings. The nature of this process of decay is described in various ways. If we hope to penetrate to the kernel of the story, perhaps it is best to begin with the simplest and most easily understood versions before we proceed to the more enigmatic ones. The following African myth provides an apt and picturesque starting point.

According to the Barotse of Zambia, the Creator, Nyambi, once lived on Earth with his wife, Nasilele. Nyambi had made fishes, birds, and animals, and the world was full of life. But one of Nyambi's creatures was different from all the rest. This creature was Kamonu, the first man. Kamonu was special because he was able to imitate everything Nyambi did. If Nyambi was making something out of wood,

Kamonu would do the same. If Nyambi was creating in iron, Kamonu would work in iron as well.

This state of affairs continued for some time, with Kamonu serving as Nyambi's apprentice, until one day Kamonu forged a spear and killed an antelope. Despite Nyambi's protest, Kamonu went on killing; the Creator, realizing that he had lost control of his creature, grew angry. "Man, you are acting badly," said Nyambi to Kamonu. "These are your brothers. Do not kill them." Nyambi found he could no longer trust Kamonu and began to fear him.

Nyambi drove Kamonu out of Litoma, his sacred realm, but Kamonu pleaded to be allowed to return. Nyambi gave the man a garden to tend, hoping thereby to keep him happy and out of mischief. But when buffalo wandered into Kamonu's garden at night he speared them, and when other animals came close he killed them, too. But after a while Kamonu discovered that the things he loved were all leaving him: his child, his dog, and his pot (his only possession) had all disappeared. He went to Nyambi's sacred realm to report what had happened, and there he found his child, dog, and pot. They had fled Kamonu and returned to their real home. Kamonu asked Nyambi for magical powers that would enable him to keep his things—implying that he had no intention of changing his murderous behavior, which was the real cause of his losses. Nyambi refused.

Then Nyambi called his counselors together to consider the matter. "Kamonu knows too well the way to this place. We shall have no peace. What are we to do?" Nyambi tried to flee from Kamonu by moving first to an island, then to the peak of a high mountain. But Kamonu would always find his way to Nyambi. Meanwhile, Kamonu's descendants were spreading over the Earth, killing the animals and creating an awful din.

Nyambi decided to move away from the Earth altogether, so he sent birds in search of a new site for Litoma. The birds failed to find a suitable place. At last Spider succeeded in finding an abode in the sky for Nyambi and his court and spun a thread stretching from Earth to the new heavenly home. After Nyambi and all his court had ascended by the thread, Nyambi blinded Spider so that he could never find the way to Litoma again.

Meanwhile, Kamonu and his descendants had resolved to build a tower to reach Litoma. They cut down many trees for logs and built their structure higher and higher. But it finally became top-heavy and collapsed, and Kamonu never again found his way to Nyambi's abode. But every morning when the Sun rose, Kamonu would greet it, saying, "Here is Nyambi." At night he and his descendants likewise greeted the Moon, calling on Nasilele, Nyambi's wife.[1]

The story of Nyambi and Kamonu, like nearly all African myths of the Fall, tells of the disappearance of God into the sky because of human depravity. The Ngobe say that in the beginning the Creator lived on Earth among human beings, but because of the people's quarrelsomeness he left them to themselves. Nobody has seen him since, so people today do not know what he is like. In Angola, Nzambi is "the name of one great, invisible God, who made all things and controls all things. . . . Tradition says men have offended him, and he has withdrawn his affection from them."[2]

Similarly, according to the myths of the Bantu and Yao of equatorial southern Africa, God was long ago driven away by humanity's cruelty. The Bantu say that after the first man and woman were created by Mulungu,

> all the animals watched to see what the people would do. . . .
> They rubbed two sticks together in a special way and thus made fire. The fire caught in the bush and roared through the forest and the animals had to run to escape the flames.
>
> The people caught a buffalo and killed it and roasted it in the fire and ate it. Then the next day they did the same thing. Every day they set fires and killed some animal and ate it.
>
> "They are burning up everything!" said Mulungu. "They are killing my people!"
>
> All the beasts ran into the forest as far away from mankind as they could get. . . .
>
> "I'm leaving!" said Mulungu.[3]

Thus, according to the Africans, it was people's cruelty, quarrelsomeness and insensitivity to Nature that caused the Fall.

The Native Americans agree. The Yurok of the northern California coast say that when the Earth was new it was inhabited by the Immortals, myth-time beings who lived in accordance with cosmic law. When people were created, the Immortals went away: "While the world itself remained perfect and beautiful, human beings had the capacity to violate and disrupt that beauty, to throw off the balance of Creation through, especially, their greed."[4] Similarly, the Hopi say that long after the time of creation people began to depart from the instructions of the Great Spirit:

> [They] began to divide and draw away from one another—those of different races and languages, then those who remembered the plan of creation and those who did not. There came among them a handsome one . . . in the form of a snake with a big head. He led the people still further away from one another and their pristine wisdom. They became suspicious of one another and accused one another wrongfully until they became fierce and warlike and began to fight one another.[5]

The Indic peoples describe the fateful change in human character by emphasizing the First People's loss of saintliness:

> In the Treta Yuga [the second age] sacrifices began, and . . . virtue lessened a quarter. Mankind sought truth and performed religious ceremonies; they obtained what they desired by giving and doing.
>
> In the Dwapara Yuga . . . religion lessened one-half. . . . Mind lessened, Truth declined, and there came desire and disease and calamities; because of these men had to undergo penances. It was a decadent Age by reason of the prevalence of sin.
>
> In the Kali [present] Yuga . . . only one quarter of virtue remaineth. The world is afflicted, men turn to wickedness; disease cometh; all creatures degenerate; contrary effects are obtained by performing holy rites; change passeth over all things.[6]

The Greek poet Hesiod, in his enumeration of world ages, described the degeneration of humanity in similar terms:

> Then they who dwell on Olympus made a second generation. . . . They could not keep from sinning and from wronging one another, nor would they serve the immortals. . . . For now truly is a race of iron, and men never rest from labour and sorrow by day, and from perishing by night.[7]

Later Greek and Roman philosophers elaborated on the loss of self-sufficiency and peace of mind suffered by human beings following the

A snake-encircled tree. From a fourth-century Thyrean relief. Athens, National Museum.

end of the Golden Age. In his eulogy of Diogenes, Maximus Tyrius wrote:

> By thus pursuing pleasure they fell into misery. When they sought after wealth, they always considered what they already possessed as mere poverty in comparison with what they lacked, and their acquisitions always fell short of their ambitions. Dreading poverty, they were incapable of being content with sufficiency; fearing death, they took no care of life; seeking to avoid disease, they never abstained from the things that cause it. Full of mutual suspicions, they plotted against most of their fellows. . . . They hated tyranny and themselves desired to tyrannize; they blamed base actions but did not refrain from them. Good fortune they admired but not virtue; misfortune they pitied but knavery they did not avoid. When luck was with them they were bold, when it turned against them they were in despair. They declared that the dead are happy, yet themselves clung to life; and on the other hand they hated life, yet were afraid to die. They

denounced wars and were incapable of living in peace. In slavery they were abject, in freedom insolent. Under democracy they were turbulent, under tyranny, timid. They desired children, but neglected them when they had them. They prayed to the gods, as to beings able to assist them, and they scorned them, as unable to punish; or again, they feared them as avenging powers, and swore falsely, as if the gods had no existence.[8]

In sum, nearly every tradition ascribes the loss of Paradise to the appearance of some tragic aberration in the attitude or behavior of human beings. While in the Golden Age they had been "truth-speaking" and "self-subdued," living "with no evil desires, without guilt or crime," they now succumbed to suspicion, fear, greed, mistrust, and violence.

But how did this change of character come about? Though purporting to describe a historical event, the ancients' descriptions of the cause of the Fall were nearly always cast in metaphors and allegories. As noted earlier, among these stories the most frequently encountered themes are disobedience, the eating of a forbidden fruit, and forgetting (spiritual amnesia).

Disobedience

The idea that the first people committed a crime of disobedience is reiterated in countless myths. In the Eden story in Genesis, the Lord warns Adam and Eve not to eat of the Tree of the Knowledge of Good and Evil. But the serpent, who "was more subtil than any beast of the field," tempts Eve, saying, "Ye shall not surely die, for God doth know that in the day ye eat thereof, then your eyes shall be opened, and ye shall be as gods."

And when the woman saw that the tree was good for food, and that it was pleasant to the eyes, and a tree to be desired to make one wise, she took of the fruit thereof, and did eat, and gave also unto her husband with her; and he did eat. And the eyes of them both were opened, and they knew that they were naked; and they sewed fig leaves together, and made themselves aprons (Genesis 3:6-7).

The ancient Greeks had two stories of the Fall. The first was contained in the tradition of the world ages; in the second, the origin of evil was attributed to the actions of a mortal woman. Pandora (whose name comes from two Greek words meaning "all" and "gift") was given gifts from all the gods, including not only beauty and grace but also the capacity for persuasion and trickery. In her time, human beings led happy lives, all plagues and troubles having been contained in a jar by the farsighted gods. But when Pandora arrived on Earth, she pried everywhere and eventually came upon the jar. Though she had been warned not to open it, she let her curiosity get the better of her and, raising the lid, inadvertently released a horde of plagues upon humanity.

In the following myth from the Gilbert Islands of the South Pacific, the disobedience relates to sex:

> Nakaa, the primordial judge, ruled even the great gods, the spirits of the Tree of Matang. He lived below a mountain in the paradisal land of Matang, where he planted two pandannus palms, one in the north for men, the other in the south for women, and all the people lived, each under their own tree, ageless and undying.
>
> One day, Nakaa called them all together to tell them he was going on a journey. He ordered them to disperse again, each to their own tree, and they did, but the sight of the others had unsettled them and eventually the men joined the women under the tree, and so their hair began to turn grey. When Nakaa returned and saw this sign of their disobedience, he expelled them from Matang forever.

Nakaa let the people choose one of the trees to take with them. They chose foolishly, and so the tree they departed with became for them the tree of death, while the tree of life remained with Nakaa in Matang. He told them that their ghosts would find him at the juncture of the lands of the living and the dead and would be judged by him. Nakaa stripped the leaves from the tree of death, wrapped all kinds of illnesses in them, and threw them at the people as they fled Matang.[9]

Ethnologist Paul Schebesta relates the following tradition of the Fall held by the Bambuti Pygmies of Zaire, in which the nature of the disobedience is unspecified:

The "paradise" in which God first placed man was the primeval forest. He put it at man's disposal together with all that it produced. God had, however, also given one commandment on the keeping or breaking of which man's further fate depended. He had threatened the severest punishment if man should disobey. The whole of creation would enter into league against the rebellious subject. Animals, plants and elements, which had so far been man's friends and servants, would then become his enemies. Toil and misery, sickness and death would follow in the wake of his rebellion.[10]

In this, as in so many other instances, the punishment—death, the need to labor, and the loss of the divine presence—seems out of proportion to the crime. For an act whose nature is obscure, or one seemingly equivalent to a child's raid on the cookie jar, all humankind is condemned to suffering, generation after generation. Yet, as is typical of disobedience stories, the punishment is here regarded as having been *deserved*. According to Schebesta,

> The Pygmy myths contain no expressions that might indicate resentment against God for having decreed such punishment for the transgression of his law. The consequences must, therefore, have been felt to be deserved and the original command must have been a matter of serious moment.[11]

Both the divine command and the human disobedience, for all their fateful significance, are as yet ambiguous. But as we explore more images common in myths of the Fall we begin to perceive the nature of the crime.

The Forbidden Fruit

Many myths describe the original disobedience as the eating of the fruit of a sacred tree. The best-known example of this theme is the Hebraic account, in which Adam and Eve disobey Yahweh by partaking of the fruit of the Tree of the Knowledge of Good and Evil. But elsewhere we find astonishingly close parallels to the Genesis story. The Masai of Tanzania say that the first man came down from

Impression from the so-called Temptation Seal (2500 B.C.). On the left, the Sumerian goddess Gala Bau, behind her the serpent, representing the power of the Great Mother. On the right of the sacred tree sits her son-lover Dumuzi, the ever-dying, ever-resurrected god of vegetation, "son of the Abyss, Lord of the Tree of Life." British Museum.

Heaven, while his wife came forth from the Earth. They were forbidden to eat from a certain tree, but the woman was tempted to do so by a serpent. As a punishment, she and her husband were made to leave Paradise.

According to some myths, the eating of the earthly fruit immediately diminishes the powers of celestial beings. A version from Nepal, for example, says that the Earth was once inhabited by heaven-dwellers who at a certain point desired to eat the fruits of the Earth. Once they had tasted the fruits they lost their ability to return to the higher world. A similar story—in which grain is substituted for fruit—is told by the Burmese, who say that the first nine inhabitants of the world descended from the skies and were sinless and sexless. But as they became accustomed to their new home their appetites grew. When they took to eating a particular sort of rice, they became gross and heavy. Being unable to return to their blissful heavenly home, they developed sex and became subject to toil and suffering. Thereafter, they had to work for their living, and they occasionally resorted to crime.[12]

What was this fruit, the eating of which brought Paradise to an end? Clearly, we are not speaking here of ordinary apples or pears. The image is undoubtedly intended as a metaphor—and a profound one at that, considering its centrality to the story. While for the most part we are postponing a consideration of the meaning of the Paradise myth until later in the book, in this case the mythic imagery fairly cries out for some preliminary deciphering.

In nearly all languages, the word *fruit* is used metaphorically to refer to the result of any creative process. Fruit is the ultimate product of the vegetative cycle of reproduction and growth upon which we depend for our survival, and so it is natural for people in every culture to speak of the end result of human labor, or of any constructive activity, as its fruit. Since all creative processes—from the growth of a tree or an embryo to the invention of a new technology—begin invisibly and end with a completed physical form, the image of fruit is metaphorically applicable to any finished product.

To eat is to take something into oneself and allow it to become a part of one's body. But there are analogous emotional, mental, and spiritual processes: we speak of devouring literature and of feasting on the sight of our beloved. Whatever fascinates us we incorporate mentally and emotionally into ourselves. The eating of the mythic fruit, then, was a fascination or union with the result, or end product, of creation, which is the manifest form of things.

Adam and Eve were stewards of the creative process, enjoined to tend and keep the Garden. The story implies that human beings were originally concerned with the entire process of creation rather than merely with its end products. The wise gardener—metaphoric or literal—cares for all phases of the creative cycles at hand. But when he becomes fascinated merely with the fruit, neglecting or distorting other parts of the process, the whole continuum is thrown out of balance. As we are discovering throughout the world today, the farmer who is interested only in increasing crop yield and who ignores the health of the soil will eventually drain the land of its ability to provide nourishing food.

This teaching is explicitly expressed in some Paradise myths, as well as in the core religious teachings of most cultures. Many Native American tribes (the Hopi and the Yurok, for example) tell us that the First People were instructed in the ways to maintain the balance of the forces of Nature. The Fall came with their ancestors' abandonment of the responsibilities of stewardship. In one way or another, nearly all the world's scriptures warn against the "sweet, soft sinfulness," as the *Bhagavad Gita* calls it, of obsessive desire for an end product in form. "Want not! ask not!" Krishna commands. "Find full reward of doing right in right! Let right deeds be thy motive, not the fruit which comes from them."[13]

In ancient Iranian, *Adam* means "I," and in Old Sanskrit, a related language, *aham* means "I" or "the self." Indo-Iranian mysticism says that the pure, untainted self—Adam—fell from perfection in its spiritual habitations because of attraction to Earth, which in all Western traditions is equated with physical form.[14] The early Christian Gnostics similarly believed that human consciousness is inherently of Heaven, and that evil is the result of the heavenly Self's emotional involvement with the earthly end product of the creative process.

According to the Gnostic writings attributed to Hermes Trismegistus, man is an emanation of the mind of God—*Nous*—and has become tragically ensnared in matter. The *Poimandres of Hermes* tells how the Nous, Father of all, Life and Light, created man in his own image. Man wished also to be a creator, and this was permitted by the Nous. Man was given full power over the world of created things and over the irrational animals, and he revealed to Nature the form of God. Nature smiled in love upon him, and he, seeing himself reflected in Nature, loved her and desired to dwell with her. Immediately, the wish became reality, and man found himself trapped in the world of form and devoid of reason. Nature, having received her beloved into herself, embraced him wholly, and they mingled, inflamed with love.

> And this is why alone of all the animals on earth man is twofold, mortal through the body, immortal through the essential Man. For though he is immortal and has power over all things, he suffers the lot of mortality, being subject to the Heimarmene [Destiny]; though he was above the Harmony [i.e., the law of the interrelations between the Cosmos and the psychological principles in human beings], he has become a slave within the Harmony; though he was androgynous, having issued from the androgynous Father, and unsleeping from the unsleeping one, he is conquered by love and sleep.[15]

The eating of the forbidden fruit, and other metaphors used in describing the Fall, suggest that the spiritual degeneration of human beings came about because of their excessive involvement with the end product of creation, the manifest world of things and forms. Moreover, as we examine these metaphors more closely, we begin to see how and why this fascination with form was believed to have eclipsed humanity's original sense of divine identity and awareness of its duty of stewardship for the total process of creation.

The Knowledge of Good and Evil

As we have seen, the Genesis account attributes the Fall to the eating of the fruit of a specific tree—the Tree of the Knowledge of Good and Evil. This tree "was pleasant to the eyes, and a tree to be desired to make one wise." The act of eating its fruit caused Adam and Eve's eyes to be opened, "and they knew that they were naked."

> And the LORD God said, Behold, the man is become as one of us, to know good and evil: and now, lest he put forth his hand, and take also of the tree of life, and eat, and live for ever: Therefore the LORD God sent him forth from the garden of Eden, to till the ground from whence he was taken. So he drove out the man; and he placed at the east of the garden of Eden Cherubims, and a flaming sword which turned every way, to keep the way of the tree of life (Genesis 3:6-24).

Few passages in world literature have provoked more speculation than this. Why was the Tree of the Knowledge of Good and Evil forbidden? One might think God wished human beings to remain ignorant. This interpretation inspired certain Gnostic sects, as well as philosophers such as Kant and Schiller, to suggest that the serpent was in reality the benefactor of humanity, the bringer of knowledge. But what kind of knowledge is it? Is it, as many theologians have suggested, the knowledge of sex (which causes the original couple to recognize their nakedness), or is it a general discriminative knowledge of right and wrong?

The story implies the existence of two kinds of evil—one inherent in Nature, embodied in the Tree of Knowledge itself, and one created by the act of disobedience of eating from the tree. It is the latter evil that causes Adam and Eve to hide themselves from the presence of the Lord. Moreover, when the Lord calls out to them, asking "Where art thou?" they seek to evade responsibility: Adam blames Eve, and Eve blames the serpent. The serpent, having no one to blame, receives the first curse.

The first kind of evil—that which grew as fruit on the tree—exists prior to moral choice. It is the evil to which Job refers when he says, "What? Shall we receive good at the hand of God, and shall we not receive evil?" Hindu theology acknowledges the complementarity of this premoral good and evil by equally revering Brahma the Creator and Shiva the Destroyer. The traditions of the Native Americans, Chinese, and Japanese, in their various ways, also agree that in Nature both growth and decay, completeness and incompleteness exist as essential partners in the creative process.

The second kind of evil—the moral evil that is unique to humanity—arises from judgment between the qualities and pairs of opposites inherent in Nature and from emotional attachment to categories and distinctions. Existence in the physical world in and of itself occasionally produces suffering, but it is a suffering that is contained in the ebb and flow of natural cycles and processes. It is a suffering contained entirely in the present moment. The human mind produces another kind of suffering, one that has its basis in expectation and memory, greed and fear. It is the suffering of separateness and alienation, arising from the mind's attachment to its own artificial categories of discrimination and its projection of those categories onto the world. This second evil is unnatural; its origin was the Fall.

This understanding of the nature of the act of eating from the forbidden tree appears in the Judeo-Christian exegetical literature by way of the Gnostic *Gospel of Philip*, in which the author traces the origin of death to the original couple's attempt to gain knowledge by dividing experience into false categories consisting of mutually exclusive pairs of opposites: "Light and darkness, life and death, right and left, are brothers of one another. They are inseparable."[16] But it is in Hinduism, Buddhism, and Taoism that the fundamental error—and psychological consequences— of false discrimination are most clearly explicated. For the Taoists, for example, the Golden Age of Grand

Unity was the time before human beings had knowledge of the pairs of opposites. Chuang Tzu writes:

> The knowledge of the ancients was perfect. In what way was it perfect? They were not yet aware that there were things. This is the most perfect knowledge; nothing can be added. Then, some were aware that there were things, but not aware that there were distinctions among them. Then, some were aware that there were distinctions, but not yet aware that there was right and wrong among them. When right and wrong became manifest, the Tao thereby declined.[17]

Since it is the making of false distinctions that produces illusion, then enlightenment and liberation—the experience of Paradise—must arise from the abandoning of artificial categories of human judgment and emotional attachment to the qualities of form.

At the heart of the Buddha's teachings are the Four Noble Truths, which affirm that all human suffering arises from desire and fear based on attachment to form and the vagaries of human discrimination. Buddhist doctrine describes nirvana—the paradisal condition of peace, wisdom, and absorption in the oneness of all being—as the natural condition of human consciousness before attachment arises and after it has ceased. While Buddhism does not acknowledge the Fall as a historical event, passages such as the following (from the *Lankavatara Sutra*) could be said to express the Buddhist analysis of the nature of "fallen" human consciousness and how it may be clarified:

> False-imagination teaches that such things as light and shade, long and short, black and white are different and are to be discriminated; but they are not independent of each other; they are only different aspects of the same thing, they are terms of relation not of reality. Conditions of existence are not of a mutually exclusive character; in essence things are not two but one. . . .
>
> When appearances and names are put away and all discrimination ceases, that which remains is the true and essential nature of things and, as nothing can be predicated as to the nature of essence, it is called the "Suchness" of Reality. This universal, undifferentiated, inscrutable "Suchness" is the only Reality, but

it is variously characterized as Truth, Mind-essence, Transcendental Intelligence, Noble Wisdom, etc. . . .

But the cessation of the discriminating-mind can not take
place until there has been a "turning-about" in the deepest seat
of consciousness. The mental habit of looking outward by the
discriminating-mind upon an external objective world must be
given up, and a new habit of realising Truth itself within the
intuitive-mind by becoming one with Truth itself must be established.[18]

Attachment and false discrimination produce a condition in which
our awareness of the fullness and magic of the present moment are
drowned out by the mind's restless machinations. Then, as the *Gita*
says, "memory—all betrayed—lets noble purpose go, and saps the
mind, till purpose, mind and man are all undone."[19]

Forgetting

A final allegorical image of the Fall is contained in the metaphor
of forgetfulness. According to Gnostic, Hindu, and Buddhist traditions, it is the act of forgetting one's true identity and purpose, because
of distraction with the physical world, that produces the misery of the
fallen condition.

According to Platonic philosophy, Lethe ("forgetfulness") has
erased not only temporal memory, but also the Ideas—that is, the
absolute knowledge of universal principles. In the process of being
born, the soul forgets the Ideas, its own past and identity, and the
collective past of humankind. This forgetting, according to Plato, is
the primary cause of human illusion and suffering.

The central myth of the early Christian Gnostics, as preserved in
the *Acts of Thomas*, also revolves around forgetting and remembering.
A prince from the East comes to Egypt seeking "the one pearl, which is
in the midst of the sea around the loud-breathing serpent." The
Egyptians make the prince a captive and give him food that makes him
forget who he is. "I forgot that I was a son of kings, and I served their
king; and I forgot the pearl, for which my parents sent me, and because
of the burden of their oppressions I lay in a deep sleep." But his
parents, learning of his captivity and amnesia, send a letter:

From thy father, the king of kings, and thy mother, the mistress of the East, and from thy brother, our second [in authority], to thee our son. Call to mind that thou art a son of kings! See the slavery—whom thou servest! Remember the pearl, for which thou wast sent to Egypt!

The letter turns into an eagle and flies to the prince. Alighting beside him, it speaks and turns again into a letter.

At its voice and the sound of its rustling, I started and rose from my sleep. I took it up and kissed it, and I began and read it; and according to what was traced on my heart were the words of my letter written. I remembered that I was a son of royal parents, and my noble birth asserted its nature. I remembered the pearl, for which I had been sent to Egypt, and I began to charm him, the terrible loud-breathing serpent. I hushed him to sleep and lulled him into slumber, for my father's name I named over him, and I snatched away the pearl, and turned to go back to my father's house.[20]

This story may be seen as an allegory for the process of incarnation. Prior to birth, the human spirit lives in the eternal realms of light, but in birth—the journey to Egypt—it enters a sleep of forgetfulness. The pearl is the purpose for which the spirit incarnates; the serpent is a metaphor for the mind's powerful addictions. The letter is *gnosis*—spiritual knowledge that brings wakefulness and remembrance.

The Gnostics often described this ontological forgetfulness as a state of sleep or drunkenness into which the soul has fallen by its involvement with form. "Burning with the desire to experience the body," the spirit has forgotten its real nature. "She forgot her original habitation, her true center, her eternal being."[21]

If the images of forgetfulness and sleep are powerful metaphors for the Fall, remembering and awakening likewise serve as apt descriptions of the goal of all spiritual practices in every cultural setting: the object of meditation and ritual is always to *remember*, to *awaken*.

Awakening implies a return to the awareness of the soul's celestial origin, and the messenger who brings this awakening offers life, salvation, and redemption. A Manichaean text exhorts: "Awake, soul of splendour, from the slumber of drunkenness into which thou hast fallen . . . follow me to the place of the exalted earth where thou dwelledst from the beginning."[22] The injunction is not merely to remember who one divinely *is*, but to remember also the commission with which one has incarnated: "Slumber not nor sleep, and forget not that which thy Lord hath charged thee."[23]

Being "awake" means maintaining a consciousness of Heaven while living on Earth. Hinduism and Buddhism regard the true Self (*purusha*) as an expression of the divine ground of Being, individualized in human form. Sin consists of forgetting one's true Self; all suffering ensues from this. The core teaching of the Upanishads, *Tat tvam asi* (That thou art) corresponds to the letter in the Gnostic myth quoted above, sent by the King of kings (Brahman) to the prince (Atman) to remind him of his royal heritage.

The Effects of the Fall

Whatever the causes of the Fall, its effects are described similarly in almost all traditions. With disobedience, attachment, and forgetting come the loss of contact with the sacred Source; death and the necessity for reproduction; and limitations of various kinds, such as the loss of luminosity and the abilities to fly and to communicate with the animals. Human beings must now labor to obtain what they need to survive, must invent technologies to compensate for the diminution of their various natural abilities, and must wander through life unaware of their real nature, purpose, and collective past.

Of all the results of the Fall, the most grievous was the loss of the divine presence. Paul Schebesta writes that for the Pygmies' first ancestors,

> what caused . . . the most suffering was God's departure. God disappeared. He withdrew and was no longer perceptible. . . . In the opinion of the Pygmies who spoke of these things, God's withdrawal was undoubtedly the greatest catastrophe that ever befell mankind; the other consequences of sin were less keenly felt.[24]

In all traditions, as Eliade points out, the longing for Paradise is first and foremost the longing for the immediate communion with Deity:

"The nostalgia for origins is a *religious* nostalgia. Man desires to recover the active presence of the gods."[25]

We have already considered several myths that attribute the origin of death to the transgressions of the earliest human beings. Whereas human beings once lived forever, could fly, and could visit Heaven at will, they have now become earthbound creatures who are, in Eliade's phrase, "limited by temporality, suffering, and death."

The *Books of Adam and Eve* tell how the original couple's very flesh was changed. Prior to the Fall, Adam and Eve glowed with visible light; now their bodies were dense and animal-like.

> And, indeed, when Adam looked at his flesh, that was altered, he wept bitterly, he and Eve, over what they had done. . . . And Adam said to Eve, "Look at thine eyes, and at mine, which before beheld angels in heaven, praising; and they, too, without ceasing. But now we do not see as we did: our eyes have become of flesh; they cannot see in like manner as they saw before." Adam said again to Eve, "What is our body to-day, compared to what it was in former days, when we dwelt in the garden?"[26]

Like the First People of the Mayan tradition—who could see "equally well what is far and what is near"[27]—Adam and Eve had lost a "bright nature" that had allowed them to stretch their gaze to encompass Heaven and Earth:

> Then God the Lord said unto Adam, When thou wast under subjection to Me, thou hadst a bright nature within thee, and for that reason couldst see things afar off. But after thy transgression thy bright nature was withdrawn from thee; and it was not left to thee to see things afar off, but only near at hand; after the ability of the flesh, for it is brutish.[28]

According to the text, the human being is by very nature light: "For I made thee of the light; and I willed to bring out children of light from thee and like unto thee."[29]

> And when he was in the heavens, in the realms of light, he knew naught of darkness. But he transgressed, and I made him fall from heaven upon the earth; and it was this darkness that came upon him. And on thee, O Adam, while in My garden and obedient to

Me, did that bright light rest also. But when I heard of thy transgression, I deprived thee of that bright light. Yet, of my mercy, I did not turn thee into darkness, but I made thee thy body of flesh, over which I spread this skin, in order that it may bear cold and heat.[30]

In the myths of the Greeks, Native Americans, and Africans, the cruelty of human beings causes them to forfeit their friendship with the animals. But then, having lost their divine powers, the people are reduced to a condition materially equivalent to that of the animals, with whom they can no longer communicate.

Substitutes for their former magical abilities must be developed, and these substitutes take the form of inventions and institutions— the rudiments of civilization. The Greek and Roman Stoic and Cynic philosophers describe the emergence of civilization as a process of moral decline. Ovid, for example, tells us that after humanity's loss of its original Golden condition,

There broke out . . . all manner of evil, and shame fled, and truth and faith. In place of these came deceits and trickery and treachery and force and the accursed love of possession. Sails were spread to the winds, for not yet had the sailor known them. . . . And the land, hitherto a common possession like the light of the sun and the breezes, the careful surveyor now marked out with long-drawn boundary line[s]. Not only were corn and needful foods demanded of the rich soil, but men bored into the bowels of the earth, and the wealth she had hidden and covered with Stygian darkness was dug up, an incentive to evil. And now noxious iron and gold more noxious still were produced: and these produced war—for wars are fought with both—and rattling weapons were hurled by blood-stained hands.[31]

Innocence has gone. Human beings are estranged both from the gods and from Nature, and are caught in an addictive round of fear and desire that saps both memory and vital powers. Already, they know the dulling sense of shame and loss. Not only their subjective experience, but the very substance of their physical bodies is changed. Moreover, their new mode of existence is destined to have effects reaching far beyond themselves.

The Deluge

According to the traditions of innumerable cultures, the change of character that overcame humanity had catastrophic consequences for the entire planet. The Yurok Indians say that "because people constantly broke the law, death threatened to outweigh life in the world. As violations of the law and deaths built up, their weight began to tip the earth-disk in the seas upon which it floated."[32]

Virtually every culture remembers at least one world-destruction, which is usually explicitly associated with the Fall. The most widespread story of this kind recalls a worldwide Flood, and of all the Flood stories the most familiar is that of Noah and his ark:

> And GOD saw that the wickedness of man was great in the earth, and that every imagination of the thoughts of his heart was only evil continually. And it repented the LORD that he had made man on the earth, and it grieved him at his heart. And the LORD said, I will destroy man whom I have created from the face of the earth; both man, and beast, and the creeping thing, and the fowls of the air; for it repenteth me that I have made them (Genesis 6:5-7).

One man, Noah, found grace in the eyes of the Lord. God gave Noah the dimensions of a boat, which he built; into it he took his family, and "of every clean beast . . . by sevens, the male and the female: and of beasts that are not clean by two. . . . Of fowls also of the air by sevens, the male and the female; to keep seed alive upon the face of all the earth." Then the fountains of the deep and the windows of heaven opened simultaneously, and "rain was upon the earth for forty days and forty nights. . . . And all flesh died that moved upon the earth, both of fowl, and of cattle, and of beast, and of every creeping thing . . . and every man." But God remembered Noah, and the rains abated. Noah sent out a raven and a dove to look for dry land. When the dove returned seven days later with an olive leaf, Noah left the ark with his family and made an offering. The Lord promised that "while the earth remaineth, seedtime and harvest, and cold and heat, and summer and winter, and day and night shall not cease."[33]

The Babylonian story of Utnapishtim, part of the Epic of Gilgamesh, is believed by many scholars to be the prototype of the biblical

account of the Deluge. In the Utnapishtim narrative, as in the story of
Noah, the Flood is brought about because of the violence of humankind. Enlil gives Utnapishtim the dimensions of the ship he is to
build. Then,

> *The anunnaki [judges in the underworld] raised (their) torches,*
> *Lighting up the land with their brightness;*
> *The raging of Adad [god of storms and thunder] reaches unto heaven*
> *(And) turns into darkness all that was light.*
> *(. . .)the land he broke (?) like a pot*
>
> *. . . .*
>
> *No man could see his fellow.*
> *The people could not be recognized from heaven.*
> *(Even) the gods were terror-stricken at the deluge.*[34]

Again, "the seed of all living creatures" is taken into the boat. In
the Babylonian version, the Flood lasts seven days; a raven, a dove,
and a swallow are sent out to find land. After emerging from the boat,
Utnapishtim makes a thanksgiving offering, and Enlil promises that
no flood shall again destroy the world. Then Utnapishtim and his wife
receive a blessing from Enlil.

The Greeks remembered three floods: the flood that destroyed
Atlantis, the flood of Deucalion and Pyrrha, and the flood of Ogyges.
Of the Atlantean cataclysm we have only Plato's account; of the latter
deluges several versions survive.

According to Greek myth, Deucalion was the son of Prometheus;
he married his cousin Pyrrha, the daughter of Epimetheus and Pandora. When Zeus decided to destroy the human race (Hesiod's Bronze
Race, who were violent and vicious), Prometheus advised Deucalion
to build a box and furnish it with the necessities of life. In it, Deucalion and Pyrrha survived while the rest of humanity perished. Perhaps the most widely read version of the Deucalion flood is Ovid's:

> *At his command the mouths of fountains opened*
> *Racing their mountain waters to the sea.*
> *Under the blow of Neptune's fork earth trembled,*
> *And a way was opened for a sea of water:*
> *Where land was the great rivers toppled orchards,*
> *Uncut corn, cottages, sheep, men, and cattle*

Albrecht Dürer, *The Deluge* (1525). A page from his notebooks. Beneath the drawing, the artist wrote: "In the night between Wednesday and Thursday after Whitsunday [May 30, 31] 1525, I saw this appearance in my sleep—how many great waters fell from heaven. The first struck the Earth about four miles away from me with terrific force and tremendous noise, and it broke up and drowned the whole land. I was so sore afraid that I awoke from it. Then the other waters fell and as they fell they were very powerful and there were many of them, some further away, some nearer. And they came down from so great a height that they all seemed to fall with an equal slowness. But when the first water that touched the Earth had very nearly reached it, it fell with such swiftness, with wind and roaring, and I was so sore afraid that when I awoke my whole body trembled and for a long while I could not recover myself. So when I arose in the morning I painted it above here as I saw it. God turn all things to the best. Albrecht Dürer."

Into the flood. Even stone shrines and temples
Were washed away, and if farmhouse or barn
Or palace still stood its ground, the waves
Climbed over door and lintel, up roof and tower.
All vanished as though lost in glassy waters,
Road, highway, valley, and hill swept into ocean,
All was a moving sea without a shore.[35]

After the couple emerged, they offered a sacrifice to Zeus and proceeded to repeople the Earth. But civilization did not immediately reappear: according to Plato, "for many generations the survivors died with no power to express themselves in writing."

The flood of Ogyges, the legendary king of Thebes in Boeotia, was of a different era than that of Deucalion. The early Christian chronicler Julius Africanus wrote that "Ogygus . . . who was saved when many perished, lived at the time of the Exodus of the people from Egypt, along with Moses."[36]

In Hindu traditions Manu, the First Man, is warned by a great fish of a coming Deluge. He is told to build a ship and to take aboard it all manner of seeds, together with the seven Rishis (mind-born sons of Brahma and the traditional composers of the Vedas). The waters come, and a fish guides the boat to the highest peak of the Himalayas. "To this he ties the ark. He then sacrifices. Out of the oblation a woman arises. The two then create mankind afresh."[37]

In their version of the story of the Fall, the Gypsies of Transylvania tell of a time when people lived forever and knew neither worry nor sickness. Food was plentiful, and rivers flowed with milk and wine. Not only human beings, but the animals as well lived happily and without fear. One day a peculiar old man came to the home of a couple, asking for lodging. As he was departing the next day, he gave his hosts a jar containing a small fish, saying, "Take care of this fish; do not eat it. I will come back in nine days. When you return the fish to me I will reward you."

The wife wanted to eat the fish, but her husband forbade it. But when the man was away, the wife grew hungry. Just as she was about to place the fish on hot coals, she was killed by lightning, and it began to rain. On the ninth day the strange man returned and told the husband: "You have kept your word by not killing the fish. Take a new wife, gather your kinfolk, and build a boat. All men and creatures shall perish, but you shall live. Take with you animals and seeds." The boat was built, and the rain continued for a year. The man, his new wife, his relatives, and the animals survived, but now they had to struggle to live. Sickness and death were their lot, and they multiplied only very slowly.[38]

From the mountains of Yunnan in southwest China, the Lolos— an aboriginal race of people who who have a pictographic script of their own in which they have recorded their legends and songs—say that the divine patriarchs who now live in the sky once dwelt on Earth, where they lived to great ages. The most famous was Tse-gu-dzih, who brought death to the world by opening a forbidden box. At the time, human beings were wicked, and Tse-gu-dzih sent them a messenger asking for some flesh and blood as tribute. Only one man, Du-mu, would comply. Tse-gu-dzih was wrathful and locked the rain gates, so that water began to mount to the sky. But Du-mu and his four sons were gathered into a hollow log, together with otters, wild ducks, and lampreys. These were the only survivors; from Du-mu's sons are descended all the peoples of the world.

The Aborigines of central Australia say that many ages ago there was a disastrous Flood that brought famine to the land. People and animals survived only by clinging to mountain ridges. When the waters abated, the survivors resorted to cannibalism. Then Baiame, the great totemic Ancestor, resolved to incarnate in order to teach the people how to live in their new environment.[39]

In the Americas, Flood traditions are widespread and, in the case of Earth Diver myths, are often interwoven with stories of Creation. We frequently encounter a hero and several animals surviving the Deluge on a raft, from which one or a series of the animals is sent to discover soil, vegetation, or a landing site on a mountain. Often, the story goes on to describe the construction of a ladder to Heaven, the confusion of tongues, and the dispersal of humanity.

The North American natives held the belief that all people originated together in one place and were scattered only after the Flood. The Chelahi of the Pacific Northwest called the early French explorers and traders the "drift people," believing that they were Chelahi people who had been carried away during the great Flood and were now returning.

The Navajo say that they were warned of the approaching Deluge. They took soil from the four corner mountains of the world and placed it on top of the mountain that stood in the north, and all went there, humans and animals. The waters rose, and the people climbed higher. They planted a reed and entered into the hollow of it; the reed grew every night, ultimately growing up to the floor of the present world. There the people found a hole through which they passed to the surface.

The Papago Indians of Arizona preserve a story of Creation, Paradise, and Fall in which Montezuma and a coyote are the sole survivors:

> The Great Spirit first made the earth and its creatures. Then he came down to look at his handiwork. Digging in the ground he had made, he found some clay. He took this back into the sky with him and let it fall back into the hole he had excavated.
>
> Immediately there came out man, in the form of Montezuma, the hero of this legend. With his help there also came forth all the Indian tribes in order. . . . Peace and happiness [were] in the world those first days. The sun being nearer to the earth than it is now, all the seasons were warm, and no one wore clothing. Men and animals shared a common tongue, and all were brothers.
>
> Then a fearful catastrophe shattered the golden days. A great flood destroyed all flesh wherein was the breath of life, except Montezuma and a coyote who was his friend. The coyote had prophesied the flood's coming, and Montezuma, his friend, had believed him. . . .[40]

The Algonquin Indians said that at first the Earth was in a state of peace and happiness. But when a powerful snake came among the people, they became confused and began to hate one another. The snake resolved to destroy all living beings by flood. The waters spread over the land and destroyed everything alive. On Turtle Island dwelt Manabhozo, the grandfather of living things; only his prayer saved a few of the people.

According to the Hawaiians:

> Twelve generations from the beginning of the race, on the genealogy of Kumuhonua, during the so-called Era-of-overturning

(Po-au-hulihia), occurs the name of Nu'u. . . . [I]n his time came the flood known as Kai-a-ka-hina-li'i, which may be translated as 'Sea caused by Kahinali'i' or as 'Sea that made the chiefs (ali'i) fall down. . . .'[41]

The idea that Nu'u built a big boat in which to survive the Flood is probably indigenous, and not a product of contact with missionaries: "Old people on Hawaii [said] that they were informed by their fathers that all the land had once been overflowed by the sea, except a small peak on Maunakea, where two human beings were preserved from the destruction that overtook the rest, but they said they had never heard of a ship or of Noah."[42] It is said also that at the time of the Flood an ancient homeland called Hoahoamaitu sank beneath the waves.

Other Catastrophes

While the Deluge is the most widely and vividly remembered catastrophe of ancient times, most cultures retained traditions of other world-destructions as well. The Greeks, for instance, believed that the four expired ages of the world had each ended in a catastrophe. In his *Theogony*, Hesiod described the end of one of the ages thus: "The life-giving Earth crashed around in burning . . . all the land seethed. . . . It seemed even as if Earth and wide Heaven above came together; for such a mighty crash would have arisen if Earth were being hurled to ruin, and Heaven from on high were hurling her down."[43]

In his *Timaeus*, Plato recalls an ancient memory of recurring catastrophes; here, the Egyptian priest is speaking to Solon of Athens:

"You are all young in your minds," said the priest, "which hold no store of old belief based on long tradition, no knowledge hoary with age. The reason is this. There have been and will be hereafter, many and divers destructions of mankind, the greatest by fire and water, though other lesser ones are due to countless other causes. . . . with you and other peoples again and again life has only lately been enriched with letters and all the other necessities of civilization when once more, after the usual period of years, the torrents from heaven sweep down like a pestilence, leaving only the rude and unlettered among you. . . ."[44]

Like the Greeks, the Tibetans and Hindus also remembered four completed ages, each of which ended in a conflagration, flood, or hurricane. The Chinese called the period between world-destructions a "great year." Each great year ends "in a general convulsion of nature, the sea is carried out of its bed, mountains spring out of the ground, rivers change their course, human beings and everything are ruined, and the ancient traces effaced."[45] In nearly all world-ages traditions, the end of the era is believed to be brought about by the corruption of the human population.

The Arawak of Orinoco say that there were two destructions of the Earth, one by water and the other by fire. Both took place because men disobeyed the Dweller-on-High, Aiomun Kondi. The Arawak also have a Noachian hero, Marerewana, who saved himself and his family during the Deluge by tying his canoe to a large tree with a rope.[46] One of the early explorers of Latin America, Cardim, reported:

> It seemeth that this people had no knowledge of the beginning and creation of the world, but of the deluge it seemeth they have some notice: but as they have no writings nor characters such notice is obscure and confused; for they say that the waters drowned all men, and that one only escaped upon a Janipata with a sister of his that was with child and from these two they have their beginning and from thence began their multiplying and increase.[47]

In the Hopi account of the four worlds, the first three end in destruction. When the First World is about to be destroyed, Sótuknang says to the people:

> You will go to a certain place. Your *Kopavi* (vibratory center on top of the head) will lead you. This inner wisdom will give you the sight to see a certain cloud, which you will follow by day, and a certain star, which you will follow by night. Take nothing with you. Your journey will not end until the cloud stops and the star stops. . . .
>
> When they were all safe and settled Taiowa commanded Sótuknang to destroy the world. Sótuknang destroyed it by fire because the Fire Clan had been its leaders. He rained fire upon it. He opened up the volcanoes. Fire came from above and below

and all around until the earth, the waters, the air, all was one element, *fire*, and there was nothing left except the people safe inside the womb of the earth.[48]

The Hopi account of the second world-destruction contains a description of the onset of an Ice Age:

> So again, as on the First World, Sótuknang called on the Ant People to open up their underground world for the chosen people. When they were safely underground, Sótuknang commanded the twins, Poqanghoya and Palongawhoya, to leave their posts at the north and south ends of the world's axis where they were stationed to keep the earth properly rotating.
>
> The twins had hardly abandoned their stations when the world, with no one to control it, teetered off balance, spun around crazily, then rolled over twice. Mountains plunged into seas with a great splash, seas and lakes sploshed over the land; and as the world spun through cold and lifeless space it froze into solid ice.[49]

Many ancient peoples seem to have believed that the Deluge and other catastrophes were associated with changes in the motions of the sky—and therefore, in modern astronomical terms, with alterations in the axial direction and orbital motion of the Earth itself. Plato wrote in the *Timaeus*:

> At certain periods the universe has its present circular motion, and at other periods it revolves in the reverse direction. . . . Of all the changes which take place in the heavens this reversal is the greatest and most complete. . . . There is at that time great destruction of animals in general, and only a small part of the human race survives.[50]

In their book *Hamlet's Mill*, Giorgio de Santillana and Hertha von Dechend explored the astronomical basis of myth and concluded that

> the theory [of the ancients] about "how the world began" seems to involve the breaking asunder of a harmony, a kind of cosmogonic "original sin" whereby the circle of the ecliptic (with the zodiac) was tilted up at an angle with respect to the equator, and the cycles of change [the seasons] came into being.[51]

Many ancient cultures instituted rituals and ceremonies for the purpose of forestalling yet another catastrophe. Among the Yurok Indians, for instance, it is said that

> there was always a struggle to keep the world balanced upon the waters, the rhythms of abundance steady, in accord with the law and despite human beings' breaches of it. Knowing that this would be so, before they left the wo·gey [the Immortals, or myth-time beings with pure spirits] instructed certain people in what to do to put the world back in balance when the weight of human violations grew too great for it.[52]

Other cultures merely memorialized the catastrophes, or tried to emulate their destructiveness through sacrifice and ritual warfare. Eighteenth-century scholar Nicholas-Antoine Boulanger, after analyzing the cosmologies of the ancient Germans, Greeks, Jews, Arabs, Hindus, Chinese, Japanese, Peruvians, Mexicans, and Caribs, concluded that the ceremonies and myths of all these peoples resulted to a large extent from the effects of global catastrophes and the fear engendered by those catastrophes. That fear, according to Boulanger, has been passed from generation to generation:

> We still tremble today as a consequence of the deluge and our institutions still pass on to us the fears and the apocalyptic ideas of our first fathers. Terror survives from race to race. . . . The child will dread in perpetuity what frightens his ancestors.[53]

More recently, psychoanalyst Immanuel Velikovsky found in the worldwide memories of global cataclysms a source for the collective delusional systems that, as Freud and Jung had earlier concluded, afflict the entire human race. In his *Mankind in Amnesia* (1982), Velikovsky traced the psychological and social effects of the ancient mass trauma:

> The agitation and trepidation preceding global upheavals, the destruction and despair that accompanied them and the horror of possible repetition all caused a variety of reactions, at the base of which was the need to forget, but also the urge to emulate. Astrologers and stargazers, as well as soothsayers, divined; conquerors excelled in wanton and cruel devastation, invoking and

imitating planetary models. Prophets and seers exhorted and priests propitiated.[54]

It is worth noting briefly the existence of physical evidence—signs of ocean-level changes and of the simultaneous extinctions of large numbers of plant and animal species—that suggests that relatively recent, worldwide destructions have indeed taken place. Geologists and archaeologists are generally undecided about the interpretation of this evidence and often refer to it as "mysterious." But for the mythologist and the psychologist, there can be no question: the *memory* of catastrophe is universal, and the terror persists.

ॐ

In these first five chapters we have surveyed the stories of Creation, Paradise, Fall, and catastrophe, as they have been told and retold in the literature and oral traditions of peoples from every part of the world. Here, according to the ancient sages of all cultures, is the explanation for the present condition of human beings, and of the world.

But Paradise is not entirely contained in mythology. It appears in other aspects of human culture as well. And if it is the object of nostalgic regret, it is also the fuel for revolutionary and prophetic longing. Therefore, we will turn our attention next to the eruptions of the paradisal image in prophecy, literature, and utopian thought, as we progress from a consideration of memories of an original Paradise to visions of its eventual return.

PART TWO

Vision

For now we see though a glass darkly; but then face to face: now I know in part; but then shall I know even as also I am known.

I CORINTHIANS 13:12

CHAPTER · 6

Prophecy: The Once and Future Paradise

ARADISE IS NOT JUST THE STUFF of mythic memories. People of virtually every civilization and tribal culture, in every era, have nourished dreams of a golden world to come. In religious cultures these visions of Paradise have taken the form of prophecies, while in the modern secular West they have tended to be expressed in fictional or poetic literary works and in utopian social theories. In Part Two we will explore these various manifestations of the Paradise vision, beginning with prophecies of an eventual return of the Golden Age.

In the End as in the Beginning

Prophets of every spiritual tradition have envisioned an eventual dramatic end to the present human state and a general renewal of the world—a return of the original Paradise. The term *eschatology*, referring to doctrines of the end of history and the world to come, was originally applied to Jewish and Christian prophecies of the Last Judgment and the appearance of Christ's paradisal Kingdom, but historians of religion now use it to refer to similar themes in other traditions as well. Eschatological speculation seems to thrive in times of crisis. And though the imagery varies—from the Malaccan Pygmies' anticipation of a final great flood from which men's bones will miraculously rise and live again, to the Marxist doctrine of the ultimate revolutionary triumph of the proletariat in a paradisal communist

115

commonwealth—the underlying message is remarkably constant. Humanity's moral or spiritual decline must eventually culminate in a catharsis of cataclysmic dimensions, from which will emerge the seed of a restored age of peace and perfection. This seed is frequently embodied in the person of a messiah or reincarnated culture hero.

In an early Babylonian text we can already see the essential elements of the later and more familiar Hebrew and Christian eschatologies: there will be signs in Heaven, and the world will fall into confusion; "the people will sell their children for gold, the husband will desert his wife, the wife her husband."[1] But this era of chaos will be followed by a universal renewal, when a divine King will be enthroned.

The ancient Iranians also believed in an ultimate confrontation between good and evil, when the last of the spiritual descendants of Zoroaster will appear to raise the dead and to rehabilitate humanity and Nature. A consuming fire will make way for "a new world, free from old age, death, decomposition and corruption, living eternally, increasing eternally, when the dead shall rise, when immortality shall come to the living, when the world shall be perfectly renewed."[2]

The Greeks and Romans had their own eschatologies—no doubt influenced by those of the Babylonians, Hebrews, and Iranians—to which they added speculations about the recurrence of cosmic cycles. The fifth-century Roman writer Nemesius, for example, described the belief still current in his time concerning a periodically repeated destruction and renewal of the world:

> The Stoics say that the planets will be restored to the same zodiacal sign, both in longitude and latitude, as they had in the beginning when the cosmos was first put together; that in stated periods of time a conflagration and destruction of things will be accomplished, and once more there will be a reconstitution of the cosmos as it was in the very beginning. And when the stars move in the same way as before, each thing which occurred in the previous period will without variation be brought to pass again.[3]

In his "Messianic" *Eclogue*, Virgil presented a conception of the future repetition of the Golden Age, which would follow upon the present era without an intervening world destruction. His poem faithfully preserved the literary traditions of Hesiod and found readers among the early Christians. The child of the future, according to Virgil,

> shall be born to a godlike life, and shall see heroes mingling with the gods, and shall himself be seen amongst them, and shall rule a world restored to peace by his father's virtues. On thee, oh child, shall Earth, untilled, bestow thy earliest playthings— trailing ivy with foxgloves and lilies with acanthus. . . . The serpent shall disappear, and deceitful poisonous herbs. The Assyrian balsam shall spring up on every roadside.[4]
>
> Begin thy great career, dear child of the gods . . . the time is now at hand. See how the world trembles beneath its massive vault, the lands and ocean wastes and lofty sky: see how all rejoices at the age that comes to birth.[5]

Unlike Virgil, the Teutonic Norse said that a renewal of the world would come only after a great destruction. According to their legends, *ragnarok*, "the doom of the gods," will be preceded by a period of anarchy in which human beings will perform every kind of foul crime. Then the sky will be rent, the stars will fall, and the mountains will be shattered in earthquakes. All the gods will die, with the exception of Surtr, who will cause the Earth to be engulfed by flames, destroying all humankind. As the flames rise to Heaven, the Earth will sink into the sea. But then it will rise from the waters renewed, fresh and green, to be repeopled. The final stanzas of the *Völuspá*—the "Sibyl's Prophecy"—paint an idyllic picture of the restored Paradise:

> *Now do I see the earth anew*
> *Rise all green from the waves again;*
> *The cataracts fall, and the eagle flies,*
> *And the fish he catches beneath the cliffs.*
>
> *The gods in Idavoll meet together,*
> *Of the terrible girdler of earth they talk.*
> *And the mighty past they call to mind,*
> *And the ancient runes of the Ruler of Gods.*
>
> *In wondrous beauty once again*
> *Shall the golden tables stand mid the grass,*
> *Which the gods had owned in the days of old.*

Then fields unsowed bear ripened fruit,
All ills grow better, and Baldr comes back; . . .

More fair than the sun, a hall I see,
Roofed with gold, on Gimle it stands;
There shall the righteous rulers dwell.
And happiness ever there shall they have.[6]

The belief in the world's devastation by water and fire prior to its renewal also existed among the Celts, long before the arrival of Christianity. Native Irish documents, for example, attest to it: the prophecy of the war-goddess Babd and that of Fercertne in *The Colloquy of the Two Sages* resemble somewhat the tales of *ragnarok* in the Norse *Völuspá* in their descriptions of a world-consuming fire.

Muslims look toward the Day of Doom, which is the subject of many *suras*, or chapters, of the Koran. On that day,

when the Trumpet is blown with a single blast and the earth and the mountains are lifted up and crushed with a single blow,

Then, on that day the Terror shall come to pass, and heaven shall be split. . . .

On that day you shall be exposed, not one secret of yours concealed.[7]

Then the "Companions of the Right" will be "brought nigh the Throne, in the Gardens of Delight . . . a recompense for that they laboured. Therein they shall hear no idle talk, no cause of sin, only the saying 'Peace, Peace!' "[8] The Shia sect of Islam looks toward the arrival of the *mahdi*, "the divinely guided one," the hidden twelfth *imam* who will reappear in the Last Days. And the Egyptian Druzes believe that the Egyptian caliph al-Hakim, who reigned during the period 996–1021 and whom they regard as the last prophet and divine incarnation, will return at the end of the world—which they expect to occur at the close of the twentieth century.

The doctrine of the world ages in the *Mahabharata* is not without parallel in the apocalyptic passages in Iranian, Jewish, Christian, and Islamic literature. The end of the present *Kali Yuga*, the age of destruction, is described as follows:

And when men will begin to slay one another, and become wicked and fierce and without any respect for animal life, then will the Yuga come to an end. And even the foremost of the best classes, afflicted by robbers, will, like crows, fly in terror and will speed and seek refuge in rivers and mountains and inaccessible regions. And always oppressed by bad rulers with burdens of taxes, the foremost of the best classes will, in those terrible times, take leave of all patience and do improper acts. . . . And the low will become high, and the course of things will look contrary. And renouncing the gods, men will worship bones and other relics deposited in walls. . . . These all will take place at the end of the Yuga, and know that these are signs of the end of the Yuga. And when men become fierce and destitute of virtue and carnivorous and addicted to intoxicating drinks, then does the Yuga come to an end. And when flowers will be begot within flowers, and fruits within fruits, then will the Yuga come to an end. . . . And the course of the winds will be confused and agitated, and innumerable meteors will flash through the sky foreboding evil. And then the Sun will appear with six others of the same kind. And all around will be din and uproar, and everywhere there will be conflagrations. . . . And fires will blaze up on all sides. . . . And, when the end of the Yuga comes, crows and snakes and vultures and kites and other animals and birds will utter frightful and dissonant cries. . . . And people will wander over the Earth, uttering, "Oh father! Oh son!" and such other frightful and heart-rending cries.[9]

But the end of the *Kali Yuga* presages the recapitulation of the paradisal *Krita Yuga*.

Always—whether in Oriental or Western prophecies—the collapse of the old order signals the emergence of a restored Paradise. Nichiren, a thirteenth-century Japanese religious teacher, foretold that "the golden age, such as were the ages under the reign of the sage kings of old, will be realized in these latter days of degeneration and corruption, in the time of the Latter Law."[10]

The Tibetans say that we are now living at the end of a 26,000-year period of darkness. A series of global catastrophes, accompanied by political strife, will initiate a Purification and a new era of spirituality and light. The Shambhala tradition of Tibet—preserved in numerous sacred texts and oral teachings—tells of a mystical kingdom hidden behind snow peaks somewhere to the north. There, a line of enlightened kings is guarding the innermost teachings of Buddhism for a time when all truth in the world outside is lost in war and greed. Then, according to prophecy, the King of Shambhala will emerge with a great army to destroy the forces of evil and bring in a Golden Age.[11] The final battle is to be expected shortly after the barbarians of the outer world fly over the protective snow mountains in "vehicles made of iron" in an attempt to invade Shambhala.

Waiting for the Millennium

While the expectation of cosmic disruptions and unprecedented human misery leading to the return of Paradise is nearly universal, the prophecies most familiar to Westerners are those of the Judeo-Christian messianic tradition. With its powerful imagery of a coming apocalypse and the dawning of a new age of peace, the prophetic tradition in the West has shaped not only religion, but social and literary movements as well.

The Hebrew prophets consistently foretold that, following a great cosmic catastrophe that would both rout the heathens and purify the remnant of the Children of Israel, the righteous would assemble once again in the land of their fathers and God would dwell among them as ruler and judge. Deserts would blossom; the Moon would shine as the Sun, and the Sun's radiance would increase sevenfold; there would be an abundance of every kind of food; disease and sorrow would vanish; the people would live in perpetual joy and peace.

It was around the time of their nation's decline, beginning in the eighth century B.C., that the Hebrew prophets began to foretell that the restoration of Paradise would hinge on the appearance of a miraculous hero, the Messiah. While at first envisioned as a powerful monarch of Davidic descent who would lead his people to victory and prosperity, the Messiah was later pictured in superhuman terms as the Son of Man, who would appear riding on the clouds of Heaven.

According to the Syriac *Apocalypse of Baruch*, composed in the first century A.D., the Messiah will come only after a period of terrible hardship, the time of the last and most oppressive empire. He will destroy the enemy, taking its leader captive and bringing him in chains to the summit of Mount Zion. The Messiah will then inaugurate a kingdom of peace and an age of bliss wherein hunger, pain, violence, and eventually death itself will be abolished. It was under the spell of belief in the imminent advent of this savior-king that the Jews launched their suicidal war against the Romans, which ended in the capture of Jerusalem and the destruction of the Temple in A.D. 70.

Many early Christians interpreted Jesus' sayings according to the then-current Jewish messianic eschatology, and believed that his advent portended a swift and cataclysmic end to all things. His prophecies, couched as they were in the same language as the apocalyptic literature of the time, did little to dampen such expectations:

> And ye shall hear of wars and rumours of wars: see that ye be not troubled: for all these things must come to pass, but the end is not yet.

> For nation shall rise against nation, and kingdom against kingdom: and there shall be famines, and pestilences, and earthquakes, in divers places. . . .

> For then shall be great tribulation, such as was not since the beginning of the world to this time, no, nor ever shall be. . . .

> Immediately after the tribulation of those days shall the sun be darkened, and the moon shall not give her light, and the stars shall fall from heaven, and the powers of the heavens shall be shaken:

> And then shall appear the sign of the Son of Man in heaven: and then shall all the tribes of the earth mourn, and they shall see the Son of Man coming in the clouds of heaven with power and great glory.

> And he shall send his angels with a great sound of a trumpet, and they shall gather together his elect from the four winds, from one end of heaven to the other (Matthew 24:6, 7, 21, 29-31).

But Jesus had not appeared as a mighty warrior, throwing off the Roman oppressors and establishing a renewed, Edenic Jewish kingdom. The early Christian church was thus faced with a problem: many of the prophecies of Ezekiel, Isaiah, and Daniel had been left unfulfilled. Though the anointed one had come, events were unfolding not through apocalyptic divine intervention but according to familiar human political and economic processes. This problem was solved

Albrecht Dürer, *St. John before God and the Elders*,
from the woodcut series *Apocalypse* (1498).

through the doctrine of the Second Coming: the new age had indeed dawned, but it would not prevail in human affairs until Jesus returned to Earth in power and glory.

This second-advent doctrine was formulated in the latter part of the first century and was embodied in the Book of Revelation, probably the single most influential piece of prophetic literature in history. Combining Jewish and Christian elements in a poetic and immensely powerful eschatological scenario, the Apocalypse of John (as the book was also known) established images and archetypes—the New Jerusalem, the woman clothed with the Sun, the dragon, the beast with seven heads and ten horns, the Lamb standing on Mount Sion, the whore of Babylon, the sea of glass, the seven golden candlesticks, the four beasts and seven angels—that would dominate the prophetic imagination for centuries to come.

Chapter 20 of Revelation describes Satan as being bound and thrown into a bottomless pit, and Christian martyrs being raised from the dead and reigning with Christ for 1,000 years in a restored Paradise. After this Millennium there is to follow a general resurrection of the dead and the Last Judgment, when those whose names are not recorded in the Book of Life will be cast into the lake of fire. Then the New Jerusalem will descend from Heaven:

> And I saw a new heaven and a new earth: for the first heaven and the first earth were passed away; and there was no more sea.
>
> And I John saw the holy city, new Jerusalem, coming down from God out of heaven, prepared as a bride adorned for her husband.
>
> And I heard a great voice out of heaven saying, Behold, the tabernacle of God is with men, and he will dwell with them, and they shall be his people, and God himself shall be with them, and be their God.
>
> And God shall wipe away all tears from their eyes; and there shall be no more death, neither sorrow, nor crying, neither shall there be any more pain: for the former things are passed away.
>
> And he that sat upon the throne said, Behold, I make all things new (Revelation 21:1-5).

The Book of Revelation was the quintessential expression of the deep prophetic current from which Christianity itself sprang. But as the early church grew from a small band of persecuted visionaries to become the official state religion of the Roman Empire, millenarianism, with its visions of the collapse of all temporal authority, came to be seen as a dangerously revolutionary and mystical doctrine. The third-century Hellenic theologian Origen was the first of the church fathers to reject a literal reading of the apocalyptic prophecies of Revelation. From his time onward, Christianity has been divided between the establishment allegorists, who see the Millennium as a spiritual state into which the church entered at Pentecost, and innumerable radical millenarian sects that have insisted on taking biblical prophecies literally.

From the Montanian heresy of the second century, to the widely believed predictions of the imminent dawning of an age of love (originating with Joachim of Fiore in the Middle Ages), to the millenarianism of Charles Taze Russell and the Jehovah's Witnesses in our own era, Western civilization has been periodically swept by radical prophetic and messianic movements. Today, visions of a restored Paradise, based on Old and New Testament prophecies, continue to shape the worldview of millions of Christians everywhere. The events of the twentieth century have done nothing to dampen such expectations, and the millenarian movement in the United States continues to grow as books, magazines, and television and radio programs devoted to the interpretation of biblical prophecy feed the keen interest of a large audience.

The Great Purification

Apocalyptic thought is by no means unique to scriptural religions. Tribal peoples in every part of the world have preserved their own unwritten traditions telling of an eventual end to the present world, to be followed by the restoration of the original Paradise.

During the last few centuries, these ancient indigenous beliefs have been augmented and transformed through contact with missionaries, and hundreds of new tribal religious movements—often dramatically eschatological in character—have sprung up. While it is sometimes difficult for anthropologists to distinguish between indigenous and borrowed elements in these new religions, in nearly every instance tribal peoples themselves believe that their

Quetzalcoatl, the Plumed Serpent and the civilizing god of the Toltecs, was associated with the planet Venus and was considered the god of magic.

prophecies—whether ancient or recent—are being fulfilled by events surrounding the collision of their relatively small and defenseless cultures with the gargantuan momentum of civilization. It is as though their world were being rent by supernatural forces, setting the stage for a final universal destruction and the appearance of an entirely new mode of being. In many instances, the cultural upheavals that tribal peoples have faced during the past few centuries seem only to confirm their ancient prophecies of a time when human beings would become so greedy that the gods would destroy them to make way for a new Creation.

According to the Andaman Islanders, the world will come to an end in a great earthquake, which will destroy the barrier between Heaven and Earth. The spirits of the dead will then be reunited with their souls, and human beings will lead happy lives without sickness, death, or marriage. Even now, they say, the impatient spirits of the underworld are beginning to shake the roots of the palm tree that supports the Earth, so as to bring the end more quickly.

The Aborigines of Australia believe that the end of the world will come when the Dreamtime Law—the code of rituals established by the Creator-Ancestors—is no longer kept. Among many Aboriginal tribes, the last members initiated into these codes of ritual are growing old, with no young initiates to take their place. The Dreamtime Law is being forgotten, and the elders anticipate dire consequences for the entire world.

The Mortlock Islanders of the South Pacific likewise foretell that when the day comes in which people no longer worship the Creator-God Luk, when they wage wars and commit sins, the Lord of the World will put an end to them. Everything will go to ruin; only the gods will live on in their heavenly Paradise.

The Gabonese Pygmies of West Africa say that in the beginning Kmvum, the archetypal progenitor of the human race, lived on Earth with all his progeny in a Golden Age. But the people betrayed him, and the day of separation came. The Pygmies say that at the end of the present age Kmvum will return, bringing with him joy, abundance, and happiness.

The Altaic Tartars similarly believe that Tengere Kaira Khan, the "graceful emperor of Heaven" who once dwelt among men, will return at the end of the world.

The Toltecs and Aztecs of Central America remembered the prophecies of a priest born about A.D. 950, whom they regarded as the reincarnation of Quetzalcoatl, who appears in their mythology variously as culture hero, Christ figure, and celestial plumed serpent. The primordial Quetzalcoatl was said to have taught agriculture, astronomy, mathematics, and theology to the Maya at the beginning of their history. The tenth-century reincarnated Quetzalcoatl told the Toltecs that one like himself in appearance—bearded and light-skinned—would one day come from the east, wearing a feathered plume and clothing that would shine like the Sun, and traveling in a canoe with huge wings. In 1519, when Hernán Cortés arrived in a sailing ship, wearing shining armor and a plumed helmet, the Aztec emperor Montezuma immediately recognized the fulfillment of the prophecy. Quetzalcoatl had foretold that the arrival of the bearded white man would initiate a period of nine "hells"—fifty-two-year cycles of spiritual darkness. At the end of the nine hells would come a time of supreme cleansing and purification, when cities and mountains would collapse and most of the world would be reduced to rubble by fire. Quetzalcoatl promised to return at that time to initiate a Golden Age of spiritual renewal.

The Salish Indian tribes of the Pacific Northwest say that before the Creator-God left the Earth, he promised to return at the end of time. The world will then be reborn, and all human beings will live together in peace and happiness. The land of the spirits will no longer be separate from the physical world, and all things will be made right.

According to Pawnee myth, there will come a termination to all earthly life, which will be preceded by horrifying portents: the Moon will turn red, and the Sun will die. The North Star will preside over the great destruction. "When the time comes for all things to end," say the Pawnee prophets, "our people will turn into small stars and will fly to the South Star, where they belong."[12]

The prophets of the Mesquakie tribe said that there would come a time when many animals would become extinct and when people would sit and look into a box, seeing things happening far away and hearing the voices of people not present. These tribal seers foresaw floods and earthquakes as the means of cleansing the Earth of all that human beings have made, so that the original condition of the world can be restored.

The Hopi say that their prophets long ago told of the coming of wheeled boxes rolling over "black snakes" stretched across the land. They also spoke of special "cobwebs" by means of which people would be able to communicate over great distances. Hopi prophets say that within the next few decades humankind will either destroy itself or enter into a new spiritual age, the Fifth World. They foresee wars, famines, and natural disasters as steps in this Great Purification.

As noted earlier, many tribal eschatologies are of recent origin, having appeared as a response to contacts with civilization, and particularly with Christian missionaries. A famous and tragic example is the Ghost Dance movement of the Plains Indians of central North America. The movement originated with the Paiute around 1860 and spread westward until about 1873; a resurgence, inspired by Wovoka, a Paiute messiah-prophet, spread eastward in the late 1880s and culminated in the massacre of the Lakota (Sioux) Indians at Wounded Knee Creek in 1890.

According to the prophets of the movement, at the time of the fulfillment spiritual power would flood the Earth. The faithful were to dance for five days until a deep trance was induced, and they were to repeat the procedure every six weeks. The priests of the dance could heal by touch and were said to be able to see into the spirit world. The Lakota, led by Sitting Bull, were told that through the actions of the white race the Great Spirit had chastened them, and that deliverance was at hand. Their meager ranks would be augmented by the ghosts of their ancestors, and the white man's bullets would no longer be able to pierce Indian flesh. It was this sense of invincibility that led to the suicidal attack by the Lakota at Wounded Knee.

James Mooney, an ethnologist writing at the time of the Ghost Dance movement, described it this way:

> The great underlying principle of the Ghost Dance doctrine is that the time will come when the whole Indian race, living and dead, will be reunited upon a regenerated earth, to live a life of aboriginal happiness, forever free from death, disease and misery. On this foundation each tribe has built a structure from its own mythology, and each apostle and believer has filled in the details according to his own mental capacity or ideas of happiness, with such additions as come to him from the trance.[13]

The Ghost Dance, in which many tribes (such as the Navajo and Hopi) did not participate, was neither the first nor the last new Native American eschatological movement. The circumstances that gave it birth—the destruction of the Indian peoples and their ceremonial traditions—have hardly improved. Modern Native American spiritual leaders remember with sorrow the tragedy of Wounded Knee and have no desire to resurrect the illusions of warrior invincibility associated with the Ghost Dance. Yet they cannot but reiterate the same fundamental prophecy that fired that ill-fated movement: the greed and heartlessness of the modern world must end in a cathartic time of purification, when not only white people but Indians as well will face, en masse, the results of their attitudes and actions. Afterward, life will be permitted to continue only if people return to the original sacred way.

One of the most eloquent modern enunciations of the Native American vision is contained in these words of Hopi elder Dan Katchongva:

> Hopi is the bloodline of this continent, as others are the bloodline of other continents. So if Hopi is doomed, the whole world

will be destroyed. This we know, because the same thing happened in the other world. So if we want to survive we should go back to the way we lived in the beginning, the peaceful way, and accept everything the Creator has provided for us to follow. . . .

My father, Yukiuma, used to tell me that I would be the one to take over as leader at this time, because I belong to the [Clan of the] Sun, the father of all the people on the Earth. I was told that I must not give in, because I am the first. The Sun is the father of all living things from the first creation. And if I am done, the Sun Clan, then there will be no living thing left on the Earth. So I have stood fast. I hope you will understand what I am trying to tell you.

I am the Sun, the father. With my warmth all things are created. You are my children, and I am very concerned about you. I hold you to protect you from harm, but my heart is sad to see you leaving my protecting arms and destroying yourselves. From the breast of your mother, the Earth, you receive your nourishment, but she is too dangerously ill to give you pure food. What will it be? Will you lift your father's heart? Will you cure your mother's ills? Or will you forsake us and leave us with sadness, to be weathered away? I don't want this world to be destroyed. If this world is saved, you all will be saved, and whoever has stood fast will complete this plan with us, so that we will all be happy in the Peaceful Way.[14]

A new Paradise awaits, but humanity must first undergo a cathartic cleansing. Few prophets have looked beyond the day of Purification to describe the events of the restored Golden Age, for the world to come will be inconceivable in terms of the present one. With the return of Paradise, history—as a chronicle of wars and intrigue, of plots and villains—will be finished. Humanity and Nature, Heaven and Earth will once more be joined in peace and harmony as a new Creation-Time begins.

. . . the golden age, the most improbable of all dreams that ever existed, but the one for which men gave their lives and all their strength, for which prophets died and were slain, without which peoples do not wish to live and cannot even die!

FYODOR DOSTOEVSKY

CHAPTER 7

Paradise as a Force in Human Culture

HE VISION OF PARADISE fires human imaginations as few other ideas, images, or dreams have ever done. Our greatest desire is for a state in which all our interactions are based in a free, mutual, and noble exchange of love. Everyone wishes to be in a condition of relaxed, yet intimate and purposeful harmony with the whole of life. And so it is understandable that the quintessential expression of those longings, in the mythic image of Paradise, should naturally evoke a profound response. It is an image of transcendence, of radiance, of mystical flight, and of the union of humankind, Deity, and Nature. It both describes and explains the essence of human evil, and it culminates in the image of the heroic journey leading from the present fallen human condition back to the original state of perfect union.

In this chapter we will explore three of the many ways in which the paradisal image has shaped the course of civilization. First, we will trace the theme of Paradise in Western literature from the Middle Ages to the present. Then we will see how the longing for an earthly Paradise has produced the phenomenon of the American Dream. Finally, we will follow the current of Edenic vision running through history's most important social theories and experiments.

Paradise in Literature

Literature, as all forms of art, is usually evaluated critically in terms of the subtlety or delicacy with which it is wrought. But formal considerations alone do little to explain why one poem or novel achieves immortality while others pass into oblivion. A surer guide to the potency of literature is its ability to evoke and satisfy universal archetypal longings.

This view is confirmed by the findings of a relatively new school of literary analysis known as archetypal or mythic criticism. Its pioneers, Maud Bodkin (author of *Archetypal Patterns in Poetry*) and Northrop Frye (author of *Anatomy of Criticism*), have sought the source of universal attraction in literature not in form or content per se, but in universal patterns of imagery and narrative, such as those that shaped ancient myths and rituals. And the patterns that the mythic critics have found spring almost entirely from images of Paradise and its loss or the heroic quest for its renewal. In their detailed and scholarly studies, mythic critics have shown that much of the greatest and most profoundly moving literature in history owes its inspirational power to the paradisal myth.[1]

The subject of Paradise in literature is so vast that we cannot hope to do it justice in a few pages. The only solution is to limit the scope of our survey, and I have therefore chosen a small core of examples from European and American literature.

The Divine Comedy of Dante Alighieri (1265–1321) is generally considered to be the greatest single literary work in the Italian language. This epic poem of three grand divisions—the *Inferno*, the *Purgatorio*, and the *Paradiso*—describes Dante's imaginary journey through hell and the misery of sin to the mountain of purgatory, where souls struggle to learn virtue. From there, Beatrice—Dante's personification of otherworldly enlightenment—conducts the poet through nine heavens toward the all-encompassing, spaceless Empyrean, where he is allowed a brief vision of God himself:

> *Forth from the last corporeal are we come*
> *Into the Heaven, that is unbodied light;*
> *Light intellectual, replete with love;*
> *Love of true happiness, replete with joy;*
> *Joy, that transcends all sweetness of delight.*

In finding words to convey the experience of the infinite, Dante used vivid religious imagery—derived, certainly, from Medieval Christian sources, but perhaps also from Zoroastrian and Islamic folklore, which it closely resembles.

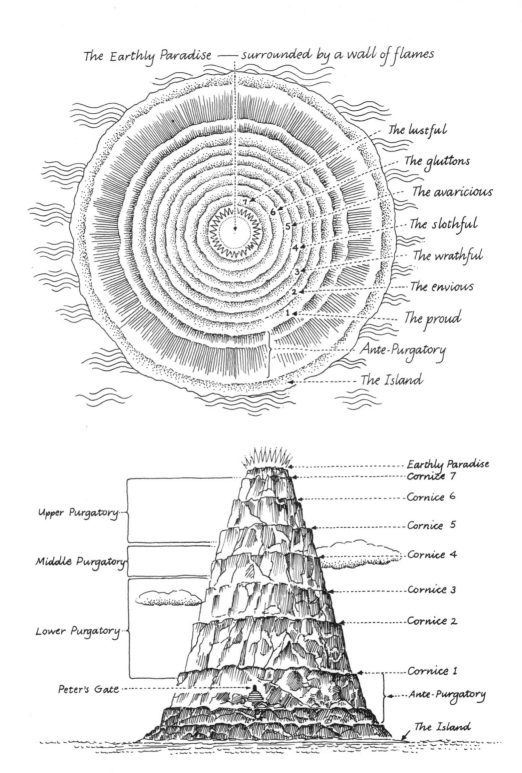

The Earthly Paradise — surrounded by a wall of flames

The lustful

The gluttons

The avaricious

The slothful

The wrathful

The envious

The proud

Ante-Purgatory

The Island

Earthly Paradise
Cornice 7

Cornice 6

Cornice 5

Cornice 4

Cornice 3

Cornice 2

Cornice 1

Ante-Purgatory

The Island

Upper Purgatory

Middle Purgatory

Lower Purgatory

Peter's Gate

The plan of Dante's Mount Purgatory

Dante's description of a journey to Paradise was, as Howard R. Patch showed in *The Other World According to Descriptions in Medieval Literature* (1950), a masterful recasting of what was probably the most widespread theme in pre-Renaissance European literature and folklore. In romance, allegory, and didactic treatises, medieval imagination again and again attempted a description of either an earthly or an otherworldly garden of delight filled with fountains and fruit-laden trees, sweet-songed birds, and pavilions decked with flowers, crystals, and jewels. Dante's accomplishment lay not just in his power of literary expression, but also in his ability to penetrate to the core of the longing that suffused his world. In so doing he created a poem that, in the eyes of nearly every literary critic of the past three centuries, was not to be equaled until the appearance of Milton's *Paradise Lost*.

In his supreme work, the brilliant English poet John Milton (1608–1674) set before himself the problem of evil: Why, if there is a God, and he is benevolent, does he permit the torture and destruction of humankind by war, disease, and famine? Milton's answer epitomized the spiritual vision of Protestant Christendom. Humankind suffers because of an innate perversity that originated with the first couple. Adam and Eve were created perfect and were given a scope of freedom no human beings have known since.

> *Then was not guilty shame, dishonest shame. . . .*
> *So passed they naked on, nor shunned the sight*
> *Of God or angel, for they thought no ill:*
> *So hand in hand they passed, the loveliest pair*
> *That ever since in love's embraces met,*
> *Adam the goodliest man of men since born*
> *His sons, the fairest of her daughters Eve.*

Yet our first parents chose forbidden knowledge and death instead of obedience and life. It was only fitting punishment that God then deprived them of their freedom and drove them out of the Garden to die in a world made hostile by their own failure. The futility and sorrow of present humanity, otherwise unexplainable in a world created by a God of mercy, are the result of the original crime. Evil desires gnaw at human beings from within, and unforgiving Nature attacks from without. However, through sober conduct, integrity in living, and God's grace, human beings can again hope to attain liberty of spirit and perfection of soul—though only individually and to a limited degree.

The impact of Milton's poem on English literature has been comparable to that of Dante's on the Italian. Between 1700 and 1800, *Paradise Lost* was published more than 100 times; in contrast, during the same period Shakespeare's works appeared in only 50 editions. Milton himself felt that he was writing—or rather, dictating, since he was blind when the poem was composed—from direct inspiration. It is perhaps to the quality of this inner vision that *Paradise Lost* owes its continuing influence.

Not long after Milton's death, a popular Baptist preacher named John Bunyan (1628–1688) recast the quest for Paradise in the language of Puritan England. Bunyan's book *The Pilgrim's Progress from This World to That Which Is to Come* was an allegorical portrayal of his own inner journey, which began with his childhood as the dissolute son of a country tinker and embraced his dramatic religious conversion, success as a minister, soldiering on the side of the Parliamentarians in the civil war, and eventual imprisonment—a circumstance that Bunyan used to advantage in writing his masterpiece, which in its time attained a popularity second only to that of the Bible.

The chief character of the novel is Christian—symbolically, Bunyan himself—who at the beginning of the story finds himself burdened with sin. He meets a man named Evangelist, who urges him to leave the City of Destruction and make for a distant light that will guide him to the Wicket Gate, where his journey must begin. Obstinate and Pliable try to dissuade him from his path, but their arguments are of no effect. Pliable even offers to join Christian, and on the way they fall into the Slough of Despond, from which they escape only with difficulty. Christian continues to meet obstacles by way of such characters as Mr. Worldly Wiseman (who lives in the town of Carnal Policy), Mr. Legality, Mr. Civility, Simple, Sloth, Presumption, Formalist, and Hypocrisy. He must make his way over the Hill of Difficulty and through the valleys of Humiliation and of the Shadow of Death. Eventually, he reaches the Delectable Mountains, but must still cross the River of Death before arriving at his goal—the Celestial City. Bunyan's description of Heaven is itself a fountain of paradisal imagery:

It was built of pearls and precious stones; also the streets thereof were paved with gold; so that, by reason of the natural glory of the City, and the reflection of the sun-beams upon it, Christian with desire fell sick.

As they near the City, Christian and his companion Hopeful meet "shining men" and leave behind their "mortal garments."

You are going now, said they, to the paradise of God, wherein you shall see the Tree of Life, and eat of the never-fading fruits thereof: and when you come there you shall have white robes given you, and your walk and talk shall be every day with the King, even all the days of eternity. . . . In that place you must wear crowns of gold, and enjoy the perpetual sight and vision of the Holy One: for there you "shall see him as he is."

The eighteenth and nineteenth centuries saw literature turning away from overtly biblical imagery toward more realistic and psychologically penetrating descriptions of the human state. During this period, which embraced the Age of Reason and the rise of the Romantic school, there were few attempts to depict Paradise directly. Instead, writers strove with the universal problem of evil and the heroic quest for love, happiness, and justice. These trends, exemplified in the works of Defoe, Dickens, and Melville, came full circle to the vision of a paradisal world in the works of the Russian novelist Fyodor Dostoevsky.

Dostoevsky, whose fictional explorations of the human mind and spirit influenced the development of both depth psychology and existential philosophy, had an unhappy and contentious life even after arriving at his own unorthodox, mystical brand of Christianity while in his thirties. In his short story "The Dream of a Ridiculous Man," he brought the Paradise myth to life as perhaps no other modern author has done. The narrator of the story is on the verge of suicide when he falls asleep in an armchair and dreams that he has shot himself. Instead of experiencing pain followed by oblivion, he finds himself witnessing his own funeral and burial. From the grave he is transported by some "dark and unknown being" through space to another world, like the Earth geographically but very different in other respects:

I suddenly, quite without noticing how, found myself on this other earth, in the bright light of a sunny day, fair as paradise. . . . The grass glowed with bright and fragrant flowers. Birds were flying in flocks in the air, and perched fearlessly on my shoulders and arms and joyfully struck me with their darling, fluttering wings. And at last I saw and knew the people of this happy land. They came to me of themselves, surrounded me, kissed me. The children of the sun, the children of their sun—oh, how beautiful they were! Never had I seen on our own earth such beauty in mankind. Only perhaps in our children, in their earliest years, one might find some remote, faint reflection of this beauty. The eyes of these happy people shone with a clear brightness. Their faces were radiant with the light of reason and a fullness of serenity that comes of perfect understanding, but those faces were gay; in their words and voices there was a note of childlike joy. Oh, from the first moment, from the first glance at them, I understood it all! It was the earth untarnished by the Fall; on it lived people who had not sinned. They lived just in such a paradise as that in which, according to all the legends of man-kind, our first parents lived before they sinned.

Dostoevsky goes on to describe the way of life of the inhabitants of this dreamworld Paradise:

They had, for instance, no science like ours. But I soon realised that their knowledge was gained and fostered by intuitions differ-ent from those of us on earth, and that their aspirations, too, were quite different. They desired nothing and were at peace; they did not aspire to knowledge of life as we aspire to understand it, because their lives were full. But their knowledge was higher and deeper than ours; for our science seeks to explain what life is, aspires to understand it in order to teach others how to live, while they without science knew how to live; and that I under-stood, but I could not understand their knowledge. They showed me their trees, and I could not understand the intense love with which they looked at them; it was as though they were talking with creatures like themselves. And perhaps I shall not be mis-taken if I say that they conversed with them. Yes, they had found their language, and I am convinced that the trees understood them. They looked at all nature like that—at the animals who lived in peace with them and did not attack them, but loved them, conquered by their love. They pointed to the stars and told me something about them which I could not understand, but I am convinced that they were somehow in touch with the stars, not only in thought, but by some living channel. . . .

There was no quarrelling, no jealousy among them, and they did not even know what the words meant. Their children were the children of all, for they all made up one family. There was scarcely any illness among them, though there was death; but their old people died peacefully, as though falling asleep, giving blessings and smiles to those who surrounded them to take their last farewell with bright and loving smiles. I never saw grief or tears on those occasions, but only love, which reached the point of ecstasy, but a calm ecstasy, made perfect and contemplative. One might think that they were still in contact with the departed after death, and that their earthly union was not cut short by death. They scarcely understood me when I questioned them about immortality, but evidently they were so convinced of it without reasoning that it was not for them a question at all. They had no temples, but they had a real living and uninterrupted sense of oneness with the whole of the universe.

Dostoevsky's protagonist inadvertently brings about a Fall by introducing lying, shame, war, crime, and slavery—as well as science, which merely enables the people to rationalize these new evils. The half-mad narrator sees the results of this corruption and repents, preaching forgiveness and redemption. His formula for the return of the Golden Age is summed up in the Golden Rule: ". . . in one day, *in one hour*, everything would be settled at once. The main thing is—love others as you love yourself. . . . Right away you will find out what to do."

If the description of an earthly Paradise has occasionally seemed naive to modern, sophisticated adult readers, it has nevertheless remained a staple device in children's literature. One thinks immediately of the Emerald City in *The Wizard of Oz*, Never-Never Land in *Peter Pan*, and the talking animals in *Through the Looking Glass*.

Superman, as all comic-book readers and film-goers know, was sent to Earth as an infant by his parents from the paradisal planet Krypton, which was about to be engulfed in a cataclysm. In the guise of mild-mannered journalist Clark Kent, the hero uses his powers of flight and X-ray vision to defeat the forces of evil on behalf of "truth, justice, and the American way."

Some archetypal fiction, while failing to achieve greatness as literature because of flaws in form or style, nevertheless attains wide popularity. One of the best-selling novels of the 1930s was James Hilton's *Lost Horizon* (which Frank Capra made into a classic film). The setting for the story is a remote and secluded Himalayan Paradise called Shangri-La, created in the early eighteenth century by a Capuchin friar who, near death, accidentally stumbled upon the valley of the Blue Moon. *Lost Horizon* is the story of a twentieth-century hero named Conway, who, with his brother and a planeload of British and American sophisticates, is kidnapped and taken to the hidden city. After a time Conway realizes he is being groomed to be the successor of the now-ancient Capuchin friar, who still presides over the community. Instead of accepting the commission, Conway chooses to escape with his brother, to whom Shangri-La is hell on Earth. The story ends with Conway's struggle to return to Paradise.

Much of the popular literature of the past few decades has taken the form of science fiction, a genre that offers unlimited scope for the rehearsal of mythic themes. Space travel can itself be seen as but a new expression of the ageless longing for a Paradise beyond the bounds of mundane existence. In science fiction one often finds descriptions of paradisal planets or of worlds destroyed by catastrophe following some moral decline. Striking examples appear in the works of Frank Herbert (*God Emperor of Dune*) and Ursula Le Guin (*The Dispossessed*).

Within the vast and uneven corpus of science fiction, some of the best-written and most mythologically penetrating works are the novels of Doris Lessing. *Shikasta* (1981) tells of an Edenic planet, Rohanda, that succumbs to disobedience and the resulting Degenerative Disease. Lessing breathes new life into the images of ancient Paradise; her description of Rohanda evokes visions of Stonehenge and of the pyramids when they were new. Just as the ancient Druids and Egyptians built their monuments to blend and mediate the forces of Heaven and Earth, the Rohandans used their geometric cities and stone alignments to maintain constant contact with a cosmic source of order and control, the star Canopus.

> Canopean strength was beamed continually into Rohanda. Rohanda's new, always deepening strengths were beamed continually back to Canopus. Because of this precise and expert exchange of emanations, the prime object and aim of the galaxy were furthered—the creation of ever-evolving Sons and Daughters of the Purpose.[2]

But Rohanda suffers an internal failure and becomes Shikasta. "To identify with ourselves as individuals—this is the very essence of the Degenerative Disease, and every one of us in the Canopean Empire is taught to value ourselves only insofar as we are in harmony with the plan."[3]

Dreams of Earthly Paradise

Fiction shades into nonfiction. For millennia, people of all cultures assumed that in some geographically remote region a place of beauty, peace, and abundance actually existed, awaiting discovery and exploration. Many early Greek authors specialized in the genre of the fantastic traveler's tale: from the voyages of the Argonauts in search of the Golden Fleece, to Hecataeus' and Diodorus Siculus' descriptions of the Hyperboreans—a race who lived in a Golden Age condition in a place "beyond the North Wind"—readers were regaled with stories of journeys to magical lands. Some of these stories were exaggerated reports of actual expeditions, in which the primitive life of tribal peoples was romanticized as a survival of Hesiod's Golden Race. In other instances the tales were entirely fictional—for example, in Diodorus' description of the voyage of Iambulus to a "happy island" in the south, where the people are tall and beautiful and have rubber bones and forked tongues, which allow them to carry on two conversations simultaneously.

Such stories of a still-existing earthly Paradise are by no means a phenomenon of Western culture alone. We have already noted the Tibetan legend of Shambhala, which, according to popular belief, is hidden in a remote valley in the Himalayas. Certain Buddhist texts purport to give directions to the lost kingdom, while others describe its way of life and form of government in elaborate detail. According to one legend Shambhala dematerialized long ago, when all of its inhabitants became enlightened, but the Rigden kings of Shambhala still maintain watch over the world and will return at a strategic time to save humankind from destruction. Modern scholars are divided between the belief that Shambhala is completely mythical, and the opinion that it corresponds to one of the historically documented kingdoms of central Asia.[4]

Some tribal cultures likewise believe in the continuing existence of an earthly Paradise. The Guarani tribes of Brazil, for instance, remember a former world that was utterly destroyed, and they expect the present world to be consumed in the near future. Some of the tribes foresee an end by flood, others by raging fire, still others by prolonged darkness or by monsters. With this expectation in mind, sometime before the arrival of the Portuguese the Guaranis began to migrate in search of a Land-without-Evil, in hopes of finding it before the destruction comes. This magical goal, "the land where one hides," is the only safe place; it is a land without fear, hunger, sickness, or death. The Land-without-Evil is difficult to reach, the Guaranis believe, but it is surely located in this world.

Throughout the Middle Ages and well into the Age of Discovery, most Europeans were confident that the biblical Garden of Eden still physically existed. Authorities debated its location in all earnestness. St. Augustine held that it was at the top of a great mountain reaching almost to the Moon and was therefore inaccessible to mortals. St. Basilius wrote rapturously of the sacred homeland, elevated to the "third region of the air" and filled with every pleasurable sight and sound one can imagine. There, the climate is uniformly pleasant, the flowers always bloom, and waters well up in crystal fountains. All of Nature enjoys perpetual youth and joy, and nothing decays and dies. St. Ambrosius, whose fourth-century writings achieved great popularity, likewise rhapsodized on the verdure and beauty of the still-existing Garden.

Thus, in the fifteenth century—when techniques of navigation and shipbuilding began to enable ever-longer sea voyages, and economic and political interests began to press the search for new trade routes—explorers had more than economics in mind as they set sail for the ends of the Earth. The greatest of the discoverers, Christopher Columbus, was apparently acquainted with the writings of Basilius and Ambrosius and, according to his own statements, undertook his voyages more for religious reasons than for any economic or scientific purpose. Moreover, he believed that the islands he found were in close proximity to the very gates of Eden.

Columbus was obsessed with the prophecy in Matthew 24:14 that states, "And this gospel of the kingdom shall be preached in all the world for a witness unto all nations; and then shall the end come." In his *Book of Prophecies*, he wrote that the conquest of the new continent and the conversion of the heathen would be the penultimate events leading to the destruction of the Antichrist and the end of the world. In this apocalyptic drama he assumed for himself no minor role: "God made me the messenger of the new heaven and the new earth." Columbus told Prince John that the location of Paradise had been revealed to him, in fulfillment of prophecies in Isaiah: "He showed me the spot where to find it."[5]

The confusion of the newly found continent with the earthly Paradise hardly ended with Columbus. Throughout Europe there flowed a deep current of longing for the renewal of Christianity, and the discoveries across the Atlantic fueled hope that perhaps a longed-for spiritual renaissance might be brought about by migration to Eden. Ulrich Hugwald, a sixteenth-century utopian Humanist, prophesied that following the colonization of America humanity would return "to Christ, to Nature, to Paradise"—to a state without war, want, or luxury.

While Catholic explorers from Spain and Portugal sought to subdue the "Indian" heathens in fulfillment of biblical prophecies, representatives of the Protestant Reformation rejoiced in the belief that they had found their own promised land, where the reform of the Church could be completed and perfected. The doctrine was broadcast in the colonies that America, among all the nations of the Earth, had been chosen as the place of Christ's Second Coming. The Millennium would bring with it a physical transformation of the world. As the Puritan Increase Mather, president of Harvard University from 1685 to 1701, put it, "When this kingdom of Christ has filled all the earth, this earth will be restored to its Paradise state."[6]

Early European colonists, and the hordes of immigrants who

followed, journeyed to the New World in expectation of beginning life anew, of finding a new birth. Everything in America was considered bigger, stronger, and more beautiful than anything in the decaying Old World, which was often equated with Hell. The colonists considered themselves the chosen people, and their return to simplicity was a moral triumph. "The more cultured and intelligent you are," wrote Cotton Mather, "the more ready you are to work for Satan." America provided an escape from the oppression and extravagance of the European aristocracy, and an opportunity to return to a purified Christianity. The colonists considered the inferiority of their clothes and culture in comparison to those of Europeans to be a sign of their moral superiority.

The frontier, which was the rudest and most primitive place of all, was correspondingly the most paradisiacal: the vast forests, the open range, and the rugged simplicity of pioneer life were set in contrast to the demonic vices of the urban environment. The revivalist movement began on the frontier and spread eastward, carrying with it the conviction that urban iniquities, of European origin, were the cause of the decline of Christianity; only a return to the vigor and simplicity of the "old-time religion" could recall the happy, moral, Edenic way of life.

Many of the American pioneers considered industrialism a European evil. However, another view gradually gained prominence: instead of threatening the hope of achieving an earthly Paradise, the combined forces of capitalism and scientific invention were seen as ensuring its fulfillment. Thus, in the nineteenth century the idea of unending progress became a kind of religion in itself, promising the ultimate achievement of a Golden Age of leisure and wealth for all. J. A. Eltizer's 1842 book *The Paradise within the Reach of All Men, by Power of Nature and Machinery* expressed this new Yankee dream—a way of life perfected by automation—in language every American could understand.

Meanwhile, American philosophers and poets were giving a more sublime outlet to their Adamic yearnings. Ralph Waldo Emerson and Henry David Thoreau called for what amounted to a return to innocence, which was to be accomplished through a casting aside of the dusty spiritual and intellectual traditions of Europe in favor of a renewed and immediate perception of the universal and the sacred.

Edward Hicks, *Peaceable Kingdom with Seated Lion* (1833–1834). Hicks, an American primitive artist, frequently depicted the paradisal situation described in Isaiah 11: "and the leopard shall lie down with the kid; and the calf and the young lion and the fatling together; and a little child shall lead them." Hicks regarded William Penn's treaty with the Indians as an event foreshadowing the Millennium, which he saw as a return to the "peaceable kingdom."

Walt Whitman, who spoke of himself as a "Chanter of Adamic songs," declared, "Divine am I, inside and out, and I make myself holy whatever I touch." The past was dead, and humanity had been granted a new beginning, a second primordium in the Paradise of America. A generation later, however, the New World was already running out of frontier, already beginning to struggle against its own revolutionary institutions. While the American Dream would live on well into the twentieth century, it would now be dogged with the suspicion that Paradise had once again slipped away.

Utopia: Paradise Made to Order

In their attempts to organize their collective affairs, human beings seem to come under the periodic influence of two opposing psychological drives. One is the longing for Paradise—the yearning for a state of individual and collective happiness, purpose, and harmony. This compulsion, when it reaches fever pitch, typically drives people to revolution, reform, or bold social experiments. The other drive is the desire for stability, power, and domination. When given full rein, this second drive inevitably seems to result in some kind of despotism. Most of history can be seen as a series of oscillations between periods of the relative dominance of one or the other of these two drives. And sometimes—as was the case in 1793 in France and again in 1917 in Russia—the oscillations can be so quick and violent that totalitarianism and indiscriminate slaughter are justified in the name of universal love and brotherhood.

It is commonly thought that some forms of government are inherently paradisal or idealistic while others are inherently oppressive. It is perhaps more reasonable to suggest that the influence of both the visionary and bureaucratic drives can be traced in every form of social order. Kingship, for example, originated as a way of commemorating the reign of the World King of the Golden Age, and the benevolent monarch was regarded as the conduit of the forces of life. But of course, in the hands of a megalomaniacal autocrat, the institution of kingship can serve instead the forces of death and oppression. Democracy also had idealistic beginnings as a means of realizing individual freedom and equality. According to the democratic ideal, human nature is fundamentally trustworthy and, given the opportunity, the majority of people will collectively make wise and just decisions. But in a democracy there is always the danger that the nation will tend morally and intellectually toward its lowest common denominator, leading to control by powerful special interests and clever demagogues.

History shows that it is in the early, idealistic phase of a social order that the visionary drive tends to predominate. The promise of Paradise fires the emotions of the masses, often inspiring them to deep personal sacrifice. Sooner or later, however, some group finds a way to manipulate this paradisal idealism to further its own interests. Those in power then seek to instill in the people a fear of losing whatever bit of Paradise they seem to have gained. Greed and fear lead to corruption and bureaucracy, which in their extremes then sow the seeds for another visionary revival.

Thus, if we wish to isolate and examine the paradisal impulse in the social psyche, we can perhaps best do so by exploring the idealistic premises that spawn new social orders. And there is no more instructive or economical way to do this than to make a historical study of utopian dreams and visions.

The belief that a perfect society can be built by human beings, given sufficient foresight and industry, has exercised thinkers since the time of the ancient Greeks. In his *Republic*, Plato outlined his vision of an ideal state ruled by philosopher-kings, with the military protection of a class of guardians. It would be a communist republic, with all property shared without regard to status of birth. In the *Republic*, communism extends even to marriage, with wives and children held in common. Everything is ordered rationally, by law.

If the type of society envisioned by Plato could be said to foreshadow national socialism, another early *Republic*—this one by the Stoic philosopher Zeno—prefigured modern anarchism by advocating the abolition of the state. Zeno taught that human institutions breed laziness and corruption, and that the greatest good comes from the individual cultivation of strength of character. If people live according to the dictates of their own innate sense of reason and integrity, everything will run smoothly, without the need for armies, governments, or laws. Plato and Zeno thus represented the two poles of utopian thought—on one hand, the belief that Paradise can be attained through an imposed social order; on the other, the belief that only the assumption of absolute individual responsibility will result in any ultimate state of peace and fulfillment. Historically, most utopians have followed Plato.

The word *utopia* (from Greek, with the double meaning of "good place" and "no place") was coined by St. Thomas More (1478–1535) as the title for his fictional account of an imaginary state where social life is governed by principles similar to those advocated by Plato. The text of *Utopia* is written as the report of a Portuguese sailor, Raphael Hythlodaye, who has made three voyages to the New World with Amerigo Vespucci. Though Hythlodaye tells of travels through various wild and unexplored lands, the centerpiece of the narrative is his description of the island of Utopia, founded by King Utopos. The island contains fifty-four well-planned cities, where the population is kept constant, crops are controlled, food is freely distributed, money and finery are scorned, everyone works a six-hour day, and education is compulsory. Rulers are chosen from the learned class by secret ballot, and laws are so few and so simple that lawyers are unnecessary. The Utopian way of life, according to More,

> provides not only the happiest basis for a civilized community, but also one which, in all human probability, will last for ever. They've eliminated the root-causes of ambition, political conflict, and everything like that. There's therefore no danger of internal dissension, the one thing that has destroyed so many impregnable towns. And as long as there is unity and sound administration at home, no matter how envious neighboring kings may feel, they'll never be able to shake, let alone shatter, the power of Utopia.[7]

Unlike Plato's *Republic*, More's perfect community is described as though it already exists. His implication is clear: utopia is realizable if people will only make it so.

If More's *Utopia* doesn't seem so paradisal to modern readers—after all, what is the advantage of a six-hour workday, we would ask, when slavery is condoned, leisure is strictly regulated, and people are forbidden to assemble to discuss politics?—it was nevertheless considered visionary in its own time. During the Middle Ages the entire social hierarchy, from king to serf, was regarded as divinely ordained and immutable. Following the appearance of *Utopia*, political theory was again open to discussion. People began to ask whether inequality, oppression, and poverty were indeed part of God's inscrutable plan, or whether they might instead be simply the consequences of human stupidity, greed, and neglect. Perhaps the application of reason and ingenuity might make it possible to create, if not Paradise, at least a new social order in which everyone would be better off.

Following More, utopian fantasies and proposals proliferated. Francis Bacon's unfinished *New Atlantis* (1627) was an attempt to add technology to utopia's attractions. On the imaginary island of Bensalem, science is applied to nature by a learned society called Solomon's House (after which the British Royal Society was later patterned), and inventions such as aircraft, submarines, radio, and telephone make the island a place of ease and plenty. It is in Bacon's ideal community that we see the first expression of the modern idea of scientific and technological progress as the road to Paradise.

By the end of the eighteenth century the feudal system had collapsed throughout much of Europe, to be replaced by unbridled capitalism, which brought its own unique set of opportunities and evils. Economic necessity forced peasants from the countryside and into crowded cities, where they competed for dreary factory work. It was in this context that Comte Henri de Saint-Simon (1760–1825) laid the groundwork for socialism with his writings attacking unbridled individualism. As an alternative to laissez-faire economics, he proposed a new industrial administration. Like Bacon, Saint-Simon saw salvation in the advent of science and technology and advocated rule by scientific experts. The future utopian society would be run like a huge workshop, with the state—as a coercive institution—virtually eliminated.

Karl Marx and Friedrich Engels, the fathers of communism, appropriated and developed Saint-Simon's ideas of class struggle. They called Saint-Simon's ideas utopian socialism to distinguish them from their own scientific socialism, which they based on a strictly materialist interpretation of history. But communism was nevertheless clearly utopian in its goals: Marx predicted that the struggle of proletarians (the working class) against their capitalist taskmasters in the modern industrial state would eventually end in the formation of a socialist society in which associated producers would cooperate, free of economic and social restraints. Thus, not only class struggle but the tyranny of history itself would ultimately be brought to an end.

Engels, at the end of his critique of the writings of socialist Eugen Düring, outlines his vision of what the perfected future society will be like. Monetary value will have no connection with the distribution of goods, and the economy will be coordinated by production plan; the division of labor will disappear with the "suppression of the capitalist character of modern industry." With factories located throughout the country, opposition between urban and rural interests will dissolve, to the benefit of both industry and agriculture. At the end of the process the state itself will be abolished, and religion will wither.

As Bertrand Russell pointed out, Marxism, despite its dogmatic atheism, is modeled on the messianic pattern of history. In Marx's writings the redemptive role of the "just," the "anointed," and the "innocent" in eschatological Christian writings is taken up by the proletariat, whose sufferings change the world. Marx predicts a final struggle between good and evil—personified in the proletariat and the capitalists, respectively—that is analogous to the beginning of the Millennium. Paradise, in the communist canon, is a classless society in which most work is done by machines, and all goods are held in common.

By the early twentieth century, the number of utopian proposals and fantasies in print numbered in the hundreds, with most writers elaborating on communistic and technocratic ideas traceable to Plato, More, and Bacon. A theme that appeared more than once was the biological engineering of the human race into a breed of wise, talented, and incorruptible patricians. Other theorists identified Paradise merely with the ideal city, a cosmopolitan Eden to be achieved through enlightened design and engineering.

But all of this enthusiasm for the potential of technology as humanity's savior provoked a backlash. Some authors began exploring the literary form of the dystopia—a utopia in reverse. One notable example was George Orwell's *Nineteen Eighty-Four* (published in 1948), in which all of humanity languishes under the rule of the ultimate totalitarian state. Was the future technological society—in which even human reproduction would be supervised by machines and scientists—truly a vision of Heaven, or was it instead a very Hell on Earth? In one way or another, the question has extended to every utopian plan ever devised: one person's *Paradiso* is another's *Inferno*.

The Power of Example

While some utopians have tried to change society through revolution, referendum, or reform, others have chosen the quiet path of building a model of an ideal community in the hope of influencing the rest of the world by example. By distancing themselves from the rest of society, these experimenters have opened to themselves the possibility of pursuing ideals far more radical than those that any modern nation could likely be persuaded to voluntarily accept. While many such communities have sought a shared religious experience through contemplation and meditation, others have championed equality of sex and color and the abolition of private property or of the institutions of monogamy and marriage. While some have tried to attain a more natural way of life through nudism or vegetarianism, others have emphasized nonviolence or the development of character through hard work and scrupulous craftsmanship. In one way or another, whether explicitly or implicitly, every one of these experiments has sought to actualize some aspect of the archetypal vision of Paradise.

One of the first recorded communal social experiments was the Pythagorean community, established in the sixth century B.C. in Crotona, on the instep of the Italian boot-heel. In addition to being an institute of education and an academy of science, Pythagoras' school was a small model city. It was ruled by the Council of Three Hundred, a kind of political, scientific, and religious order that was made up of initiates and whose recognized leader was Pythagoras himself. The Pythagorean Order, which had as its goal the initiation of a new Golden Age of wisdom and peace, was so successful in governing that it gained control over most of the western Greek colonies. Wherever Pythagoras and his societies appeared, order and concord followed. Around 500 B.C., however, a man named Cylon, who had been rejected from the school in Crotona, organized a mob at whose hands Pythagoras and forty leaders of the Order died. The Order itself survived for two centuries afterward before disappearing.

At about the same time in India, Gautama Buddha and his disciples—who at the time of his death numbered 1200, of both sexes and all castes—were creating a sort of nomadic utopian village. In the rainy season they stayed in one place, listening to Gautama's lectures and studying, but the rest of the year they followed their master on his travels. The aim of the Buddha and his followers was, in the words of Nasaru, "to produce in every man a thorough internal transformation by self-culture and self-conquest."[8] If the Buddha could be called a utopian, then he was clearly of the school of Zeno. After the Buddha's death, his community continued and formed the basis for Buddhist monasticism. Buddhist monks were the great civilizers of China and southeast Asia: they led the people in the transformation of wastelands into rice fields, in the production of art, and in the development of medicine, science, and education.

The Essenes, a religious brotherhood that flourished in Palestine from about the second century B.C. to the end of the first century A.D., held all property in common, ate their meals together in silence, and lived ascetic lives of ritualistic purity, apart from society. Like the Pythagoreans, the Essenes admitted only those who had qualified through a process of initiation. Their communal lifestyle set the pattern for later Christian monasteries, the first of which was established by the ascetic Pachomius of Thebaid.

From the beginning of the fifth century on, monasteries sprang up throughout Christendom. With the decline of the Roman Empire came social crises of every kind; paradoxically, while the Church was responsible for the destruction and suppression of ancient spiritual and scientific knowledge, it occasionally acted as preserver as well. In the medieval monastery, books were written and copied, crafts developed and maintained, and new technologies invented. Monks opened schools, distributed food to the poor, and traded goods. All of this activity was an articulation of their longing for Paradise: just as the monks' walled gardens were intended to recall the original Edenic Garden, the towered cathedrals they helped build were designed to embody a vision of the celestial City of Revelation.

Utopian America

America, as we have already seen, was from the time of its discovery through the period of its colonization the object of the paradisal longings of the entire Western world. It was also the site of scores of communal experiments. Most were religious in nature, such as the Bruderhof communities—the Mennonites and their subsequent offshoots, the Hutterites and Amish—and the Quakers, Shakers, and Mormons. All of these groups valued hard work and simplicity of lifestyle. While most flourished for only a few decades, some continue to do so. The Amish of Pennsylvania, for example, shun modern agricultural technology with its expensive equipment and chemicals, and yet are among America's most successful farmers.

But not all of the American experimental communities had a religious basis. During the nineteenth century, many of the more than 150 cooperative communities founded in America were attempts to prove the social theories of the European utopian theorists Robert Owen and Charles Fourier.

In his book *A New View of Society, or Essays on the Principle of the Formation of the Human Character,* British socialist Owen set forth his theory that character is formed by environmental influences, from the earliest years of childhood. A perfect society, therefore, should begin with enlightened education. Owen argued for the subordination of machinery to humanity and for the establishment of villages of "unity and cooperation," of about 1200 people each, in which competition would be eliminated and people would be free to improve themselves physically, mentally, and morally.

In 1825, Owen came to America to test his theories. He was able to purchase the site of a previous communal experiment, Harmonie (a religious community founded in 1815 by Georg Rapp), which came complete with a town of 160 houses, a brick kiln, and mills, vineyards, and factories. Owen then addressed the United States Congress, describing his theories of educational and industrial reform and opening the community of New Harmony to prospective members. These soon arrived by the hundreds. Although the people who responded to Owen's appeal were a heterogeneous lot—consisting of idealists and scholars seasoned with more than a few fanatics, loafers, and crooks— life at New Harmony was, for a time, idyllic. Concerts, dances, discussions and lectures enlivened the leisure time of the inhabitants. An Owenite poem expressed their shared paradisal vision:

> Ah, soon will come the glorious day,
> Inscribed on Mercy's brow,
> When truth shall rend the veil away
> That blinds the nations now.

The face of man shall wisdom learn,
And error cease to reign:
The charms of innocence return,
And all be new again.

Soon, however, the community succumbed to disagreements over forms of decision making and the role of religion. Though the controversies were carried on in an "admirable" spirit, Owen withdrew in 1828, having invested and lost most of his fortune in the project. New Harmony had remained in existence only two years, but during that time it had produced the first kindergarten, the first trade school, the first free public library, and the first community-supported public school in the United States. The scientists Owen had brought from Europe—who had suffered opposition from the Church in their native countries and were eager to join the experiment—brought the beginnings of geology, zoology, botany, and chemistry to America.

In the 1840s and 1850s, more than two dozen communities were established in the United States and Canada to implement the ideas of the French social visionary Charles Fourier. Fourier was a prolific writer who had the knack of making the most outrageous proposals seem plausible and even compelling. He prophesied, for example, that when the release of human passion finally brings the world together in a harmonious and noncoercive order, the oceans will turn to lemonade and wild beasts will magically transform themselves into antilions and antitigers who serve humanity. Fourier drew up plans for model communities in which drudgery would be abolished, and people would be free to develop their talents; they might, for example, work in gardens in the morning and sing in the opera in the evening.

Among the Fourierist experiments was Brook Farm in Massachusetts. Established in 1841 by a group of intellectuals and idealists led by the Reverend George Ripley, the community was at first simply an exercise in combining education and industry. Its school sought to prepare students for college, while at the same time offering farm employment and experience in working beside skilled craftsmen. Ripley managed to attract some of the finest minds in New England as members or associates; among these were Ralph Waldo Emerson, Bronson Alcott, Margaret Fuller, and Nathaniel Hawthorne. For most of the five years of its existence, Brook Farm was probably the most intelligent and enlightened community in New England, and the happiest as well. Members worked, wrote, discussed, played, sang, and danced. But as Ripley turned the community increasingly toward doctrinaire Fourierism, many of its transcendentalist supporters backed off. In 1846 a fire destroyed the main meeting hall, whose construction had already strained the available financial resources. Creditors grew impatient, residents drifted away, and after a few months the community simply dissolved.

Members of the Oneida Community, begun in New York State in 1848 by John Humphrey Noyes, called themselves "Perfectionists," believing that true socialism could never be achieved apart from religion. They considered selfishness and jealousy the greatest of evils and regarded common ownership and common responsibilities as the way to root out exclusiveness. The principle extended even to marriage. To be devoted to a singular spouse, they taught, breeds possessiveness. As an alternative, the community developed a system of "complex marriage," reminiscent of certain of Plato's proposals in the *Republic*. The words of an Oneida song expressed the sense of complete communality that pervaded their affairs:

> *We have built us a dome*
> *On our beautiful plantation*
> *And we all have one home*
> *And one family relation*

In deference to public sentiment, complex marriage was discontinued in 1879, and the community ceased to pursue the perfectionist philosophy. Oneida was incorporated into a joint stock company in 1880 and still operates as a successful industry.

The New Communal Spirit

The early twentieth century saw a lull in the formation of alternative communities. Higher land prices in the first decade made such experiments more difficult to organize. Then came the First World War, followed by the cynical and hedonistic 1920s. In the 1840s, when Emerson wrote that "not a reading man but has a draft of a new community in his waistcoat pocket," there had seemed plenty of room and time for individualistic experimentation. Now the public's attention was fixed on the problems and opportunities of society as a whole—the Great Depression, the march of technology, and the horrors of another World War.

But with the 1960s came the greatest burgeoning of visionary social experiments in history. Many of them, products of the drugs-and-revolution counterculture, were formed with little serious forethought. Some were purely economic cooperatives, while others sprang from a universalist spiritual philosophy whose lineage could be traced to the transcendentalism of Emerson and the early days of Brook Farm.

One of the earliest—and certainly the most highly publicized—of the new communities was begun not in America, but in Findhorn, Scotland in 1963. Drawing its initial inspiration from spiritualistic guidance received by founders Peter and Eileen Caddy, the community was located in a sandy and forbidding caravan park outside a small coastal village. After several years of bare survival, the original group of three adults and two children began trying to establish communion with the local Nature spirits. Soon their garden was producing giant vegetables, which were celebrated in newspaper and magazine articles and in a popular book, *The Magic of Findhorn* by Paul Hawken. Spiritual seekers began to arrive at Findhorn from around the world, and the community was soon being described as the capital of the planetary New Age culture.

Those who flocked to Findhorn in the early 1970s brought plenty of idealism, but not always as much commitment or willingness to persevere. The community's ensuing growing pains brought changes in leadership, as well as disillusionment among many of those who had come merely on the basis of romanticized press accounts. Gradually, however, a natural sorting process occurred, and today Findhorn is stable and thriving.

Following the example of Findhorn came a plethora of hippie and New Age communes, most of them located in North America but some in Europe, Australia, and New Zealand as well. The largest was The Farm, founded on the down-home Zen philosophy of Stephen Gaskin, a former college professor from Los Angeles who in 1973 took his Monday night class on a permanent field trip to Tennessee. Traveling in old schoolbuses painted with psychedelic emblems, the long-haired pilgrims stopped in towns and cities along the way. There, at impromptu camp meetings, Gaskin spoke, musicians played, and jugs of peyote tea were passed through the audience.

When they arrived at the parcel of land they had purchased near Summertown, Tennessee, the Californians—whose ranks were now swelled by enthusiastic hippies who had joined the caravan along the way—began setting up a village, which included publishing facilities for the printing and distribution of Gaskin's books. The Farm, which soon boasted a population of 1100, also began an outreach program that included a touring rock-and-roll band and disaster-relief crews that were sent to Guatemala and New York City. In recent years The Farm's population has decreased significantly, and now hovers in the range of 200–300.

One of the most fertile of the twentieth-century experimental spiritual communities is Sunrise Ranch, founded in 1945 by Lloyd Meeker (1908–1954), a visionary with a modest formal education but a wealth of experience in motivating and inspiring people. Meeker, who used the pen name Uranda, underwent a dramatic personal transformation in 1932, which he later described as the dissolution of his hereditarily and environmentally generated human personality and the revelation of a transcendent inner source of absolute knowing. He spent the next dozen years traveling throughout North America, spreading his message of spiritual regeneration and gathering followers in an association known as Emissaries of Divine Light. Seeing the potential usefulness of a permanent setting where they could bring their vision into practical expression, Uranda and his small core of associates in 1945 purchased a desolate, abandoned farm near Loveland, Colorado. Their express purpose was to plant a seed of restored Eden.

The community of Sunrise Ranch received little public attention and as a result grew slowly, though consistently. Over the years, Emissaries founded eleven sister communities in North America, Europe, Australia, and Africa. Today, Sunrise Ranch has a stable population of 150 living on miraculously revitalized farmland, and serves as the headquarters for international organizations devoted to the demonstration of spiritual principles in agriculture, education, business, health care, and the communication arts.

Recently *Newsweek* magazine estimated that there are currently some 3000 cooperative intentional communities in the United States. Extrapolating from statistical studies of past communal experiments, one can safely predict that most of these present experiments will persist for no more than one to three years before dissolving. If a community's success is to be measured simply by longevity, then the vast majority will ultimately be considered failures. Yet the dissolution of a community as an entity may not mean failure for the individuals involved. The effort of creating and maintaining an intentional community, even for a few years, brings with it a kind of experience that is unattainable in the ordinary urban environment. In the best instance, communal life offers the chance to associate closely with a few friends who share a commitment to living consistently according to their highest vision.

What makes some communities thrive and others dissolve? There are a few essential issues that inevitably arise in every communal group—questions of leadership and decision making, of the division of labor, and of the distribution of material goods—whose resolution requires an ongoing compromise on the part of the egos of all concerned. The communities that survive the longest are those in which members are somehow motivated to transcend their own wants and fears for the good of the whole. In the great majority of cases, that motivation arises from a shared paradisal vision and a shared sense of the sacred. Every sociological study of cooperative communities has come to essentially the same conclusion: when the vision dies, the community dies.

However we measure their individual successes, intentional communities have in any case provided laboratories for the discovery and pioneering of a paradisal way of life, and they have benefited society as a whole in countless ways. From the Pythagoreans and their profound effect on Greek philosophy and political theory, to the Buddha's community of followers and the spread of their gentle, contemplative way of life throughout Asia, to the cultural greenhouses of the medieval monasteries, to the influence of the Fourierists and Owenites of nineteenth-century America on the development of public institutions, to the New Age communes of the present, experimental communities have been a quiet but potent historical force, with an influence on civilization far out of proportion to the numbers of people involved.

We have seen how pervasive and deep is the memory of an original Golden Age; we also have seen how compelling is the vision of its return. But we have yet to penetrate to the core of these archetypal dreams. The stereotypical image of Paradise is a perennial focus for human yearnings. *But where does it come from? And what does it mean?*

PART THREE

Search

They have no wool cloth, nor linen, nor cotton, because they do not need any. Also they have no private goods; all things are in common. They live together without King, without Emperor, and each one is Lord of himself. . . . Beyond that, they have no churches and keep no law, and yet they are not idolatrous. What shall I say, except they live according to nature?

AMERIGO VESPUCCI

CHAPTER 8

Paradise as History

E ARE FACED WITH SOME EXTRAORDINARY FACTS. In virtually every culture on Earth we encounter a myth telling how humankind originated in a time of peace, happiness, and miraculous power and, because of some mistake or failure, degenerated to its present condition. Moreover, nearly every tribe and nation reveres the sayings of some ancient prophet who foretold that the corrupt human world will one day be consumed in a purifying cataclysm to make way for a renewed Golden Age. And, as if the similarities of all these ancient myths and prophecies were not remarkable enough, we are confronted with the additional fact that much of our civilization's greatest literature and many of its most inspiring social theories and experiments seem to derive their vitality and appeal from these mysterious memories and visions of Paradise.

But what is the *meaning* of these stories? Are they indeed—as they purport to be—recollections and predictions of historical events, or are they instead allegories describing some subtle spiritual or psychological process? We are not, of course, the first to wonder about the source and significance of universal myths and prophecies of Paradise, and so we may now proceed to consider the opinions of scholars and scientists who have gone before. We cannot attempt an exhaustive survey here, but we can familiarize ourselves with the principal avenues of interpretation that have been pioneered through the centuries by theologians, psychologists, mythologists, and archaeologists.

In this chapter we will investigate the possible historical content of these myths through the investigations of archaeologists and anthropologists. In the following chapter we will examine a few of the principal allegorical interpretations that have been applied to the Paradise story. Then, having a working knowledge of both the myths themselves and what others have said about them, we will be in a position to explore Paradise from a perspective opened only recently by some new and still-controversial findings about the frontiers of human consciousness.

Did It Really Happen?

Is sacred history *factual* history? Was there an actual Golden Age, was there a Fall, and did global catastrophes occur within the range of human memory? In Part One we considered a certain kind of evidence—that of comparative mythology—which, because of its peculiar consistency from culture to culture, suggests at least the possibility of a historical Paradise. But few of us base our ideas about the past on mythology alone. What other evidence is there, and what does it tell us?

Perhaps the best proof of the reality of the Golden Age would be to uncover unequivocal archaeological evidence—ruins of crystal cities whose golden streets are strewn with the remains of goddesses and gods, their miraculously preserved bodies still giving off glimmers of light. I will not keep the reader in suspense: no such cities have been discovered. But what can we *realistically* expect to find? What have archaeologists already found? Do their discoveries rule out or support a paradisal interpretation of history?

While physical artifacts are important as evidence, they are not the only nonmythological vestiges of a Golden Age we might hope to find. We might also investigate the existence of cultural artifacts: Could aspects of an original paradisal way of life survive in any of the world's cultures? Do anthropological studies of "primitive" societies, for example, suggest that they are in some way holdovers from a prehistoric Eden?

Any investigation of the relationship between myth and history opens both sacred and secular ideas about the past to reassessment, and so the subject we are exploring is a sensitive and controversial one. Of all the fields of science, paleoanthropology—the study of what human beings were like in the distant past—is perhaps the most speculative. The kinds of raw data that are available can almost always be interpreted in several different ways. Therefore, in our exploration of the evidence for a historical Paradise we will consider as many divergent views as possible. And while we will begin with a look at what more traditional archaeologists say about the possibility of a past Golden Age, we will also consider opinions that are, from the standpoint of the present scientific consensus, outright heresy.

Biblical Archaeology

Archaeologists are generally reluctant to make use of mythic sources as a guide for their research. However, because of its immense popularity, one piece of ancient literature—the Bible—has proved an exception to this unwritten rule. Biblical archaeologists from a half dozen countries have been digging throughout the Near East for more than a century, and many significant discoveries have resulted from their investigations—the uncovering of the walls of Jericho, the excavation of Solomon's stables at Megiddo, and the discovery of the Nag Hammadi texts and the Dead Sea scrolls, to name a few. These finds have repeatedly confirmed the historicity of events and characters in both the Old and New Testaments. According to Harvard Bible scholar William F. Albright, "Archaeology . . . has finally corroborated biblical tradition in no uncertain way."[1]

Since archaeologists have investigated nearly every place named in the Bible, one might expect that the first geographical location mentioned in Genesis—the Garden of Eden—would have yielded important finds. But such is not the case, and it's not difficult to see why archaeologists have come up empty-handed. After all, what should they look for? There is nothing in Genesis to lead us to assume that Adam and Eve left behind walls, pottery, or even stone tools. The recovery of Edenic artifacts is almost out of the question; the most we can hope to do is locate the site itself on the basis of whatever clues are provided in Genesis. But even this is problematic. The geographical situation of the Garden is described only in terms of four rivers:

> And a river went out of Eden to water the garden; and from thence it was parted, and became into four heads. The name of

the first is Pison: that is it which compasseth the whole land of
Havilah, where there is gold; And the gold of that land is good:
there is bdellium and the onyx stone. And the name of the
second river is Gihon: the same is it that compasseth the whole
land of Ethiopia. And the name of the third river is Hiddekel:
that is it which goeth toward the east of Assyria. And the fourth
river is Euphrates (Genesis 2:10-14).

Three of the rivers' names are unfamiliar. The Hiddekel is usually
interpreted as being the Tigris, and the Gihon, which "compasseth the
whole land of Ethiopia," has often been equated with the Nile. Jewish
historian Josephus Flavius of the first century A.D. considered the fourth
river, the Pison, to be the Ganges. In this case, Eden would have
encompassed the entire region from eastern Africa to mid-Asia. But the
identification of the Gihon is not without difficulties—for example,
the King James translators seem to have been mistaken in rendering
the Hebrew *Kush* as "Ethiopia." As a result, later scholars considered
only the Tigris (Hiddekel) and Euphrates to be certain of identification, which left the identities of the Gihon and Pison a mystery.
Nevertheless, throughout the last century theories were plentiful.

By the beginning of the twentieth century, most scholars had set
aside the problem of locating Eden's rivers and were concentrating
instead on the analysis of the biblical text itself, aided by the discovery
and translation of Sumerian and Akkadian documents. As we saw in
chapter 3, many liberal Bible scholars adopted the theory that the
Eden story had been derived from an earlier Mesopotamian source,
perhaps from the Dilmun texts of the Sumerians. This view was
strengthened as more and more parallels between biblical and
Sumerian literature were discovered. Like the ancient Hebrews, the
Sumerians told of the emergence of the world from a primeval sea; of
the creation of human beings from clay; of a universal Flood; of the
rivalry between two primordial brothers; and of a tower to heaven
whose destruction caused the dispersion of humanity. Thus, while the
similarities between the Hebraic Eden and the Sumerian Dilmun were
debatable, many scholars simply assumed that by locating Dilmun they
would find Eden as well. But the identification of Dilmun was itself a
problem: while some researchers claimed to have discovered it in
Bahrain or on the western coast of the Persian Gulf, other authorities

suggested areas as far removed as Pakistan and India. In short, the attempted equation of Eden with Dilmun accomplished nothing.

Recently, however, the Genesis passage describing the four rivers of Eden has inspired another round of speculation and research. In 1980, following a decade of fieldwork in Saudi Arabia, archaeologist Juris Zarins of Southwest Missouri State University decided to apply himself to the old problem of locating the original Garden. Zarins began with the textual account, and he then familiarized himself with the geology and hydrology of the Near East and the language patterns of its ancient inhabitants. But his crucial clue was to come from space-age technology: satellite survey images show that the Tigris and Euphrates were once met by two other rivers, one of which is now dammed, the other a dry bed. Moreover, the valley where the rivers meet was once rich in bdellium, an aromatic gum resin, and in gold, which was still being mined there until the 1950s. As we saw earlier, both of these substances are mentioned in Genesis. On the basis of this new evidence, Zarins concluded that Eden was a relatively small area south of the spot where the four rivers met, a region now covered by the tip of the Persian Gulf.[2]

Paleontologists agree that around 5000–6000 B.C., southern Mesopotamia was a forager's dream. While the region had previously been arid, there was now abundant rainfall and diverse plant and animal life. Agriculture had been developed at least two millennia earlier, and settlements were appearing in the valley. As the climate changed and people began to migrate into the region, competition must have arisen between farmers and gatherer-hunters for the fertile land. Zarins theorized that the Eden myth originated in that era of competition and change: "The whole Garden of Eden story . . . could be seen to represent the point of view of the hunter-gatherers."

> It was the result of the tension between the two groups, the collision of two ways of life. Adam and Eve were heirs to natural bounty. They had everything they needed. But they sinned and were expelled. How did they sin? By challenging God's very omnipotence. In so doing they represented the agriculturalists, the upstarts who insisted on taking matters into their own hands, relying upon their knowledge and their own skills rather than on His bounty.[3]

In the Eden story we find Adam and Eve naked and unashamed, eating the fruits of trees. It requires little stretching or twisting of the story to read this as a description of the lives of primitive foragers. After all, it was only after the Fall that God sent Adam forth to till the ground. The author of the passage seems to be telling us that human beings were innocent and happy as long as they simply lived off the bounty of Nature. Once they began to eat the fruit of the Tree of the Knowledge of Good and Evil—once they began to bend the cycles of Nature to their own presumed benefit—their innocence was lost. It was only then that the symbolic original couple realized their naked-ness and were cast out of the Garden.

Of Foragers and Farmers

The idea that preagricultural life could be considered Edenic seems peculiar at first to those of us who have grown up with a belief in the desirability and inevitability of technological progress. We in the civilized world have been taught to think that agriculture was the greatest advance in prehistoric human society: by freeing human beings from dependence on an uncertain food source, it made possible the development of the arts and sciences. Our stereotypical image of primitive foragers is of bands of half-starved savages, usually exhausted from searching for roots and berries or hunting wild animals, engaging in periodic bloodthirsty raids on one another's camps, and living in superstitious terror of the capricious and mysterious natural forces controlling their lives. The myths instead portray the lives of the First People as supremely happy. Surprisingly, the recent findings of anthro-pologists and archaeologists tend to support the primitivist rather than progressivist view.

Both from archaeological studies of ancient sites and from ethno-logical studies of surviving gathering-and-hunting peoples (such as the Bushmen of Africa and the Aborigines of Australia), researchers are finding that agriculture may have been, as physiologist Jared Diamond puts it, "the worst mistake in the history of the human race."[4] We see evidence for this assessment in comparative studies of diet and nutri-tion, for example. Most agricultural societies tend to adopt a diet based on relatively few foods—usually, two or three starchy grain crops that by themselves do not provide a sufficient variety or balance of nutrients. Foragers, on the other hand, know how to obtain a wide range of foods. The !Kung Bushmen of the Kalahari Desert, for instance, consume seventy-five or so different wild plants; the Aborigines of the Cape York region of Australia only a few generations ago knew at least 140 edible species. Paleopathologists, who study evidence of disease in prehistoric human remains, find that the skeletons of ancient gatherer-hunters tend to be larger and more robust and show fewer signs of degenerative disease and tooth decay than do those of the later agriculturalists.

Likewise, with regard to the question of labor versus leisure time, agriculture may have been a step backward. As Michigan University anthropologist Marshall Sahlins pointed out in his *Stone Age Economics*, and as anthropologist Marvin Harris confirmed in his *Cannibals and Kings: The Origins of Cultures*, gatherer-hunters may devote only twelve to twenty hours per week to obtaining food. The rest of their time is given to family and friends, art, music, and storytelling. Australian anthropologist Max Charlesworth writes that

> while technologically and materially Aboriginal culture is of extreme simplicity, religiously and spiritually that culture is of extreme complexity and subtlety. Indeed, it has even been argued that the Aborigines deliberately chose a simple technology and style of economic life so that they could devote themselves to the elaboration of a rich and intricate social and religious life.[5]

Moreover, among primitive peoples activities we might think of as labor—foraging and hunting—tend to be regarded as sacred and highly enjoyable, and are surrounded by the spirit of adventure. In fact, among many tribes it is difficult to find any indigenous idea corresponding to our civilized concept of "work." Anthropologist Elman R. Service writes,

> We think of a time to work and a time to play, and [complain of] the lack of time for as much play or rest as we want. In all primitive communities I have visited, work-time merges into play-time—or, better, no one really distinguishes [between] the two.[6]

Since agriculture can hardly be said to have freed human beings from unnecessary labor, neither can it be said to have been responsible for the flowering of the arts. If leisure time is the key to high culture, the foragers should have had time enough to build cathedrals and write symphonies, had they wanted to. But the key to more complex forms of artistic expression is not really leisure time so much as elaborate social organization. It is impossible to imagine a Beethoven, for example, without a piano, a symphony orchestra, and a publisher with a printing press, all of which are outgrowths of industrial civilization. It is not unreasonable to suppose, then, that there have been aboriginal Beethovens and Tolstoys who have made significant contributions to their cultures, but in ways that the civilized world cannot yet appreciate: their efforts and achievements have not been preserved through writing or artifact, but have instead been woven into an oral tradition.

The oral traditions of tribal peoples are rich and complex, often revealing a profound understanding of the workings of Nature and the human mind. Anthropologists have as yet succeeded in comprehending only the superficial aspects of these traditions, hindered by differences not only in language but also in styles of thinking. The names of the founders and shapers of these tribal oral traditions are, in most cases, lost.

Agriculture made town dwelling and social stratification not only possible but, through the centralization of food storage and the division of labor, virtually necessary. The implications of this organization and specialization of human life were, according to Sahlins and Harris, not altogether beneficial. One result was the creation of deep class divisions. Gradually, it became possible for a few individuals to live off the food seized or demanded from others in tribute. And with the differentiation of social classes and occupations came a loss of personal autonomy. As people became more dependent on the labor of others for their sustenance, the survival of the individual came to depend increasingly on society as a whole.

Another result of the introduction of agriculture was the development of the concept of property. Primal peoples have difficulty understanding the civilized system of land ownership, since they are not owners of land; rather, the land "owns" them. To these peoples, the land is not merely soil or territorial boundaries, but also the spirits of sacred places and of the animals and plants associated with those places. The people are a part of the land and cannot imagine being alienated from it. Having no concept of property, tribal peoples do not practice trade in the sense that civilized peoples do. The native Ghanaians, for example, merely give without thought of what they will receive in return; the act of giving in itself brings honor. Such an attitude can be frustrating to civilized missionaries and anthropologists: the native who regards giving as natural and a blessing to the giver has no inclination to say "thank you."

Among tribal peoples who have been studied by anthropologists, there is no warfare in the mechanized or impersonal sense as we know it. As anthropologist Stanley Diamond puts it, "The contrast is not merely in the exponential factor of technology multiplying a constant, homicidal human impulse; in primitive society, taking a life was an *occasion*; in our phase of civilization it has become an abstract, ideological compulsion."[7]

Cultural historian Lewis Mumford wrote:

> What is conspicuous in neolithic diggings is . . . the complete absence of weapons, though tools and pots are not lacking. This evidence, though only negative, is widespread. Among such hunting peoples as the Bushmen, the older cave paintings show no representation of deadly fighting, whereas later pictures, contemporary with kingship, do.[8]

Mumford's observation is well attested in sites on all inhabited continents. Archaeologist W. J. Perry tells us that

> it is an error, as profound as it is universal, to think that men in the food-gathering stage were given to fighting. . . . All the available facts go to show that the food-gathering stage of history must have been one of perfect peace. The study of the artifacts of the Paleolithic age fails to reveal any definite signs of human warfare.[9]

Among a few tribal peoples, this innocence of warfare was maintained until recent times. Explorer and writer Sir Laurens Van der Post tells of an African Bushman tradition according to which there was once a war among their tribes, a war so terrible that eventually *one man was killed*. The parties of Bushmen involved were so ashamed of what had happened that they drew a line in the desert and agreed never to cross it, because they felt unworthy to share each other's company henceforth.[10]

In view of the studies conducted or cited by Sahlins, Diamond, and Harris, we can only conclude that primitive food-gathering societies provided good nurturance in a stable, loving community; multifaceted, supportive relationships throughout life; and the challenge of constant, direct engagement with Nature. Not only did the gatherer-hunters generally evince good health, a high esthetic sensibility, and a friendly, peaceful attitude toward others, but many anthropologists also consider them to have been intuitive ecologists. To cite but one example, until recent decades the Aborigines of Australia freely set brush fires as they went about their seasonal migrations—a practice that the European settlers forced them to abandon. Now, however, Australian ecologists are discovering that the Aborigines' fires were essential to the reproduction of indigenous eucalyptus trees, whose seeds will open only in intense heat. All of these qualities of the preagriculturalists—their physical and psychological health, their simplicity of technology and social organization, and their intimate relationship with the natural world—are reminiscent of mythic descriptions of the First People.

One might wonder why agriculture was ever adopted, given its practical drawbacks and the cultural and spiritual resistance it must have evoked. Researchers can only speculate that since agriculture feeds more people—though at a poorer level of nutrition—perhaps unchecked population growth, with its consequent overtaxing of the food source, forced certain isolated groups to resort to farming. If so, one cannot help but wonder whether this primordial population crisis could itself have been the result of some subtle disharmony between humanity and the rest of Nature. We can only speculate whether it was just such an initial alienation from Nature that gave rise to the universal myth of the Fall.

Paradise as a Garden

Not all commentators who look back to a Stone Age Paradise agree that the rise of agriculture was the downfall of humanity. In *The Recovery of Culture*, an evocatively beautiful volume published in 1949, horticulturalist Henry Bailey Stevens theorized that the Golden Age was a period of many millennia—lasting until about 5000 years ago—during which human beings lived in peace and harmony, carefully altering various wild species of grains and fruit-bearing trees. As evidence, Stevens cited archaeological discoveries showing that warfare is a relatively recent human invention, and that before the period when they began making weapons people were far more interested in art, religion, and plant domestication. Thousands of years ago wheat, rice, millet, barley, oats, and maize, as well as the apple, banana, orange, grapefruit, lemon, olive, fig, cherry, date, apricot, walnut, hazelnut, and almond, were dramatically modified from their wild state, and the people who accomplished these miracles of transformation during the early Neolithic period must have been first-rate horticulturalists.

According to Stevens, the Fall came not with the invention of agriculture but with the invasion of nomadic herdsmen whose lives were devoted to the keeping and breeding of food animals. "The people who seized power from the peaceful horticulturalists were keepers of flocks and herds," Stevens wrote. "This meant wool, hides and milk. It also meant meat. Man had gone into business as a butcher."[11] Stevens contends that it was the *breeding* of animals that made the difference.

> So long as man hunted them, he was simply another beast of prey—a part of the natural balance keeping animal life in check. But when he bred and protected vast hordes of livestock, he threw an intolerable burden upon the soil resources of the earth and has been paying for it with war ever since.[12]

Stevens's thesis has recently received support—and a feminist turn of emphasis—from the work of scholar-activist Riane Eisler, whose book *The Chalice and the Blade* posits 20,000 years of partnership between women and men in a primarily horticultural society. Like Stevens, Eisler bases her argument on archaeological finds in Europe and the Near East that challenge long-held assumptions. The new evidence, which has been accumulating since the early decades of this century, shows that long before the rise of the Sumerian culture in Mesopotamia there were people in settled towns throughout Old Europe (from the Aegean and the Adriatic to southern Poland and the western Ukraine) practicing agriculture, working metal, and using a simple script for mostly religious purposes. Says Eisler, "We now know that there was not one cradle of civilization, but several, all of them dating back millennia earlier than was previously known—to the Neolithic."[13]

> Just as in Columbus's time the discovery that the earth is not flat made it possible to find an amazing new world that had been there all the time, these archaeological discoveries—deriving from what British archaeologist James Melaart calls a veritable archaeological revolution—open up the amazing world of our hidden past. They reveal a long period of peace and prosperity when our social, technological, and cultural evolution moved upward: many thousands of years when all the basic technologies on which civilization is built were developed in societies that were not male dominant, violent, and hierarchic.[14]

In those days, according to Eisler, human relations were based on peace, cooperation, and mutual nurturance. At Catal Huyuk, in what is now eastern Turkey, the murals and sculptures of the largest Neolithic settlement yet excavated contain no scenes of fighting or warfare; fortifications and military weapons are likewise absent. Similarly, according to C. C. McCown, the Neolithic excavations at Teleilat el-Ghassul in the Jordan Valley present "no evidence that the place possessed any system of defense."[15]

Moreover, these settlements show no signs of male dominance—for example, the graves of women and men are approximately equal in size and provision—and there are few signs of the rigid, hierarchical social structure that characterized the later civilizations of Mesopotamia. Eisler writes, "What we do find everywhere—in shrines and houses, on wall paintings, in the decorative motifs on vases, in sculptures in the round, clay figurines and bas reliefs—is a rich array of symbols from nature." Decorative motifs portray the Sun, water, serpents, and butterflies, and, writes Eisler, "everywhere . . . images of the Goddess."[16]

Probably the most dramatic ruins from this peaceful, creative period have been found on the island of Crete. There, during the Minoan period—roughly, 4000–1500 B.C., according to most historians—"for the last time in recorded history, a spirit of harmony between women and men as joyful and equal participants in life appears to

[have] pervade[d]."[17] At its height, Minoan Crete had a highly developed culture, with writing, a centralized government, and cities featuring viaducts, paved roads, water pipes, fountains, reservoirs, palaces, courtyards, and gardens. Civilization here did not seem to bring with it autocratic rule and deep class divisions. "Even among the ruling classes personal ambition seems to have been unknown; nowhere do we find the name of an author attached to a work of art nor a record of the deeds of a ruler."[18]

However, on Crete—as elsewhere throughout the Old Culture—catastrophic changes began to occur about 5000 years ago. Simultaneous with catastrophes of Nature (a series of earthquakes and tidal waves), invaders from the north overran the island's undefended towns and cities and put a sudden end to the peaceful life of the inhabitants. The newcomers were tribes of nomadic herdsmen whose lives were spent in the raising and slaughtering of animals and in almost constant warfare. In India, the invaders were known as Aryans; in Mesopotamia, as Hittites; in eastern Europe, as Kurgans; and in Greece, as Achaeans and Dorians. *"The one thing they all had in common,"* according to Eisler, *"was a dominator model of social organization:* a social system in which male dominance, male violence, and a generally hierarchic and authoritarian social structure was the norm."[19]

With the invasion of the pastoralists, human evolution underwent a "massive regression," Eisler asserts.

> There will undoubtedly be those who will argue that because in prehistory there was a shift from a partnership to a dominator model of society it must have been adaptive. However, the argument that because something happened in evolution it was adaptive does not hold up—as the extinction of the dinosaurs so amply evidences.[20]

All of what we remember as human history, according to Eisler, has played itself out in the context of tragically twisted social and psychological patterns that were formed at a crucial turning point when catastrophe and invasion brought an end to the peaceful Golden Age of partnership between women and men, and between humanity and Nature.

The Paleolithic Paradise

Eisler and Stevens have the Golden Age continuing until about 5000 years ago (and, according to Eisler, in Crete until just 3500 years ago). Sahlins, Harris, and Diamond would say that Paradise ended with the invention of agriculture around 10,000 years ago, but that some primitive tribes have persisted in the "golden" state to the present.

The comparative study of mythology presents an important fact that forces us to reconsider both views. As we have already seen, Paradise myths are not restricted to agricultural peoples; surviving gathering-and-hunting tribes also have stories of an original Age of Innocence. If the Fall refers either to the first appearance of agriculture or to subsequent events, then the presence of Paradise myths among preagricultural peoples is inexplicable. The fact that the food gatherers maintain their own versions of the Paradise story suggests that the spiritual watershed remembered as the Fall must have occurred prior to the development of agriculture—and hence before the beginnings of the horticultural society described by Eisler and Stevens. Perhaps the peaceful society of Old Europe represented a survival of some aspects of an earlier, even happier time, just as the few remaining gathering-hunting societies still do in their own way.

But if the Golden Age flourished prior to the advent of the culture of Old Europe and the development of agriculture, it must have existed in the Paleolithic period, or Old Stone Age. This period, extending (according to most paleoanthropologists) from about 500,000 years ago to about 12,000 years ago, is an almost complete mystery. According to Stanley Diamond,

> we know next to nothing concerning the origins or then extant forms of language, social organization, religion and so forth; most of the formative, nonmaterial aspects of culture remain inaccessible to us. The study of contemporary primitive peoples sheds no clear light on these matters.[21]

While some anthropologists regard the surviving tribal peoples of Africa, Australia, Asia, Oceania, and the Americas as representatives of Neolithic culture, virtually all authorities agree that there are no "fossil" cultures representing humankind as it was in the Paleolithic era. The Paradise myths of the primitives (and, by inference, those of the civilized peoples as well) must therefore refer back to a state of existence that has utterly disappeared.

Although archaeological evidence reveals little about human society before the Neolithic period, the paleontological evidence provides intriguing clues about the environment of the time. Fossils show that the Earth itself *was* in some respects paradisal prior to the Paleolithic-Neolithic boundary. Paleontologists know that in the late Pleistocene epoch (which was contemporaneous with the Paleolithic period) there was a greater variety of species on every continent, including Africa. P. S. Martin writes that the pristine range of the American West was "once shared by elephants, camels, horses, sloths, extinct bison, and four-horned antelope." Australia also lost most of its large herbivores at around the same time—"overnight," in paleontological or geological terms.[22]

Prior to the late-Pleistocene extinctions, the cause of which is still debated, our world was a vastly different place. Could the Paradise myths be memories of this era when animals were more abundant and edible wild plants more plentiful?

In order to correlate the Paradise myths with a time of biological abundance, we must place the Golden Age far back in time, before the close of the Pleistocene. Doing so, we cannot help but wonder whether the late-Pleistocene extinctions were somehow remembered in myths of the Fall. Perhaps those extinctions were caused by some vast catastrophe of Nature, which also resulted in the destruction of island populations and thus in stories of great floods and sinking continents.

Evidence of such a destruction exists, but it is of a controversial nature. For the past 150 years the science of geology has been dominated by the doctrine of uniformity, which holds that all the rock formations visible today are the result of gradual, uniform processes we can still observe at work, such as erosion and the accumulation of sediment. Uniformitarianism, which effectively excludes any theory of global catastrophes, achieved dominance in the early nineteenth century not because it was supported by overwhelming evidence, but because certain influential shapers of scientific opinion wished to sever geology from the biblical tradition of the Great Flood.

Until recently, therefore, scientific discussion of global catastrophes was practically nonexistent in establishment circles. Immanuel Velikovsky and other theorists who insisted upon calling attention to the evidence of global cataclysms were ridiculed. Yet, evidence of universal catastrophes exists. The latest generation of geologists is cautiously employing a diluted form of "neo-catastrophism" to explain certain otherwise mysterious phenomena, such as the extinction of the dinosaurs and the onset of the Ice Ages. Still, signs of global catastrophes within the age of humankind—signs that could be used by Christian fundamentalists to support the literal reading of the Noah story in the Bible, or by Atlantis theorists to validate their literal reading of Plato's account of the destruction of the lost island continent—are still discounted by establishment science.

We do not have space here to consider in detail either catastrophism in general or the lost-continents hypothesis in particular. However, both are relevant to the sequence of mythic history: if worldwide myths of lost homelands destroyed by flood and fire were to gain historical validation from the evidence of geology, then the equally widespread myths of Paradise and the Fall would also become obvious candidates for historical reconstruction. A brief exploration of that evidence is therefore warranted.

Atlantis and Mu

As we saw in chapter 3, many cultures' myths describe the lost paradisal homeland as a now-sunken continent, and Plato's description of Atlantis seems to echo Hesiod's story of the Golden Age. Was the Garden of Eden, then, located where there is now only ocean?

While the subject of Atlantis is mostly off limits in establishment academia, a few capable researchers have found plausible geological, archaeological, and anthropological evidence for the former existence of at least one recently submerged continent. Dr. M. Klionova of the USSR reported in 1963 that rocks taken from a depth of 6600 feet sixty miles north of the Azores showed evidence of having been exposed to the atmosphere about 17,000 years ago. Beach sand—which is formed only along shorelines—has been found thousands of feet down in the mid-Atlantic, and sediment from the

Mid-Atlantic Ridge reveals the remains of freshwater plants, indicating that the ridge was once above sea level. In 1975, University of Miami marine scientists exploring the Mid-Atlantic Ridge found fossils and limestone containing substantial amounts of rainwater, again indicating that the ridge was once above the surface. And throughout the world's oceans there is indication that about 11,500 years ago a sudden flood of icy water caused deep-sea creatures to adapt and change so suddenly as to provide a fossil time-line for classifying sedimentary cores. Atlantis theorists insist that this icy flood was the deluge that destroyed the mythic continent.

Archaeological finds possibly related to Atlantis have been found across the Florida Strait from Miami off the island of Bimini, far from the Mid-Atlantic Ridge. Since 1956, several teams of explorers have sighted and photographed submerged artifacts, including fluted columns, a road, a possible temple platform, and a stylized marble head.

For Colonel James Churchward, inveterate adventurer and author of the controversial book *The Lost Continent of Mu* (1931), the story of the Garden of Eden was a distorted memory not of Atlantis, but of humankind's idyllic life on Mu, a now-sunken continent in the Pacific Ocean. Evidence discovered since Churchward's time has given his theory—which was based on his translations of tablets from India and Mexico—intriguing support. Soviet scientist V. V. Belousov writes in *The Geological Structure of the Oceans*: "It may be asserted that very recently, partially even in the age of man, the Pacific Ocean grew considerably at the expense of great chunks of continents which, together with their young ranges of mountains, were inundated by it. The summits of these mountains are to be seen in the island garlands of East Asia."[23] And George H. Cronwell, in a paper delivered at the Tenth World Pacific Congress, reported on the discovery of coal and ancient flora on Rapa Island (southwest of Mangareva Island), which "provides irrefutable testimony of the fact that there was a continent on that part of the ocean."[24]

According to Plato, the destruction of Atlantis occurred around 10,000 B.C. This approximate date appears also in the writings of ancient peoples on the other side of the Atlantic. Nineteenth-century Mesoamerican scholar Charles Etienne Brasseur de Bourbourg, like his successor Augustus Le Plongeon, read in early Mayan documents what seemed to be accounts of an oceanic island homeland destroyed in a great terrestrial convulsion. According to Brasseur de Bourbourg and Le Plongeon, the Mayan Troano Codex fixes the date of the cataclysm at 9937 B.C.

As we noted earlier, geologists and paleontologists date the end of the Pleistocene epoch and the beginning of the Holocene epoch, in which we are now living, at about 10,000 B.C. It was then that the last major Ice Age ended, sea levels changed, and widespread extinctions of flora and fauna occurred. Again, no cause for all these events is generally agreed upon by scientists; each is considered a mystery. Naturally, the proponents of the lost-continents hypothesis say that the flooding, climatic changes, and extinctions resulted from the cataclysm that destroyed Atlantis and/or Mu.

The geological and archaeological evidence for Mu and Atlantis is inconclusive. During thirteen years of exploration, Dr. Maurice Ewing of Columbia University found no signs of lost cities on the Mid-Atlantic Ridge. But as Ralph Franklin Walworth points out, "Locating the rubble of a city buried under yards of mud and silt in those conditions is like trying to locate a razed and buried Peoria, Illinois, by cruising over the Midwest on a cloudy and foggy night in a dirigible, trailing an [I]nstamatic camera on a three-mile long string."[25] We simply do not yet have enough geological and archaeological data to either confirm or rule out the lost-continents hypothesis.

Anthropological evidence for Atlantis and Mu is likewise inconclusive but tantalizing. The idea of a vanished source of human culture would seem extravagant and unnecessary if we could trace human origins clearly on the basis of orthodox assumptions and available data, but such is not the case. There are huge gaps in our understanding. Anthropologist J. B. Birdsell writes, "The homeland of living types of modern populations remains unknown. Their appearance in marginal areas such as Australia . . . poses real problems which existing data cannot solve."[26] And according to another anthropologist, Björn Kurtén:

There is no known transition from the Neanderthalers to those essentially modern-looking people who have been called Cro-Magnon men. Furthermore, these new Europeans are definitely not some kind of "generalized" Homo sapiens, but clearly belong to the Caucasoid, or white race. At this early date, then, man had already split up into distinct races. In the same way, the earliest modern men in China are recognizable as Mongoloid, those of Australia are related to the living Australian aborigines, and early South Africans seem to be allied to the Bushmen. Where did they all come from?[27]

Clearly, the lack of key evidence in the consensus view of human origins does not prove the correctness of any alternative theory. But the *acknowledgment* of holes and inconsistencies at least leaves the door open for fresh thinking. As James Clerk Maxwell once said, "A state of thoroughly conscious ignorance . . . is the prelude to every real advance of knowledge."

Archaeological Anomalies

Anomalies are phenomena that cannot be explained by current scientific theories. For obvious reasons, most defenders of the status quo in science are uncomfortable with anomalies and often deny their existence or try to explain them away. Scientific heretics, however, love anomalies, collect them, and call attention to them whenever they can.

As philosopher of science Thomas Kuhn has pointed out, it is the accumulation of anomalies that eventually forces the abandonment of old scientific paradigms and the installation of new ones. This was the case, for example, in early-nineteenth-century Europe, where the scientific authorities of the day held fast to the belief that meteors cannot fall from the sky because there are no stones in the sky to begin with. Widespread reports of the fall of meteors were then regarded much the way UFO sightings are today. But after enough stones had fallen—and had been seen by thousands of people, scientists included—the authorities' bulwark of denial simply collapsed.

Anomalies are defined by the nature of the theories currently held; what is anomalous to one theory may be acceptable to another. Three decades ago in America, any geological evidence of continental drift was considered anomalous. Today, any evidence that would call the theory of continental drift into question is recognized as anomalous.

In archaeology and anthropology, the current paradigm—which

has ruled for more than a century—is that human culture has evolved unidirectionally from the "primitive" to the "advanced." Any evidence that contradicts this view is, by definition, an anomaly. In this instance the anomalies are legion. On every continent there are earthworks, artifacts, and human remains that do not fit the current paradigm because they are too old, too advanced, or simply in the wrong place. For example, artifacts and human remains have been found in America that are tens of thousands of years too old to fit present theories of how and when the New World was first inhabited.[28] Objects obviously made by humans have been found encased in solid lumps of coal or in stone.[29] One could go on at great length; there are so many such anomalies, in fact, that some scientists spend their entire careers collecting and studying them.[30]

Students of archaeological anomalies often note the existence of a peculiar pattern. Everywhere we look, the scientific, artistic, and engineering accomplishments of the ancients seem to have reached their peak early on and to then have suffered a decline. In Britain, the Romans built their roads over much older pavement of unknown origin, which was often superior in construction; in America the Eskimos were once acquainted with metalworking, but were apparently later cut off from the source of their metal culture; and in Egypt some of the earliest pyramids show greater engineering skill and scientific attainment than do the monuments of any of the later dynasties.

Much of the cyclopean masonry of sites in America, Europe, and Asia is of unknown age and provenance but gives evidence of awesome skill and power. The famous wall of Sacsayhuaman, Peru, for instance, consists of blocks of stone that in some instances weigh hundreds of tons, fitted with far greater precision than one finds in most modern stone structures. In case after case, the oldest stone remains are the grandest and most perfectly executed; what followed later are crude imitations in comparison.

On the basis of such evidence, several maverick archaeologists and historians have been led to question the orthodox view that humankind has evolved steadily out of a state of barbarism over the past 10,000 years, and have concluded instead that our present civilization must have begun at the base of a descent from a former height. For example, after two decades of studying the monuments of ancient Egypt firsthand, Alsatian philosopher and mathematician

R. A. Schwaller de Lubicz concluded that Egyptian science, medicine, mathematics, and astronomy were far more advanced than modern Egyptologists have admitted. De Lubicz asserted that all the achievements of that civilization flowed from a profound philosophy of the interrelations of number, geometry, and the human spirit—a philosophy inaccessible to modern Egyptologists because of their inability to follow ancient styles of thought. Further, he concluded that since the earliest texts and monuments reveal this philosophy in its purest form, Egyptian civilization must have been a legacy from some prior, even more advanced culture. De Lubicz identified this previous, lost culture with legends of Atlantis and the Golden Age.[31]

Historian John Michell, in his popular books *City of Revelation* and *The New View over Atlantis*, has argued similarly that mysterious prehistoric monuments all over the world "were designed in accordance with one scheme of proportion in units of measurement which are everywhere the same." These, Michell claims, are "relics of a former elemental science, founded on principles of which we are now ignorant."[32] In *The New View over Atlantis*, he proposes that

> at some period, thousands of years ago, almost every corner of the world was visited by people with a particular task to accomplish. With the help of some remarkable power, by means of which they could cut and raise enormous blocks of stone, these [people] created vast astronomical instruments, circles of erect pillars, pyramids, underground tunnels, cyclopean stone platforms, all linked together by a network of tracks and alignments, whose course from horizon to horizon was marked by stones, mounds and earthworks.[33]

The straight tracks, the walls and mounds, and the stone circles and pyramids of unknown origin seem to Michell to be evidence of a way of life that does not correspond with any of our preconceptions about what constitutes an "advanced" or a "primitive" culture. The people who built this global system were not merely primitive Stone Agers inhabiting an innocent but ignorant Paradise, yet neither were they technologists in the sense that we are. Our technology is designed to promote human comfort and convenience, whereas theirs seems to have been of and for the Earth—directed, that is, toward the nourishment of the planet and the coordination of earthly cycles of germination and growth with the rhythms of the Cosmos. All of the megalithic monuments of Europe and the Americas, like the monuments of ancient Egypt, appear to have been constructed for religious purposes. All were astronomically aligned, and all were designed to embody precisely the geometric and numerical relationships, such as the golden section and the number *phi* (1.618 . . .), that govern the generation and development of living organisms.

The anomalies of prehistory are genuine and numerous, and they continue to gnaw at the base of the current theories of human cultural evolution. The present historical paradigm is in deep trouble, and the facts do not present us with a clear alternative that can easily be assimilated by current thinking. Rather, they hint at possibilities that continually frustrate our desire for simple, linear explanations.

In general, the anomalies suggest a mythic reading of history— they imply a Fall from a former universal Age of Wisdom that was divided from the present age by catastrophes of Nature. Yet the construction of a mythic paradigm of history presents its own problems. While myths describe Paradise in nontechnological terms, the earliest monuments of the Egyptians and the megalithic builders bespeak a stage of development in which human beings had both technology and complex forms of social organization. Perhaps Atlantis— whose legacy the Egyptians and the megalithic builders carried, according to de Lubicz and Michell—was itself a degenerate remnant of an age of miracles in which technology was unnecessary. It is, of course, impossible to prove such an idea on the basis of stones and bones. But the archaeological evidence of prehistory is so fragmentary that the best system of interpretation is probably the most open-ended one. And such a system, if historians and archaeologists were to pursue it, should allow for at least the possibility of a historical Paradise.

The Limits of Historical Knowledge

We tend to forget that archaeology as a science dates back only about a century, and that it was really not until after World War II that systematic excavations—as opposed to the haphazard acquisition of antiquities—began to be undertaken. Moreover, largely because of the youth of this science, and also because of certain habits of thought it has carried over from the nineteenth century, archaeology today remains a cultural phenomenon as well as an objective scientific pursuit. Anthropologist Patrick Pender-Cudlip writes,

> Most historians and anthropologists share certain ideas about possibility and probability, and it is these ideas, more than anything else, that determine how they distinguish between myth and history . . . no story has an inherent quality which makes it historical; it becomes historical not by being true but by being accepted as true. Conversely an unhistorical story or "myth" (in the popular sense of the word) is not necessarily an untrue story, but simply a story which is regarded as untrue. Neither myth nor history has any "objective" existence apart from society. . . . Historians in different societies reconstruct the past in different ways for different reasons, using different criteria to distinguish between fact and fiction, [criteria] which are a product of their cultural environment.[34]

Archaeologist Humphrey Case agrees: "Archaeology is . . . a body of myth and legend for our times, as inspiring, consoling, entertaining, and fugitive as those of the past."[35] And anthropologist Alice Kehoe writes, "Slowly there has crept into the social sciences the realization that these disciplines [anthropology and archaeology], no less than religious or political philosophies, embody axioms and values which are built into ideologies."[36]

We began this chapter with the purpose of comparing the evidence of archaeology and anthropology against two versions of human history and prehistory—the standard, unidirectional evolutionary picture, and the mythic scenario of a Golden Age followed by a general decline. At the end of our search we are perhaps more keenly aware of what the evidence does *not* show than of what it does. Nevertheless, let us sum up what we have found.

We have seen that while biblical archaeologists' attempts to locate the Garden of Eden may have succeeded in a limited sense, in that the Genesis story does seem to refer geographically to the area where the Tigris and Euphrates rivers meet, they have done little to illumine the source of other cultures' Paradise myths. We have noted the belief on the part of some anthropologists that the myths of a Golden Age refer back to the gatherer-hunter way of life that prevailed prior to the invention of agriculture.

We have also noted the paradoxical fact that tribal peoples who have maintained a nonagricultural way of life into the modern era also look back to a lost time of innocence and plenty, just as civilized peoples do. We have surveyed recent archaeological finds that suggest that in some parts of the world (Crete, Old Europe, and the Near East), the early Neolithic period was a time of general peace and creativity during which human beings developed horticulture to a degree unmatched until the present century.

We have briefly examined the paleontological record, which shows that there were catastrophic interruptions some 10,000 years ago during which great numbers of animal species suddenly succumbed to extinction. We have seen that these catastrophes may be related to the myths of lost continents.

Finally, we have noted the existence of innumerable archaeological anomalies that suggest—to some theorists, at least—that many thousands of years ago there existed a civilization with a kind of advanced knowledge that differed from our own science and technology in both method and intent.

Strictly speaking, the evidence cannot be said to rule out any theory—not the current consensus view of prehistory nor even the most extravagant alternatives, such as the lost-continents hypothesis. It neither proves nor disproves, in any absolute sense, the historical existence of the mythic Golden Age. However, we cannot escape the general trend of the data we have surveyed.

Human beings in the late Paleolithic and early Neolithic periods had technical capabilities, values, and a way of life that current theories cannot explain. Clearly, it was a time of tremendous creativity, though that creativity was directed toward projects that are not always understandable in our terms. It was also a time of peace and cooperation so pervasive as to seem miraculous by present standards. The mythic scenario of Paradise, Fall, and catastrophe does not as yet comprise a fully developed scientific paradigm capable of explaining all of the existing archaeological and anthropological data. It does, however, provide the seed from which such a paradigm might emerge.

Whether it will do may depend on the willingness of scientists to release their grip on the current paradigm of cultural evolution and to view *all* of the evidence with fresh eyes.

As we have just seen, the myth of Paradise may represent a quasi-historical memory of real events. But as we saw in chapter 1, there are two basic ways of looking at myth: as history and as metaphor. Therefore, we must also consider the possibility that the universal Paradise narrative is *other than* or *more than* history—that the images contained in the myth may have dimensions of meaning that have no relation to stones, bones, and artifacts. Is it possible that the Paradise myth, in addition to whatever historical significance it may have, is also an allegory, a story used by ancient peoples to convey a psychological or theological message? If so, what is that message?

Because the principles underlying the universe are everywhere the same, analogy is a more accurate, ultimately a more "scientific" means for arriving at an understanding of phenomena than mere measurement. This is why all sacred teachings make use of parable, analogy, myth, and symbol instead of facts. Facts do not aid understanding.

JOHN ANTHONY WEST

CHAPTER · 9

Paradise as Metaphor

NCIENT AND TRIBAL PEOPLES shared a love for metaphor. In their world, everything meant something else. According to Australian anthropologist W. E. H. Stanner, "For the Aborigines the world is a vast sign system, and their thinking is pervaded by symbolism."[1] Of the Native Americans, Jamake Highwater writes that they use symbolism in their art in order to depict the essence—as opposed to the mere appearance—of the object being represented.[2] Our modern languages are largely residues of mythic consciousness and consist of thousands of words and expressions deriving from ancient metaphors. The word *expression* itself means "what is squeezed out"; *spirit* means "breath" or "wind"; and the word *connect* means "to weave together." Moreover, as language philosopher Owen Barfield has noted, "The further back you go in time, the more metaphorical you find language becoming."[3]

Surely, then, a story as ancient and widespread as the myth of lost Paradise must harbor profound metaphoric meanings. But what, precisely, are those meanings? In this chapter we will explore this question, examining in brief the principal allegorical interpretations that have been applied to the Paradise story throughout history.

In light of the archaeological and anthropological investigations we undertook in the last chapter, we might begin by asking, *Does a metaphorical interpretation rule out a historical one?* As we shall see, the answer is *not necessarily*. Some metaphorical readings allow room for historical content in the myth; others do not. For the sake of illustration, however, let us begin our survey of interpretations and interpreters with an example of pure allegory.

The Good Old Days

Perhaps the most immediately obvious explanation for the Paradise myth is that it is simply the allegorized expression of a longing for
the "good old days"—a longing that everyone has known at one time
or another. It is not only the harried modern office worker who thinks,
"The world was a better place when I was young." We find the same
sentiment expressed by even the earliest classical authors, who, as we
have already seen, frequently complained of the general degradation of
their ancient society. "Those were the days," sighs every generation as
it reaches middle age.

In his book *Longing for Paradise*, psychoanalyst Mario Jacoby presents an elaborate and sophisticated version of this good-old-days
explanation, suggesting that myths of a lost Golden Age are merely an
expression of the universal nostalgia for the past. He argues, moreover,
that these longings have no real historical basis: "The harmonious
world which is now regarded as lost . . . never really existed."

> We project backward into the Golden Twenties, the Belle Epoch
> in Paris, the time of the *Wandervögel*, the medieval city, Classical
> Antiquity, or life "before the Fall." The world of wholeness exists
> mostly in retrospect, as a compensation for the threatened, frag-
> mented world in which we live now. "How lovely it is to be a
> child!" can be uttered only by an adult who, looking backward,
> idealizes the alleged innocence and security of childhood.[4]

The good-old-days explanation is intuitively obvious, and it ad-
dresses the universal psychological longing that the Paradise story
focuses so intensely. But it is also superficial. While good-old-days
"myths" do exist, they tend to be relatively trivial and short-lived, like
Jacoby's examples of the Belle Epoch, the Golden Twenties, and so
on. After a few generations, the nostalgia for "the medieval city" or
"Classical Antiquity" occurs only among historians. Clearly, the universal narrative of the lost Golden Age is of a far deeper stratum than
the "when I was a kid" sort of nostalgia that inspires novels, films, and
television sitcoms about happy days gone by. The myths of the First
People have a potency sufficient to have ensured their survival for
several millennia, and they possess characteristic, deeply compacted,

and intensely meaningful thematic elements. While Jacoby's examples are culture-bound, Paradise is universal.

Further, all of the ancient Paradise myths purport to be descriptions not merely of a generalized better time, but of the first time, a perfect time; not just of any earlier era, but of a specific age of magical beginnings. It was not just a time when animals were more abundant, but a time when animals and humans could understand each other's speech; not merely a time when people were happier and life was easier, but a time when there was no death or disease and human beings could commune with God face to face. In short, the good-old-days interpretation succeeds only by overlooking the details of mythic imagery, characters, and action.

In contrast, some other interpretations concentrate on detail, but at the expense of narrowing their focus to include only a single example of the narrative.

Sex and the Fall

Most Western students of the Paradise myth have confined their attention to only one version, the Eden story of Genesis. Unquestionably, the largest body of commentary on paradisal imagery has been generated not by folklorists, but by Judeo-Christian exegetes.

The earliest church fathers were already worrying over the symbolism of Eden. Philo Judaeus, who lived in Alexandria in the first century, described the fruits of the Garden as the virtues of the soul, and the working of the Garden as the observance of divine commandments. The four rivers were the four virtues of prudence, self-mastery, courage, and justice. Meanwhile, Origen, Irenaeus, and Cyprian, who lived in the second and third centuries, read the Genesis account of life in Eden as a before-the-fact description of the church, an interpretation later taken up by Augustine: "Paradise is the Church; the four rivers of Paradise are the four gospels; the fruit-trees, the saints, and the fruit their works; the tree of life is the holy of holies, Christ."[5]

To early Christian theologians, the most significant symbol in the story was the forbidden fruit from the Tree of the Knowledge of Good and Evil. The fourth-century Greek church father Athanasius reported that while some of his contemporaries assumed the fruit to have been a fig, others said it was a "spiritual" fruit—some fateful thought or attitude. He noted, however, the existence of a third group, whose members viewed the forbidden fruit as Eve's sexual attractiveness. It was this last reading that was to have the most pervasive and lasting influence.

Before the Fall, the original couple were naked and unashamed; after eating from the forbidden tree, they suddenly became aware of their nakedness and fashioned aprons of fig leaves to cover themselves. For the first time they experienced guilt and shame. The story of their loss of innocence in the primordial Garden reads like a description of the loss of innocence often experienced by children as they reach puberty. Surely—in the eyes of generations of theologians—this means that the crime itself must have had to do with knowledge of sex.

The equation of the Fall with sex can be traced back a century and a half before the Christian era to Jewish philosopher Aristobolus, for whom Adam and Eve signified reason and sensuality, respectively, while the serpent represented sexual desire. It was a train of thought that was irresistible to innumerable later Christian interpreters (for example, Clement of Alexandria and Irenaeus, the Bishop of Lyons) who concurred in regarding the Fall as sexual union. Saint Jerome taught that prior to the Fall, Adam and Eve were "virgins in Paradise," and that therefore "all sexual intercourse is unclean."[6] Seventeenth-century theologian Adriaan Beverland, in his *Original Sin*, held that the apple was the symbol of sexual love, and the word *arbor* [tree] was equivalent to *membrum virile* [male organ].[7] The Fall was no more and no less than the discovery of sex. The original crime was an act of seduction, and it was all Eve's fault.

But if Eve, the first woman and the "mother of all living," was to blame for the loss of Paradise, what has this to say for all subsequent women and for Nature herself, with whom Eve has always been identified? Generations of theologians, reading Genesis through the eyes of Aristobolus and Beverland, have drawn the conclusion that since, according to the story, woman initiated the Fall, she is therefore inherently evil—a temptress who must be chastened and mortified. The third-century theologian Tertullian may have achieved the height of misogyny when he wrote:

> And do you not know that you are each an Eve? The sentence of
> God on this sex of yours lives in this age: the guilt, of necessity,

must live too. You are the devil's gateway; you are the unsealer of that forbidden tree; you are the first deserter of the divine law; you are she who persuaded him whom the devil was not valiant enough to attack. You destroyed so easily God's image, man.[8]

Woman is the mother of all living and is thus identified with Nature, and she is the agent of the Fall as well. Therefore, Nature herself is corrupt and fallen. According to this view, first enunciated by Augustine, the world is not only degraded from its pristine state—as all Paradise traditions agree—but shares somehow in the guilt and evil of humanity, and especially of womankind. The human body, as part of fallen Nature, is evil also, and enjoyment of the body is therefore suspect, if not downright sinful.

It is probably hopeless to try to determine whether Western civilization's guilty ambivalence toward sensuality and sex, and its moral disdain of untamed Nature, *resulted from* or *caused* its blanket blame of all womankind for the Fall.[9] In any case, these attitudes are not shared by cultures whose Paradise stories take the form of an enumeration of a series of world ages. In India, for example, the degeneration of humanity described in the tradition of the *yugas* is blamed neither on women nor on men; in Hinduism the sacredness of femininity, sensuality, and Nature is extolled in canonical religious literature and in erotic temple art.

Western civilization is of two minds, in the sense that it draws its mythic inspiration from two Paradise stories, the Hebraic and the Greek. The ancient Greeks and Romans sometimes described the rule of Cronos/Saturn in moralistic, but never antinaturistic terms, and so the tradition of the Golden Age has never acquired the puritanical overlays associated with the Eden narrative. Indeed, the naturalistic primitivist poets of the Counter-Renaissance—Pierre de Ronsard, Torquato Tasso, and John Donne—went so far as to extol the Golden Age as a time of free expression of the sexual impulse, a time when love had no "regiment," when human beings were free to follow their essentially healthy natural instincts. "How happy were our Syres in ancient times," exclaims Donne, "who held plurality of loves no crime!"[10]

While the equation of the Fall with sexuality still has exponents among serious modern Bible scholars, Howard N. Wallace draws to a close his recent exhaustive survey of textual evidence and interpretations by concluding that the phrase "the knowledge of good and evil" in Genesis 2 was probably meant to refer not to sex specifically, but to "universal knowledge," including all aspects of culture and civilization.[11] But the sexual interpretation has had an incalculable effect on the lives of generations of Westerners, and it continues to be a prominent subtext in the sermons of fundamentalist preachers. Moreover, a related idea—that all of humanity's psychological distress can be traced to sexual tensions—has had its own broad sphere of influence in the ostensibly secular fields of psychoanalysis and psychotherapy.

The Oedipus Complex

Sigmund Freud did not himself publish an analysis of the myth of Paradise. Nevertheless, he believed that the collective delusions of humankind "owe their power to the element of *historical truth* which they have brought up from the repression of the forgotten and primeval past."[12] This "historical truth" was the original Oedipal drama, in which grown sons of the Paleolithic era presumably killed their fathers in order to possess their mothers. According to the founder of psychoanalysis, the great crime for which all humanity has suffered through the ages was not sex per se, but murder motivated by incestuous lust.

Freud probably would have equated Paradise with the period prior to the original patricide. This, at any rate, is the line of thought followed by several of his followers. For example, in *Myth and Guilt*, Freudian analyst Theodor Reik interpreted the sacred tree as an archaic totem and Adam's crime as the killing and eating of the father/god of the tribe. Noting the pervasiveness of tree worship in ancient times, Reik asserted that the tree was not the home of the god, but the god himself: "No doubt the god of the Hebrews was once conceived as a sacred tree."[13] Further, he identified the tree-god with the tribe's father. The crime of the First People consisted of "eating of the tree"—that is, of killing and eating the head of the primeval family. For Reik, this Oedipal cannibalistic patricide is the origin of all the food taboos found so frequently in primitive cultures. It is the real source of humanity's subsequent pathological sense of guilt.

It would be pointless to repeat here all the arguments for and against the Oedipal theory. It is perhaps enough merely to note that there is little anthropological or archaeological evidence to suggest that patricide was ever widespread, much less universal. In spite of this, Freudians have managed to interpret virtually every aspect of primitive culture in terms of this theory. Geza Róheim, for example, concludes an article entitled "Women and Life in Central Australia" with the comment "We find the Oedipus complex, transformed by repression into anxiety, at the root of all her supernatural beliefs."[14]

Theoretical expectations, if enthusiastically held, tend to confirm themselves in the mind of the researcher, even in the absence of evidence. As anthropologist W. E. H. Stanner comments (with specific reference to the Oedipal theory): "Anthropology has given many proofs that assumption and method can so dominate the effort at discovery that true discovery is not possible."[15]

In fairness to Freud, however, we must note that portions of his work suggest another, purely metaphorical interpretation of the Paradise story.

Paradise as Infancy

It is an obvious analogy: if we substitute the life of the individual for the history of all humanity, would not the Golden Age be equivalent to infancy? This, in essence, is what Freud proposed in his theory of the development of the personality—that infancy is a Paradise lost, disrupted by the impossibility of the continued free indulgence of the urge to pleasure. The parents wittingly or unwittingly impose cultural inhibitions on the forming psyche of the young child, and the enforcement of these inhibitions is experienced by the infant as Hell or, in mythological terms, as the Fall.

While Freud did not stress the mythic or historical implications of his outline of infantile development, his early collaborator Carl Jung went on to incorporate the Paradise-as-infancy concept into his theory of the archetypes. For Jung, Paradise is the positive aspect of the archetypal mother, the infant's source of security and nourishment.

The expressions "Mother Nature" and "Mother Earth" both exemplify the archetype; indeed, the English word *matter* is derived from the Latin word for mother (*mater*). The walled Garden of Paradise, the place of peace and plenty, is the symbol of a condition in which there is complete attunement with Mother Nature. For Jung, the universally shared memory of the earliest phases of infancy—in which impulses and feelings are allowed free expression, and mother and infant are so tightly bonded as to form a unitary reality—is the ground from which all the symbols and imagery of Paradise have arisen.

The idea of interpreting the Paradise myth as an analogy for the mother-infant relationship did not originate with Freud or Jung, however. Indeed, its roots go at least as far back as the Gnostics of the first century. Simon Magus, whose views are preserved (no doubt in distorted form) in Saint Hippolytus's *Refutation of All Heresies*, taught that the Garden of Eden was not a geographical place, but a metaphor for the womb: "If God forms man in his mother's womb—that is, in Paradise— then let the womb be Paradise and the after-birth Eden, 'a river flowing forth from Eden, for the purpose of irrigating Paradise.' This river is the navel."[16]

But Jung developed the analogy in a new way: the Fall is not birth—the departure from the womb of Paradise—but the growth of the independent psyche of the infant, who must gradually learn to see its mother as a separate person with human limitations and an independent existence. The Fall represents any disturbance of the primal relationship; as such, it is inevitable and necessary, but it is nevertheless the cause of neurosis if experienced too early or too traumatically.

This interpretation of the Paradise myth as an unconscious projection of memories of infancy hinges on an important question: *Can the dim recollection of individual psychological states be transformed into myths pretending to describe historical events?* This is not a problem that is amenable to a simple or unequivocal solution. And even if we assume an affirmative answer, we still have not ruled out the possibility that the myth may conceal other dimensions of meaning. The Paradise-as-infancy concept is essentially an elaboration of the good-old-days hypothesis: it helps to account for the myth's perennial appeal, but it may not be sufficient to explain its origin. Nevertheless, when we broaden the concept to include a historical component, it becomes a formidable argument.

The Evolution of Consciousness

Let us reverse the analogy we drew at the beginning of the previous section and substitute humankind for the individual. Is it possible that humanity as a whole has undergone a developmental experience analogous to that of every child? Has our species known a collective paradisal infancy and a collective weaning and separation, with Nature playing the part of the Universal Mother? Is it possible, in other words, that Paradise and Fall are allegorized descriptions of early stages in the evolution of the collective human consciousness?

This idea goes back at least two centuries. Immanuel Kant, in his *Conjectures on the Beginnings of Human History*, interpreted the Fall as humanity's coming of age with the development of reason and free will. Similarly, Hegel saw history as the process of the self-actualization of spirit: Nature is spirit fallen into matter, and evolution is spirit's method of freeing itself. Paradise, the primordial condition prior to spirit's descent, was *meant to be* left behind. Friedrich Schiller, following the same current of thought, regarded the Eden narrative of Genesis as a tale of how humanity rose from unconsciousness to reason. The first couple's disobedience of the divine commandment was humankind's initial turning from instinct, a "gigantic step of progress."[17] Schiller wrote that

> this defection of mankind from instinct, which brought moral evil into Creation but only for the purpose of making moral good possible there, is without doubt the most fortunate, the greatest event in human history. . . . Man turned from an innocent creature into a guilty one, from a perfect ward of nature into an imperfect moral being, from a happy instrument into an unhappy artist.[18]

Treading in the philosophical footsteps of Kant and Hegel, several modern writers have expanded the evolutionary view of the Paradise myth into full-blown reconstructions of the origins and development of human consciousness. Ernst Cassirer, Nicholas Berdyaev, Jean Gebser, Erich Neumann, Carl Sagan, and Ken Wilber have outlined detailed developmental schemes in which the Golden Age represents an early plateau in human awareness.[19] The Edenic consciousness was, according to Wilber, one of "primal naturic unity . . . dominated by unconscious Nature, by physiology, by instincts, by simple perception, sensations, and emotions."[20]

Neumann wrote of this as the time when "the ego germ still dwells in the pleroma, the 'fullness' of the unformed God, and slumbers in the bliss of paradise." In this collectively infantile condition,

> [Man] swims about in his instincts like an animal. Enfolded and upborne by great Mother Nature, rocked in her arms, he is delivered over to her for good or ill. Nothing is himself; everything is the world. The world shelters and nourishes him, while he scarcely wills and acts at all. Doing nothing, lying inert in the unconscious, merely being there in the inexhaustible twilit world, all needs effortlessly supplied by the great nourisher—such is the early, beatific state.[21]

Ancient oral traditions and religious documents do indeed suggest that archaic humanity experienced the world differently from the way most people do today. Their world was one filled with gods, spirits, and magical powers; every symbol derived its effectiveness from its representation of a higher, invisible reality. Where we are rational, they were nonrational; where we are concerned with economics, politics, and science, they were obsessed by ritual and myth. The question is: *Was the fundamental change from the archaic to the modern mode of being necessary and developmental?* That is, is our way of thinking and living inherently better and more highly evolved than that of the ancients, or merely *different?* We may naturally tend to assume the former, but that assumption is surprisingly difficult to support with evidence, given any sort of uniform and objective criteria. Are we, for example, happier, healthier, and more intelligent than the ancients? As we saw in the last chapter, many anthropologists doubt that this is the case.

Perhaps theorists of the evolution of consciousness have drawn more conclusions than are actually warranted by the evidence. Who can say with assurance what motives and thought processes guided our primordial ancestors, when ethnologists of the past decades have so underestimated the intelligence and cultural achievements of tribal peoples who could still be visited and interviewed in the flesh?

Human consciousness has changed in fundamental ways over the millennia, and evolution has undoubtedly played a significant part in those changes. But is it not permissible to ask whether, in addition to evolution, we have also undergone a tangential process of moral decay, as the myths universally insist? The real problem with the evolution-of-consciousness concept is that it ignores—even denies—the essential message the ancients seem to be trying to convey to us. They spoke of the Fall not as a necessary stage of development, but as a disaster. They did not suggest that we have had to give up Paradise in order to gain something more valuable, but instead lamented that what we have lost—the divine presence, the oneness of Heaven and Earth—is more precious than anything else we could ever hope to gain.

The idea that the Paradise stories describe a time when humanity knew a state of consciousness fundamentally different from the one we commonly share today does not itself contradict the message of the myths—quite the contrary. Is it possible, then, to develop this idea in the light of modern anthropological and psychological findings, in a way that respects the core of the ancients' message?

Paradise as Mystical Union

The equation of Paradise with the infantile state is attractive because it effectively relates an unknown condition of awareness (Paradise) with one that is known (infancy). But is infancy the *only* known or knowable "golden" state of consciousness? Clearly, it is not. Mystics, prophets, and saints of every tradition tell of realms of experience that are magical, peaceful, and joyous and that are characterized by oneness, knowingness, and light. Until recently, psychologists went to great lengths to explain these experiences as pathological imagination or delusion. However, as noted in chapter 1, there is a new school of thought among psychologists and mythologists, according to which the sacred dimension is not only real but is also the necessary source of spiritual nourishment and inspiration for both individuals and cultures. As also noted in that chapter, two of the earliest and most prominent exponents of this new school of thought were Mircea Eliade and Joseph Campbell. It is to their perspectives that we now turn.

One of the recurring themes in Eliade's books is that the religious experience is a window into a reality that is "higher" than the physical, mental, and emotional world in which modern humanity spends its days. That higher reality is characterized by the subjective qualities of Paradise—peace, creativity, power, and ecstatic union with the divine. Eliade writes that every historical culture has regarded the human condition as being under a temporary spell of unnatural limitation and separateness, and that the primary purpose of all religions has been to help the individual and society to break free of that spell. In *The Sacred and the Profane*, he writes that

> the existence of *homo religiosus*, especially of the primitive, is open to the world; in living, religious man is never alone, part of the world lives in him. But we cannot say, as Hegel did, that primitive man is "buried in nature," that he has not yet found himself as distinct from nature, as himself. The Hindu who, embracing his wife, declares that she is Earth and he Heaven is at the same time fully conscious of his humanity and hers.[22]

Elsewhere in the same work, he tells us that it would also be wrong to assume that "religious man" was in the infantile position of being incapable of assuming responsibility for an existence independent of Mother Nature:

> On the contrary . . . he courageously assumes immense responsibilities—for example, that of collaborating in the creation of the cosmos, or of creating his own world, or of ensuring the life of plants and animals. . . . It is a responsibility *on the cosmic plane*, in contradistinction to the moral, social, or historical responsibilities that are alone regarded as valid in modern civilizations.[23]

It is not ancient but *modern* humanity that is asleep, unconscious, or infantile, according to Eliade. For ancient and primitive peoples,

> symbols awaken individual experience and transmute it into a spiritual act, into metaphysical comprehension of the world. In the presence of any tree, symbol of the world tree and image of cosmic life, a man of the premodern societies can attain to the highest spirituality, for, by understanding the symbol, *he succeeds in living the universal*.[24]

The modern man's "private mythologies" of dream and fantasy, in contrast, never rise to the ontological status of myths, precisely because they are not experienced by the *whole man* and therefore do not transform a particular situation into a situation that is paradigmatic. In the same way, modern man's anxieties, his experiences in dream or imagination . . . do not . . . provide the basis for a system of behavior.[25]

Therefore, the modern "rational" person, though still nourished to some degree by the activity of the unconscious, is nonetheless unable to attain "a properly religious experience and vision of the world."[26]

Eliade saw the tree and mountain of Paradise as symbols of ascent and connection, of communication between Heaven and Earth. He correlated symbols of ascension and flight in oral and scriptural traditions and concluded that all are expressions of a universal compulsion to transcend the ordinary, profane plane of experience and to know again the state of ecstatic union that existed in the beginning, before human consciousness fell to its present level.

It would be absurd to minimise the differences of content that diversify examples of "flight," "ecstasy" and "ascension." But it would be just as absurd not to recognize the correspondence of structure which emerges from such comparisons. . . . [A]t every level of culture and in spite of their widely different historical and religious contexts, the symbolism of the "flight" invariably expresses the abolition of the human condition, transcendence and freedom.[27]

Eliade dealt similarly with the image of the rivers of Paradise and the Water of Life: "Living water, the fountains of youth, the Water of Life, and the rest, are all mythological formulae for the same metaphysical and religious reality: life, strength and eternity are contained in water."[28]

Joseph Campbell has likewise described Paradise as a natural, fulfilling mode of consciousness that is foreign to the modern humanity. The aim of spiritual practice is to regain that pristine condition of awareness. As Campbell put it in an interview with television journalist Bill Moyers, "Getting back into the garden is the aim of many a religion."

The Fall, according to Campbell, was and is brought about by the machinations of the separate human ego—the voice within us that tirelessly promotes the interests of "I, me, and mine" above those of the living creative process of which we are individualized expressions. We become estranged from that process, and we anxiously try to direct the course of the river of life rather than yielding to its innate wisdom and power. "We are kept out of the garden," says Campbell, "by our own fear and desire in relation to what we think to be the goods of our life."[29]

Paradise—the immaculate condition of mind and emotion that is the objective of every spiritual technique—is immediately available to every human being, according to Campbell. All of us have tasted it at some point in our lives, whenever we have allowed ourselves to be fully awake in the present moment. "The difference between everyday living and living in those moments of ecstasy is the difference between being outside and inside the garden. You go past fear and desire, past the pairs of opposites . . . into transcendence."[30]

Eliade and Campbell have opened a promising avenue of interpretation. Their acknowledgment of the reality of the sacred illuminates the common ground of all religions. Moreover, their characterization of Paradise myths as descriptions of ecstatic levels of awareness invites a discussion of the experimental findings of the psychology of alternate states of consciousness. We will undertake such a discussion shortly.

Sometimes the simplest and most straightforward approach to a problem is the best one, and yet sometimes it is the last one we see. In this case, surely the most direct approach to the universal story of the Golden Age would be to ask, *What if the Paradise myth simply means what it says—that there was a time when human beings shared a state of being in which they knew union with all life and wielded magical creative abilities, and that this state of being was somehow tragically lost?*

In the previous chapter, we saw that the findings of archaeology and anthropology by no means rule out the possibility of a historical Golden Age. We saw, on the contrary, that the mythic scenario of Paradise, Fall, and catastrophe may offer the basis for a new historical paradigm capable of integrating the backlog of anomalies accumulating around the present purely evolutionary paradigm. In this chapter we have explored the possible psychological and theological meanings of the Paradise myth. We have concluded that the most promising avenue of interpretation is one in which the myth is seen as referring

to the formerly universal experience of a state of consciousness fundamentally different from what is considered "normal" today—a consciousness of ecstatic, mystical union. These historical and metaphoric
approaches are not contradictory. Both converge on a simple but
startling idea: *There really was a Golden Age. And it was a time when, as
the myths insist, human beings were wise and innocent, and communed
with both God and Nature to a depth we can scarcely comprehend.*

Let the reader be warned: despite its simplicity and the evidence in
its favor, the idea we have just stated is so radical from the standpoint
of the present scientific consensus as to verge on heresy. The contemplation of a historical Paradise of any variety is academically unpopu-
lar, to say the least. It may be uncomfortable, as well. Many people find
it depressing to think that our modern mode of being may be deficient
compared to that of ancient peoples. As we shall see, however, this
acknowledgment may provide the key that opens a door to a beatific
state of awareness—a state that, according to the civilized, "rational"
worldview, does not even exist.

PART FOUR

Return

The ancients devoted their lives to maintaining the balance of the universe: to great things, immense, [mysterious] things.

ESKIMO SHAMAN NAJAGNEQ

CHAPTER · 10

Unfolding Images:
The Mirror of Myth

URNED AND EXAMINED from many angles, the Paradise story acts as a kind of magic mirror, reflecting back to us not our immediate appearance but our essential nature—who we are and where we have come from. While the myth speaks to the timeless core of our ultimate identity, this is not to say that we necessarily see in it what others before us have seen. The basic content of the myth may be more or less given, but as we come to know more about the human mind and spirit we may begin to perceive meaningful patterns in our reflected image where before we saw only blurred shapes. Recent developments in psychology, comparative religion, anthropology, and archaeology, for example, cannot help but influence our response to the universal image of Paradise and our ability to understand its kaleidoscopic reflections of our innermost nature.

In this chapter we will use the mirror of myth to explore the implications of the thesis we proposed at the end of Part Three—that the Golden Age actually existed, and that it was a time when all humanity shared a mystical state of consciousness. Our exploration will be directed toward answering a series of questions that this thesis naturally suggests. First, what new information does the myth give us about the nature of the mystical experience, and what does our knowledge of mystical and religious states tell us about the Paradise myth?

A second line of investigation relates to the nature of the Fall. If Paradise was characterized by a shared unitive consciousness, then how and why was that consciousness lost? Mystics throughout the ages have told us that the main impediment to the experience of Paradise is the attitude of alienation from the web of life, an attitude which brings with it both greed and suffering. Many psychologists and students of comparative religion equate this habitual stance with the human ego and the egocentric mode of function. What does the universal myth of the Fall tell us about the nature of the ego, and what does our psychological and religious knowledge of the ego tell us about the Fall?

Shamans, saints, and yogis have been known to wield miraculous powers reminiscent of the powers of the legendary First People. Therefore, we might also ask, What does the myth tell us about the nature and meaning of religious miracles? And what does the study of paranormal abilities tell us about the myth of Paradise?

Finally, we will address a question concerning our conceptualizations of the past. History as we know it has been written from a progressivist viewpoint. Virtually all historians begin with the assumption that people today are better off than their distant ancestors, and that the further back into the past we look, the poorer, more stupid, and more brutish the people were. But what if the historical and archaeological data were arranged from a paradisal perspective? Is it possible to reinterpret history in the context of the Paradise story? What does the myth mean for our understanding of the development of civilizations and institutions?

As we gaze into the magical mirror of myth, religious, psychological, anthropological, and historical perspectives converge to refocus the primordial image of a world of beauty and wonder. Since the image in the mirror is still cloudy, we will need to remember that our interpretations are speculative. However, now and then we may catch glints of light piercing the mist that illuminate a pristine and timeless memory—one that seems to live within our very cells.

The Original Mind

The psychological study of alternate states of consciousness is still in its infancy, yet it has already disclosed a vast frontier. We now know that the level of wakeful awareness we consider normal is only part of an endless range of potential conscious states.[1] Just as there are subnormal psychological conditions in which the individual is cut off, withdrawn, and unable to interact with the environment or to function effectively within it, there are also supernormal states in which an individual may attain powers and perceptions usually inaccessible, so that the present moment becomes a window to unlimited possibility.

We have already seen that the qualities of innocence and creative power universally attributed to the First People suggest not an infantile or subnormal psychological condition, but one that is supernormal. But supernormal in what way? Taken together, can the ancient myths and the findings of modern psychology (particularly the psychology of religion and of altered states of consciousness) give us some idea of what paradisal consciousness was actually like?

In 1901, psychiatric physician Richard Maurice Bucke published his classic study *Cosmic Consciousness*, in which he outlined the experiences of fifty men and women whose lives were marked by a blazing flash of insight followed by a process of inner transformation. Cosmic consciousness, according to Bucke, is "a higher form of consciousness than that possessed by the ordinary man." It is "a consciousness of the cosmos, that is, of the life and order of the universe." With this comes an "intellectual enlightenment," a "moral exaltation, an indescribable feeling of elevation, elation, and joyousness, and a quickening of the moral sense," along with "a sense of immortality, a consciousness of eternal life, not a conviction that he shall have this, but the consciousness that he has it already."[2]

In 1902, psychologist William James published another classic study along the same lines, *The Varieties of Religious Experience*. Confirming Bucke's claim of the existence of conditions of awareness as fundamentally different from normal waking consciousness as the latter is from sleep, James attempted to classify mystical states into discrete levels and categories. According to James, all have two characteristics in common: *ineffability*—that is, they defy expression, so that no adequate report of their content can be given in words; and *a noetic quality*—that is, they seem to those who experience them to be states of knowledge. They are, wrote James, "states of insight into depths of truth unplumbed by the discursive intellect."[3]

More recently, in 1975, psychiatrist Stanley Dean outlined the characteristics of what he calls "ultraconsciousness":

1. The onset is ushered in by an awareness of dazzling light that floods the brain and fills the mind. In the East it is called the "Brahmanic Splendor." Walt Whitman speaks of it as ineffable light—"light rare, untellable, lighting the very light" —beyond all signs, descriptions, languages. Dante writes that it is capable of "transhumanizing a man into a god. . . ."

2. The individual is bathed in emotions of supercharged joy, rapture, triumph, grandeur, reverential awe, and wonder— an ecstasy so overwhelming that it seems little less than a sort of superpsychic orgasm.

3. An intellectual illumination occurs that is quite impossible to describe. In an intuitive flash one has an awareness of the meaning and drift of the universe, an identification and merging with Creation, infinity, and immortality, a depth beyond depth of revealed meaning—in short, a conception of the Over-Self so omnipotent that religion has interpreted it as God. . . .

4. There is a feeling of transcendental love and compassion for all living things.

5. Fear of death falls off like an old cloak; physical and mental suffering vanish. There is an enhancement of mental and physical vigor and activity, a rejuvenation and prolongation of life. . . .

6. There is a reappraisal of the material things in life, an enhanced appreciation of beauty, a realization of the relative unimportance of riches and abundance compared to the treasures of the ultraconsciousness.

7. There is an extraordinary quickening of the intellect, an uncovering of latent genius. Far from being a passive, dream-like state, however, it can endow an individual with powers so far-reaching as to influence the course of history.

8. There is a sense of mission. The revelation is so moving and profound that the individual cannot contain it within himself but is moved to share it with all fellowmen.

9. A charismatic change occurs in personality—an inner and outer radiance, as though charged with some divinely inspired power, a magnetic force that attracts and inspires others with unshakable loyalty and faith.

10. There is a sudden or gradual development of extraordinary psychic gifts such as clairvoyance, extrasensory perception, telepathy, precognition, psychic healing, etc. . . .[4]

The mystical experience described by Bucke, James, and Dean—so clearly reminiscent of mythic descriptions of the nature and experience of the First People—has been known by many people in the modern world, but usually for only a few moments during a lifetime. One can only wonder what it would be like for an entire society to share the openness of heart, the feeling of union with all life that the great souls of history have tasted, *but on a universally shared and constant basis.* Perhaps the result would be a kind of collective mind.

As we saw in chapter 3, Paradise myths do seem to imply the primordial existence of a unified mind encompassing all of humanity. The Hebraic, Indochinese, and Mayan traditions, for example, speak of the one original language, which was shared with the animals as well. The Hopi legend of the First People says that they "felt as one and understood one another without talking." The original mind seems to have been a kind of living, pulsating web of telepathic interconnectedness, through the strands of which flowed a current of universal love.

Imagine what it would be like to live in a world in which the sense of perfect attunement we may occasionally know with our closest friends was universal. In such a condition of mutual trust—a world without secrets or fears—there could be no hatred or misunderstanding. In our present society, incalculable amounts of human energy are spent controlling the results of our feelings of isolation. We fight anxieties with drugs and entertainment or express them through competition, crime, and war. In a telepathic world, all of the energy that is now given to fighting, litigation, and peace efforts would be freed for the celebration and nourishment of our innate connections with Heaven and Earth.

The original mind seems to have included more than humanity itself. The sense of universal oneness is described in the myths as extending to the rest of Nature and beyond. Anthropologist Roger Wescott, who has contributed to the literature on states of consciousness[5] and is one of the few in his profession to have studied Paradise mythology extensively, writes:

Since, even today, many people feel that they have, at least on occasion, immediate spiritual communion with many kinds of plants and animals, it is unlikely that the more labile minds of our paradisal ancestors had less. Indeed, they may have communed with consciousnesses whose very existence we find it difficult to believe in, much less to experience. Such consciousnesses could have been associated with—if not attached to—inorganic phenomena of all sorts, from minerals to stars. Moreover, most mythic traditions concur in asserting that, in the Golden Age, human beings associated easily and often with beings that were discarnate or only intermittently incarnate, ranging from awesome cosmic deities to playful local spirits.[6]

Paradise myths seem to say that the experience of universal oneness is the *natural*, healthy condition of human consciousness, and that the customary state with which most of us are familiar—that of egocentric separateness, with all its ramifications—is *unnatural* and unhealthy. The idea that mystical or paradisal consciousness is innate and natural is also met with in the teachings of nearly every religious tradition. In Buddhism, for example, the primal condition of union with the center of all Being is called Buddha-nature, Mind-Essence, or Original Mind. It is identified with pure consciousness, which is present in everyone, though in most people it is masked by the illusion of separateness. Hindu tradition similarly holds that the individual self (Atman) is in fact identical with the Universal Self (Brahman), and that this is the case for everyone. Enlightenment is not the creation of a form of consciousness that is fundamentally new; rather, it is what automatically happens when one succeeds in dispelling certain common illusions.

We find essentially the same realization expressed—though less frequently—in the Christian tradition. For the fourteenth-century Dominican monk Meister Eckhart, for example, the "divine spark" is the possession of all human beings. Whenever any person reaches inward past the sensations, thoughts, and images of surface consciousness, divine union is realized.

If the individual experience of cosmic consciousness is profoundly elating, joyous, and uplifting, then we can probably only begin to imagine the depth of ecstasy that would have characterized the original, universally shared paradisal consciousness. But all our speculations about the subjective quality of the Edenic state of awareness—and speculations are all we have at the moment—only compound the problem: How and why was such a fulfilling mode of being lost?

Ego and the Fall

As we saw in chapter 5, despite the numerous descriptions of the primal tragedy of the Fall provided by the various mythologies of the world, the event retains an element of mystery. If we can bring myth and psychology together to clarify the nature of Paradise, can we do the same for the pivotal event that brought the Golden Age to a close?

Nearly all religions distinguish between two fundamental modes of being, or conditions of awareness. One mode is characterized by the absence of personal wants and fears and a recognition of the interconnectedness of all things; it is expressed in attitudes of responsibility, stillness, selfless caring, and compassion. This condition is identified on one hand with the object of all religious devotion and practice, and on the other hand with the original state of humankind in Paradise. The second basic mode of being consists of the assumption of individual autonomy from God and Nature; it is expressed in the attitudes of want, fear, arrogance, domination, and blame. As we have seen, some modern psychologists, as well as many religious philosophers, identify this mode of consciousness with the ego: the more egocentric we become, the less likely we are to perceive and appreciate the unified ground of being from which all diversity springs. The myths of Paradise and Fall seem to be telling us that the primal tragedy consisted of the transfer of the focus of the collective human consciousness from the condition of oneness and participation to that of separateness, greed, and fear. The Fall, in short, was the initial appearance of the human ego.

The understanding of these two essential modes of being is fundamental not just to myth and religion, but to psychology as well. Virtually all the religions of the world in one way or another equate the presence of the ego with illusion, suffering, and death, and associate the experience of universal oneness or divine union with liberation, creativity, life, and bliss. Recent discoveries in psychology and medicine tend to confirm these religious truisms. Medical experiments have consistently shown that mental attitudes and emotional states have a significant influence on health. Emotional states associated with egoic separateness—anger, blame, and feelings of isolation— tend to reduce the levels of body chemicals that serve to raise the pain threshold (endorphins) and that maintain immunity to infection (immunoglobulins). Emotions associated with transcendence of ego— for example, empathy, forgiveness, and nurturing— produce higher levels of these critical body chemicals. In one study, college students who were merely shown a film of Nobel Peace Prize winner Mother Teresa tending the sick and dying in Calcutta experienced immediate increases in salivary immunoglobulin.[7] Such findings suggest that if there was an age of shared mystical consciousness, it would also likely have been a time of relative health and painlessness.

The equation of the Fall with the origin of the ego also helps clarify, and is in turn clarified by, the mythic metaphor of the forbidden fruit. As noted in chapter 5, the story of the eating of the fruit of the Tree of the Knowledge of Good and Evil can be seen as an allegory describing what happens when human beings allow their behavior to be governed by obsessive wants or fears. When we egotistically focus our attention on our own personal desires, we become less sensitive to the needs of the larger social and ecological patterns around us. We pursue goals and end products but ignore the broader implications of our actions. We come to imagine that we can pick the "good" fruit of the tree while leaving the "evil" fruit. We imagine, for example, that we can continue cutting down forests for firewood without ever running out of trees. Because our absorption in our own wants has caused us to ignore the inevitable effects of our actions, those effects when they come seem arbitrary and undeserved. We begin to imagine that we are living in a hostile world, fear overwhelms us, and our feelings of isolation are intensified.

The egoic mode of being is today so taken for granted by nearly everyone that it is often equated with human nature. It has become a part of our universal birthright, a cage into which we are born and from which no one—apparently—fully escapes. As we saw in chapter 9, some philosophers (including Kant, Hegel, and Jung) have argued that the development of the ego was a necessary part of human evolution. The myths insist otherwise. The argument for the mythic view was expressed with characteristic clarity and insight by philosopher Alan Watts in his *Psychotherapy East and West*:

> Jung's theory of the evolution of consciousness and the ego . . . leads him to regard the egocentric mode of consciousness as a universal and historically necessary step in the development of mankind. It is the problematic but essential mechanism for regulating the primordial instincts of the swamp and the cave, for raising mankind from the merely animal level. But we should consider another alternative: that man's peculiar bestiality has little to do with beasts; that his irrationalities, inordinate appetites, mass hysterias, and deeds of shocking violence and cruelty are not historically regressive at all. . . . Does not the practice, as distinct from the theory, of psychotherapy confirm this again and again? The disturbed individual is not so much the historical throwback in whom sufficient ego strength somehow failed to develop; he is the victim of too much ego, too much individual isolation. Furthermore, one should not assume that the development of an ego is the universally necessary basis for consciousness and intelligence. The neural structures of that "enchanted loom," the brain, upon which intelligence depends are certainly not the deliberate creations of any conscious ego, and they do not dissolve into pulp when the ego is seen to be fictitious—by an act of intelligence. It would follow, then, that when the ego is dispelled there is not an "invasion" of consciousness by primordial contents from the swamp and the jungle. There is instead insight: the perception of a whole new pattern of relationships comparable to scientific or artistic discovery.[8]

Medical and psychological research suggests that the attitudes of the isolated human ego are unhealthy. Moreover, the world's great spiritual traditions tell us that the ego is unnecessary and artificial. If the creation of the ego was not an evolutionary necessity, then why did it happen? How could what was already perfect go wrong? We naturally want a rational, meaningful answer to the question. Nevertheless, it is possible that no rational answer exists. Perhaps the Fall was simply a mistake.

Mistakes do happen. although our bodies, for example, tend to function efficiently and to repair themselves in the case of sickness or mishap, nevertheless sickness and mishap are possible. Every complex system is capable of malfunction. However, imbalances are usually corrected eventually, especially in biological systems. Nature absorbs the products of disintegration and creates anew. Is it not possible that the complex system of human consciousness simply malfunctioned? While in human terms this malfunction seems catastrophic, in cosmic terms it may be a relatively local and temporary condition that will eventually be balanced and neutralized in the ebb and flow of greater cycles (although from our current perspective we can scarcely imagine how this might happen).

If the ontological nature of the Fall becomes clearer as myth and psychology reflect off each other, the historical details of the event may forever remain hazy. Perhaps the ego originated in an aberrant experiment, involving the independent thoughts or actions of a few individuals. The isolated stance may have seemed like progress to those involved. Who could have known the ultimate consequences?

The Survival of the Miraculous

As we saw in chapter 3, the myths of all cultures describe the First Time as an age of miracles and wonders in which people glowed with light and had the abilities to converse with animals and to fly. Many interpreters of Paradise myths simply ignore these images as too problematic. For us, however, they are important clues. How does our thesis shed light on the nature and meaning of miraculous phenomena? And what does a study of paranormal powers and perceptions contribute to an understanding of myth?

It would be simple enough to view the miracles of the First People as pure metaphor. We might see the magical ability to fly, for example, as a metaphor for the ability to gain access to transcendent levels of consciousness, and we might view the luminosity of the First People as an "inner light" that allowed them to "see" the workings of Cosmos and Nature. But the anthropological study of tribal peoples and the comparative study of religions suggest another, more intriguing possibility: perhaps the miraculous abilities of the First People were objectively real.

So-called miracles—displays of human abilities unexplainable in terms of our present scientific knowledge—are not unknown in the historical, postparadisal world, and they are nearly always associated with mystical states of consciousness. Moreover, we find descriptions of the exercise of "impossible" abilities on every continent and in every period of history.

For Africans, Aborigines, and Native Americans, the abilities of the shaman or medicine man to commune with animal spirits and, in some instances, to fly are legendary. The Australian "clever man," for example, is able to summon an animal "familiar" to assist him, and is even said to be able to change into an animal. He can control the elements, cure illnesses, become invisible, move through the air, or run rapidly with his feet not touching the ground.[9] And there is evidence that accounts of these abilities, if sometimes exaggerated, are not entirely imaginary. Eliade writes that "a fairly large number of ethnographic documents has already put the authenticity of such phenomena beyond doubt."[10] Examples of attested miraculous abilities from other tribal cultures include clairvoyance and telepathy among the shamans of Tonga; clairvoyance among the Zulus; levitation and communication with animal spirits among Native American medicine men; and prophecy and clairvoyance in dreams among the Pygmies.

A discussion of all paranormal powers would be out of place here. Instead, we will concentrate on reports that seem to echo mythic descriptions of the three principal miraculous abilities or characteristics ascribed to the First People.

The ability to commune with the animals is preserved in the shamanic traditions of nearly all tribal cultures. A signal part of the shaman's initiation ritual is the meeting with an animal who becomes his familiar spirit, revealing to him secret knowledge, often including the language of the animals. Among the Central American Indians, this guardian animal spirit is known as the *nagual*. Anthropologist Åke Hultkrantz writes that the "close and intimate link" between the human and the nagual—which is "at times the generalized spiritual representative of an entire animal species, at other times a single actual animal"—is expressed in the ability of the shaman to change into his animal familiar.[11]

Similar relations between humans and animal spirits were described by Australian anthropologist A. P. Elkin in his study of

Aboriginal "men of high degree." The totemic animal "warns its [human counterpart] of danger, and will also go out to do services for him, such as gaining information of events at a distance."[12] Eliade summarizes the situation by saying that "friendship with the animals, knowledge of their language, [and] transformation into an animal are so many signs that the shaman has re-established the 'paradisal' situation lost at the dawn of time."[13]

There are people in civilized societies who have shown a similar capacity to communicate with the animals. This was, for example, an ability attributed to a number of Christian saints, including St. Francis of Assisi. In 1954, Allen Boone published the classic book *Kinship with All Life,* in which he related his experiences of profound communion with members of several species—a communion based on respect, playfulness, and the expression of nobility of character. More recently, scientist John Lilly and musician Jim Nollman have written of their successful communication experiments with dolphins. Lilly and Nollman have concluded that profound levels of communication with animals are open to anyone with enough patience and openness of heart.[14]

As noted, the ability to fly is also widely attributed to medicine men and shamans in tribal societies. Officer Ray Kelly of the Australian Parks and Wildlife Service is a second-stage initiate of the Bhungutti and is reputed to know more about "clever men" than anyone else in northeast Australia. Kelly says that prior to the disruption of Aboriginal culture by white settlers, there were four stages of initiation, and that it was at the fourth stage that initiates learned to fly. At most, 10 percent of Aboriginal men reached this stage. The massacres of the 1860s and subsequent missionization of the Aborigines halted the initiations, with but a few exceptions. Kelly says the last of the fourth-stage "clever men" may have died twenty years ago. An uncle who had reached the third stage told him of having seen a fourth-stage man "fly from one mountain to another."[15]

The power of magical flight is not unknown among civilized peoples—where, again, it is nearly always associated with religious or mystical states of awareness. There is a tradition among the Chinese, for example, that the Taoist sages and alchemists were able to rise up into the air. In India, too, the tradition of magical flight is ancient and pervasive: for the yogi, levitation is only one of the *siddhis* (miraculous powers) that can be attained through spiritual exercises. And for the Buddhist, flight is a natural ability of the *arhat* (enlightened one).

Certain Christian saints are also reported to have levitated; an example is St. Joseph of Cupertino, who lived in the seventeenth century. A witness recounts: "He rose into space, and, from the middle of the church, flew like a bird onto the high altar, where he embraced the tabernacle. . . . Sometimes, too, he was seen to fly to the altar of St. Francis and of the Virgin of the Grotello."[16]

Even the myth of the original luminosity of human beings has correspondences in the experience and lore of both tribal and civilized peoples. According to ethnologist Knud Rasmussen, Eskimo shamans report a mystical experience of

> a mysterious light which the shaman suddenly feels in his body, inside his head, within the brain, an inexplicable searchlight, a luminous fire, which enables him to see in the dark, both literally and metaphorically speaking, for he can now, even with closed eyes, see though darkness and perceive things and coming events which are hidden from others.[17]

Several historical religious figures are reported to have literally glowed. Among these are Moses, upon his descent from Mount Sinai; Jesus, at the transfiguration; and several Christian saints. It is said, for example, that when Abba Sisoès was on his deathbed, with the fathers sitting around him,

> his face began to shine like the sun. And he said to them: "Here is Abba Anthony coming." Then a little later: "Here is the band of prophets," and his face shone brighter. Then he said: "Here is the band of apostles" and the light of his face shone brighter still.

Then Sisoès "gave up the ghost, and it was like a flash of lightning."[18]

In the religions of civilized peoples, miracles are often associated with great refinement of character and are seen as proof of the divine presence. In tribal societies, they are acknowledged as reminders of the original paradisal condition of humanity and Nature. According to Eliade, the shaman initiates his trance, during which his miraculous feats are performed, in order "to *abolish this human condition*—that is, the consequences of the 'fall'—and to *enter again into the condition of primordial man* as it is described in the paradisiac myths."[19] But the ability of the shamans to recall this original, miraculous condition has been diminishing, generation after generation. Eliade writes that "the Chukchee, the Koryak and the Tongans, as well as the Selk'nam of Tierra de Fuego, are all agreed that the 'old shamans' had much greater powers and that the shamanism of today is in decline. The Yakuts recall with nostalgia the time when the shaman flew right up to heaven."[20]

In sum, in both the shamanic traditions of tribal peoples and the scriptural religious traditions of East and West we find reports of supernormal abilities that are reminiscent of the miraculous powers of the First People. This suggests not only that the mythic descriptions of the wonders of the Golden Age may be more than metaphors, but also that the spiritual transformation of the present fallen human condition brings with it a return of the paradisal state, including a transcendence of many commonly accepted physical limitations.

Re-envisioning History

According to universal tradition, we human beings have exchanged the joyful, miraculous experience of universal oneness for the alienated condition of egoic separateness. From a psychological and spiritual standpoint, this hardly seems like progress. Yet, most scholars view human history as a long series of gradual improvements leading up to our present industrial civilization, which they see as the desirable and inevitable goal of cultural evolution.

Is it possible to rewrite history from the paradisal perspective? To do so in any detail would require volumes. We would have to examine the origin and development of religion, economics, political theory, and science and technology, observing how historical data realign themselves when viewed as postparadisal developments. While such a project is obviously impractical here, it is nevertheless possible to make the briefest of beginnings. The following is an initial speculative exercise in a paradisal re-envisioning of history.

Perhaps the best place to begin would be immediately before the commencement of history itself—that is, shortly after the catastrophic collapse of the original unitary culture. Following the devastation of Nature and human society recorded in the myths of the Fall and of

William Blake, *Adam and Eve Sleeping* (1808). One of twelve illustrations to Milton's *Paradise Lost*. Adam and Eve sleep peacefully in the Garden of Eden before the Fall, watched over by the angels Ithuriel and Zephan, who have just discovered Satan "squat like a toad, close at the ear of Eve," tempting her in a dream.

subsequent natural catastrophes, several generations must have lived in utter confusion. Gradually, groups of survivors would have banded together, and, depending on where they were and what their experiences had been, they would have begun to build rudimentary cultures. From this point on, I will simply describe a hypothetical course of events reconstructed from historical and archaeological data. This is what *may have happened*:

Some larger groups in relatively hospitable areas remained stationary and developed peaceful, horticultural societies. These were the people who domesticated all our present food crops and built the peaceful towns that have recently been excavated in Old Europe and the Near East.

Other, smaller groups of survivors in more devastated areas were forced to wander in search of food. Because vegetation was scarce, they had to subsist through hunting and, eventually, animal herding. Thoroughly terrorized by the unchained elements, these nomadic herdsmen began to worship a sky-god of terror and to compulsively inflict their terrific fears on any nascent cultures with which they happened to come in contact. These were the northern tribes whose conquests would instill an aggressive and warlike character into the foundations of civilization.

The people vaguely remembered the divine representatives who had presided over the Golden Age and, wherever and however they gathered, naturally looked toward whatever leaders best exemplified paradisal qualities of character. However, particularly among the nomadic tribes, a heightened state of fear called for a harsh and autocratic style of leadership. Thus in the fourth to the second millennia B.C., as the nomads overran the towns of the sedentary horticulturalists, socially stratified military city-states were born.

To the degree that the leaders of these city-states were moved by fear, greed, and hunger for power, government gradually became a secular entity whose primary purpose was the protection and extension of material privilege. Laws and crime appeared simultaneously. As social organization grew more complex, it became necessary to control the increasingly irrational behavior of *some* of the people—yet the penalties that were imposed and the compulsions that were instituted served only to restrict the natural, spontaneous actions of which *any* of the people were still capable.

In all societies and in nearly every generation, a few extraordinary individuals appeared who were able to regain and exemplify paradisal consciousness. These individuals served as priests, prophets, or shamans, preserving myth and ritual and exercising psychic and healing abilities. They provided stability and purpose for their communities and a vital link between Nature and Heaven.

But while the people might revere the sayings of the divinely anointed ones, they could no longer fully understand certain ideas and terms. When spiritual leaders used the words *Heaven, Paradise,* and *spirit,* the people could often only grope for understanding. Memories flickered momentarily and then died away. Theories and dogmas proliferated as the priesthood itself gradually lost contact with the paradisal dimension of consciousness; people compared and fought over interpretations. Most cultures degenerated into ancestor worship, which only parodied the fading memory of Heaven and the Golden Age. Thus, in most instances, religions—all of which memorialize the former existence of an earthly Paradise and attempt to revive the beatific state of consciousness once enjoyed by all people—became mere codes of dogma over which human beings quarreled endlessly.

In the beginning there had been no concept of personal property. While the thought is speculative, it is nevertheless consonant with all we know of primal cultures to suggest that money originated not as a symbol of material possession, but as a means of containing and conveying a certain spiritual substance—an energy of life and healing—that had routinely been invested in matter by paradisal humanity. But as awareness of the spiritual dimension diminished and exchanges were increasingly motivated by material want, the symbols by which those transactions were facilitated became more and more abstract: rather than using charged, inherently valuable objects and substances, people began to use convenient, inert tokens.

With physical things represented by abstract, intrinsically valueless monetary symbols, material objects could be manipulated endlessly without consideration for their uniqueness, their place within a larger context, or their inherent meaning and purpose. The marketplace came into existence as means of equating—and hence desacralizing—all things: ten monetary units' worth of cow could be exchanged for ten units' worth of iron, ten units' worth of human labor, and so on. Thus money, which had begun as a symbol of the substance of Heaven invested in the Earth, gradually became a means for the degradation and enslavement of people and the spoil and desecration of the planet.

In the First Age, knowledge was inseparable from wisdom, which is perhaps best defined as the sense of the fitness of things. Knowledge was of wholes, of organic interaction, and of the turning of systems within systems. But as human beings lost awareness of their identity and purpose, they also lost knowledge of the workings of Nature. They sought to regain this lost knowledge, but their motive for its reacquisition was to selfishly control Nature's processes, and the method used was analysis—the breaking down and tearing apart of wholes. Knowledge thus came to be divorced from wisdom.

Just as the use of abstract monetary symbols served to desacralize Nature, so did the pursuit of analytical knowledge. Eventually, it was found that the most efficient way to analyze and control Nature is to deny it any nonphysical attributes whatsoever. Hence, through analysis it became possible to know more and more about less and less, and to use that knowledge without concern for spiritual values.

As human consciousness lost contact with its internal, heavenly source of power, technology emerged as a power substitute. Its first appearance was as sympathetic magic and as the invocation of spiritual beings to change Nature for human benefit. However, as human awareness became increasingly restricted to the material world, purely mechanical technologies appeared. With the wedding of science to technology it became possible to transform energy stored in wood, coal, or oil into impressive displays of power, so that one individual, using machines, could do the work of hundreds. These capabilities were so impressive that technological discoveries began to create new desires—for example, for faster transportation and communication and for greater luxury and conveniences of every kind. Such desires soon became needs.

Meanwhile, few noticed as the servicing of the technological machine began to take more and more attention away from people's relationships with Nature and with one another. Through technology, people could construct an artificial environment in which they were thoroughly insulated by their own creations from any contact with the cyclic pulsations of the Cosmos and the deep, earthy necessities of Nature.

Not only did the memories of Heaven and Paradise fade and decay, but they were actively denied. Crisis loomed, but few would do anything to prevent it. Only a nagging whiff of memory remained—and an ancient prophecy of a time of purification when the artificial world of human contrivance would be swept away and divine representatives would return to establish a new Golden Age.

So far, we have used the mirror of myth to view the past. What we have seen may have important implications for the realization of human potential, for our understanding of the fundamental causes of our individual and societal distress, and for the recasting of the foundations of history. But if we look more deeply into the mirror, we may see the image of a Paradise that is still with us and within us, and whose ineluctable presence reaches beyond time itself.

The Heavenly is on the inside, the human is on the outside. Virtue resides in the Heavenly. Understand the actions of Heaven and man, base yourself upon Heaven, take your stand in virtue, and then, although you hasten or hold back, bend or stretch, you may return to the essential and speak of the ultimate.

CHUANG TZU

There is no death, only a change of worlds.

CHIEF SEATTLE

CHAPTER 11

Paradise Now: Between Heaven and Earth

E SAW IN CHAPTER 4 that innumerable traditions place Paradise not only at the beginning of history, but also in another, still-existing dimension of existence—the Otherworld, to which ancient peoples believed they were destined to go after death. Originally, according to myth, the earthly Paradise and the otherworldly Paradise were joined by a rainbow bridge. The First People, described as being immortal, were said to be able to ascend to Heaven at will. Later, the rainbow bridge (or a primordial rope or ladder that served to connect the two worlds) was severed or withdrawn, and since then people have rarely gained access to the heavenly Paradise while still physically alive.

While immortality and the Otherworld are central to the universal Paradise narrative and appear in nearly every version, they would seem to present the greatest problems for a historical interpretation of the myth. After all, isn't the idea of the Otherworld mere imagination, and that of immortality pure wishful thinking?

In the course of the last three chapters we have compared the findings of psychology, anthropology, and archaeology with the contents of the Paradise myth. In so doing we have found that the modern evidence does not rule out the possibility of a historical Paradise. Indeed, the findings of science may be used to clarify our understanding of the mythic imagery, while the myths themselves suggest new ways of understanding some of the data of science. In this chapter we will explore some recent discoveries in psychology relating to the questions of death and immortality. Again, science and myth reflect upon each other to yield a clearer image. Like some of the scientific data we have already cited, the discoveries we are about to consider are inconclusive and controversial. Nevertheless, they bear directly not only upon the myth of Paradise, but also upon the fundamental issues of human existence.

The Near-Death Experience

In recent years, new techniques in emergency health care have resulted in a significant increase in the number of people who are rescued from the verge of death. Frequently, a resuscitated patient will recall an experience of peace and joy and of telepathic communion with beings of light. Several physicians and psychologists, intrigued by the frequency and similarity of such reports, have undertaken to investigate them.

Two of the first published studies of near-death experiences (NDEs) were Raymond Moody's popular books *Life after Life* and *Reflections on Life after Life*. Moody, a philosopher and psychiatrist, found that NDE accounts tend to resemble the following generalized description:

A man is dying and, as he reaches the point of greatest physical distress, he hears himself pronounced dead by his doctor. He begins to hear an uncomfortable noise, a loud ringing or buzzing, and at the same time feels himself moving very rapidly through a long tunnel. After this, he suddenly finds himself outside of his own physical body, but still in the immediate physical environment, and he sees his own body from a distance, as though he is a spectator. He watches the resuscitation attempt from this un-usual vantage point and is in a state of emotional upheaval.

After a while, he collects himself and becomes more accus-tomed to his odd condition. He notices that he still has a "body," but one of a very different nature and with very different powers from the physical body he has left behind. Soon other things begin to happen. Others come to meet and to help him. He glimpses the spirits of relatives and friends who have already died, and a loving, warm spirit of a kind he has never encoun-tered before—a being of light—appears before him. This being asks him a question, non-verbally, to make him evaluate his life, and helps him along by showing him a panoramic, instantaneous playback of the major events of his life. At some point he finds himself approaching some sort of barrier or border, apparently representing the limit between earthly life and the next life. Yet, he finds that he must go back to earth, that the time for his death has not yet come. At this point he resists, for by now he is taken up with the experiences in the afterlife and does not want to return. He is overwhelmed by intense feelings of joy, love, and peace. Despite this attitude, though, he somehow reunites with his physical body and lives.

Later he tries to tell others, but he has trouble doing so. In the first place, he can find no human words adequate to describe these unearthly episodes. He also finds that others scoff, so he stops telling other people. Still, the experience affects his life profoundly, especially his views about death and its relationship to life.[1]

In descriptions of the near-death experience, as in myths of the earthly or otherworldly Paradise, we read of a realm of love and peace populated by radiant, all-knowing beings whose communication is telepathic and complete. The strength of these parallels—and the personal intensity of the experience—become even more apparent when we examine a specific firsthand account.

Following a nearly fatal automobile accident in 1976, cultural anthropologist Patrick Gallagher was comatose for weeks. His NDE was extended and vivid, typical of what researchers term a "core" experience. Here are some of the highlights of his remarkable story:

> Not only was I freed from gravity but from all other human restrictions as well. I could fly, and fly so adeptly that I felt transformed. . . .
>
> Next in sequence was the sight of a dark area ahead, void of all light, which I saw to be the entrance of a tunnel. . . . Finally I saw a circular light in the distance . . . of yellow-orange color of total beauty. . . .
>
> When I left the tunnel, I entered a dazzlingly beautiful area. . . . It was complete space, that is . . . totally and perfectly illuminated. . . . I saw [there] a number of people, some of whom

were clothed and some of whom weren't. The clothing, which seemed transparent, was adornment but not . . . shielding. . . . The people themselves [were] also of graceful beauty. . . . Every-one there, as I knew the very moment I was there, seemed to possess a knowledge as radiant, transfiguring and ideal as the luminous light. And I possessed it, too. . . . I knew that all one had to do was approach an interesting person and quite easily and almost immediately *understand his essence*. To do so completely required only a brief glance . . . into the person's eyes, without any speech . . . the result was [a] consummate exchange of knowledge. Words cannot provide a hint of such universal knowledge.

Without reflection or words, I knew them as completely as they knew me, and finally understood why poets cite eyes as the entrance to the soul. . . . I also knew that the illuminating light would never cease: no one had the need to sleep. . . . I also understood that everyone present was in a state of perfect com-passion with everyone else and everything else. . . . We were freed from all those contrivances historians often claim to be the causes of war and other conflicts, including land, food, and shelter. Love was the only axiom. These ideal conditions pro-duced a phenomenal state, for neither hate nor any other disturb-ing passion was present—only the total presence of love. . . .

I knew it was quite possible to return to my terrestrial life, and I missed . . . my children, my wife, and many others. I did decide to return, though I knew also that the price of the ticket would be gargantuan: accepting the biological, physiological, and physical needs and handicaps of my body, as well as the loss of all but a splinter of my luminous knowledge. I know nothing of any aspect of the return trip, but as soon as I decided to return and so lost the ALL of what I have ever wanted to be or to know, I was there.[2]

If Gallagher's recollection were rephrased only slightly, so as to seem to come from some ancient source, we might think we were reading yet another Paradise myth. His experience took place in a beautiful, gardenlike place; he met radiant people, with whom he shared imme-diate telepathic understanding; and both the place and its inhabitants were suffused with a sense of peace, innocence, and love.

Hieronymus Bosch, *The Ascent of the Blessed* (ca. 1500). In his depiction of the ascent of the blessed to Heaven, Bosch used imagery similar to that which is reported by modern NDErs: a bright light is approached through a long tunnel in which spirits float, weightless and free.

There are literally hundreds of thousands of people alive today who have made a similar journey to the otherworldly Paradise and returned to tell about it. Pollster George Gallup, Jr. discovered that nearly 5 percent of the adult population in North America have had an NDE.[3]
Even more striking than the frequency of the experiences is their impact on human lives. When asked to compare the NDE with dreams they remember, subjects emphasize the distinctly *undreamlike* quality of the experience. Indeed, a comment frequently heard is that ordinary waking reality seems like a dream in comparison with the NDE: "I felt as though I was *awake* for the first time in my life." Moreover, the experience seems in nearly every case to result in a drastic and immediate reorientation of values. Noting this tendency, psychologist Kenneth Ring conducted a survey among twenty-six NDErs to systematically assess changes of attitude and values following their experience. In his book *Heading toward Omega*, he concludes:

> After NDEs, individuals tend to show greater appreciation for life and more concern and love for their fellow humans while their interest in personal status and material possessions wanes. Most NDErs also state that they live afterward with a heightened sense of spiritual purpose and, in some cases, that they seek a deeper understanding of life's essential meaning. Furthermore, these self-reports tend to be corroborated by others in a position to observe the behavior of NDErs.[4]

Other studies have shown that the experiences tend to be similar in basic structure, regardless of the subject's religious training and convictions. Atheists and devout churchgoers are just as likely to have NDEs, and to experience a tunnel, a being of light, and so on. However, cultural background does appear to color the subject's *interpretation* of the experience: a Christian may view the Being of Light as Jesus, for example, whereas a Moslem may understand it as a messenger of Allah.

Nearly everyone who studies the NDE phenomenon eventually confronts the question of whether the experiences are entirely subjective hallucinations, or evidence of the objective existence of a paradisal afterlife. Most scientists assume the former. To positivist science, consciousness is a product of electrochemical processes in the brain;

when the brain dies, consciousness ceases. But, as many scientists will admit, this conclusion—or assumption, for that is what it is—is only marginally amenable to proof or disproof by material evidence. Such research as has been done by no means rules out the idea that consciousness can exist apart from the brain; quite the contrary. The evidence is such that pioneer neurosurgeon Wilder Penfield, after failing to account for consciousness through the brain's electrochemical processes, concluded late in his career that mind *must* have an independent existence from the physical brain.[5]

Penfield's conclusion is supported by the existence of a certain class of near-death phenomena called autoscopic visions. Many NDE subjects report that while floating up and out of their inert physical forms, they could *see* details of their surroundings that they could not have perceived by means of their physical senses—details that could later be corroborated by others. In his book *Recollections of Death*, cardiologist Michael Sabom details several independently confirmed autoscopic experiences. He attempts to explain the apparent accuracy of the information acquired by subjects during their NDEs "by prior general knowledge, by information passed on by another individual, and by physical perceptions of sight and sound during semiconsciousness."[6] He notes that "the details of these perceptions were found to be accurate in all instances in which corroborating evidence was available,"[7] and concludes that none of the standard explanations is adequate to account for the accuracy of the information brought back from "out of body."

Sabom also examines the range of physiological and psychological explanations for the NDE phenomenon: hallucinations based on expectation; conscious fabrication; the release of endorphins in the brain; depersonalization and other psychological phenomena known to produce hallucinations; the effects of drugs and anesthetics; and temporal lobe seizure. He finds none of these explanations sufficient, and concludes:

> I am ... aware that my arguments against the more traditional NDE explanations ... do not ipso facto prove that the out-of-body proposal is correct. Certainly other explanations for the autoscopic NDE—explanations I have not addressed—may eventually account for all these findings. I do believe, however, that

the observations . . . concerning the autoscopic NDE indicate
that this experience cannot be casually dismissed as some mental
fabrication, and that serious scientific consideration must be
given to alternative, perhaps less traditional explanations.[8]

Thus, science can do little to answer the fundamental questions of
human existence: *Does the mind, soul, or spirit have an existence apart
from the body? Is there another realm of existence, an otherworldly Paradise, that is objectively real and not merely a product of human imagination?*
It is difficult to imagine any technical or methodological breakthrough
that would enable scientists to settle these matters once and for all.
But while physical science can tell us little about the existence or
nature of the heavenly Paradise, other avenues of inquiry—such as
comparative religion and mythology—may still yield intriguing clues.

Ideas of the Afterlife

The features of the NDE that modern researchers find so intriguing were already well known to the ancient Tibetans, who compiled a
detailed account of the spirit's passage between realms, in a book they
called the *Bardo Thodol* (usually translated as *The Book of the Dead*).
This text, attributed to the founder of Tibetan Buddhism, describes
the gateways to postmortem levels of experience encountered by the
soul or spirit in the intermediate state (*bardo*) between incarnations.

According to the *Bardo Thodol*, the soul of the deceased tends to
linger around the body for several days after death. During and following this period the soul itself is experiencing, in turn, three stages of
bardo. The initial stage, Chikhai Bardo, is characterized by visions of a
Being of Clear Light in a beautiful landscape. The *Book of the Dead*
advises the dying consciousness to identify itself with the light and to
let go of all attachment to its former personality.

If it is unable to do so, it will continue to the second stage,
Chonyid Bardo, in which it begins to clothe itself with a psychically
projected body resembling its former physical body. The consciousness
encounters seven divine beings; if unable to identify with any of them,
it then meets with seven terrifying demons. The *Book of the Dead*
encourages the soul to view these grotesque beings as projections of its

own subconscious and to observe them without fear.

In the third stage, the Sidpa Bardo, the soul gains the ability to move freely and instantaneously about the physical world; it sees its family in mourning and tries in vain to convince them that it has not died. It wanders alone in misery until it perceives the Lord of the Otherworld, who has come to judge it; following a life review, it feels the torture of the demons of its own fears and desires.

The *Book of the Dead* is not a description of eternal heavens and hells, but a chronological catalog of the dimensions of reality that the soul or spirit may visit between death and rebirth. Most NDEs occur over a matter of seconds or minutes rather than days, so that—assuming the NDErs and the ancient Tibetans are describing the same experience—the entire range of phenomena usually reported in an NDE is probably contained within the first bardo.

Many traditions—particularly in Asia—distinguish between the soul and the spirit. Sometimes, as among the Yukagirs, the human being is described as having three "souls": the first is associated with the physical body, and the second with the human personality; the third is of cosmic origin, and its home is the celestial realms. The first two souls are capable of maintaining themselves outside the body for longer or shorter intervals, but eventually they decay. Only the cosmic soul, or spirit, is immortal. It is this soul that is the ultimate source of human identity and that is reborn in another body, which during the course of life develops a new personality.

Mahayana Buddhism teaches the doctrine of the *Trikaya* or "Three Bodies"—the Dharmakaya, or absolute core of being, which is the Clear Light of the Void; the Sambhgakaya, the Body of Spiritual Bliss, which is the heavenly manifestation of the Absolute in the world of space and time; and the Nirmanakaya, the material body in which the Self is incarnated. The *Book of the Dead* describes the Clear Light as "subtle, sparkling, bright, dazzling, glorious and radiantly awesome." The text urges the human personality to "be not daunted thereby, nor terrified, nor awed. This is the radiance of thine own true nature. Recognise it!"[9] But the human soul, or personality, is seldom able to do so, having become addicted to environmentally and hereditarily conditioned responses to the material world—desire and fear—during life. Instead of being drawn up into oneness with this ultimate Self, it is consigned to various disintegrative hells.

According to the *Book of the Dead*, the realms visited by the soul are objectively neither real nor unreal in our usual terms of reference. The landscape of the Otherworld is a mental projection of the human soul, yet each postmortem realm is subject to its own internal set of laws and regularities, analogous to but different from those of the physical world.

The NDE as a Form of Mystical Experience

Paradise myths insist that a "golden" consciousness of love and telepathic union was at one time known by human beings while in the flesh. We might envision the situation as being something like a continuous, waking near-death experience—without physical trauma— shared simultaneously by the entire population. Is such a condition possible? Apart from the myths, is there anything that would lead us to assume that the paradisal Otherworld is accessible to people who are alive, well, and conscious?

Toward the end of his description and interpretation of the near-death experience in *Heading toward Omega*, Kenneth Ring makes the following bold statement:

> *What occurs during an NDE has nothing inherently to do with death or the transition into death. . . .* The NDE . . . should be regarded as one of a family of related mystical experiences that have always been with us, rather than as a recent discovery of modern re-searchers who have come to investigate the phenomenon of dying.[10]

Ring is drawn to this conclusion by the similarity of all aspects of the NDE to the experiences of prophets, mystics, and saints throughout history. Meetings with beings of light, visions of heavenly landscapes, and sudden, dramatic changes of values have been known by countless people who were not in life-threatening circumstances. Some of these people have gone on to become charismatic leaders whose visions are recorded in the sacred literature of the world religions. More often, however, those who have profound mystical experiences simply de-vote the remainder of their lives to contemplation and service.

From the similarity of the descriptions of the state of mystical illumination—as supplied by Bucke, James, and Dean (see chapter 10)—to the firsthand accounts of sensations and perceptions that occur during NDEs, we can only conclude, with Ring, that both are members of a family of related experiences. Whether the NDE is evidence of survival beyond physical death is debatable, but it is unquestionably a kind of experience that is *potentially* available to everyone. If we are to call the transcendental light and the celestial landscape evidence of Paradise, then it is possible for human beings in the present to know the experience of Paradise, as described in the ancient myths, while still alive on Earth.

Yet, the fact that the paradisal experience appears so predictably when people are on the verge of death cannot help but suggest to us the existence of some deep link between mystical consciousness and the profoundly mysterious Beyond. Stories of the Golden Age in which a rainbow bridge served to connect two worlds seem to be accounts of a time when the processes of birth and death were not as mysterious as they are now. Even today the Eskimos say that "birth and death . . . are less a beginning and an end than episodes of life. Bodies are only instruments of souls—the souls that are their 'owners.'"[11] The universal myth of the immortality of the First People may simply refer to a time when life was equated with the life of the spirit rather than that of the body, and was therefore experienced as being eternal.

Imagination or Reality?

Myths of the paradisal Otherworld are often so bizarre or so fancifully embroidered that it is easy to view them as the inventions of human beings seeking an imaginary escape from the dilemma of eternal nothingness. Most anthropologists have taken the view that when primitive peoples faced the ultimate paradox of existence and nonexistence, as Arthur Koestler put it in *Life after Death*, "their minds went haywire and saturated the atmosphere with ghosts of the dead and other invisible presences who at best were inscrutable, but mostly malevolent, and had to be placated by grotesque rituals."[12]

Many would dismiss Heaven as having no place in the rational world. Then again, it can appear—as it does to those who emerge from

NDEs—as more real than what we commonly think of as reality. Is the otherworldly Paradise purely imaginary? Or is it a natural realm of experience from which we have somehow excluded ourselves? Our materialist, concrete language is simply unable to describe or define that which is neither entirely objective nor merely imaginary. Yet, no matter how elusive it is to contemplate, we cannot ignore the mythic dimension of the prophetic vision. In moments of ultimate crisis, at the verge of death, what we thought was most real and concrete slips away, and the Otherworld—which had previously seemed nonexistent—becomes suddenly more vivid than the experience of our senses ever was.

We modern Westerners have tried our best to banish the subjective realms and to live entirely in an objective, material world. Repressed, the contents of the unconscious lash out at us in the irrational compulsions of madness and prophecy. Meanwhile, the waking, objective world, loosed from its subterranean undergirding, becomes the worst kind of nightmare. Psychologists, with the exception of Jung and his followers, have tended to view the inner world as a collection of images abstracted from physical reality. Most dreams do seem to be merely the unconscious mind engaged in cleaning house, assembling fragments of emotion and thought left over from the day's sojourn in the material world. But there are occasional disquieting dreams from a level far deeper—prophetic dreams, or dreams of flying and of speaking with angelic beings—that have their source not in the mundane world, but somewhere else entirely. We have forgotten how to interpret these latter dreams, and hesitate even to acknowledge them.

Perhaps the Tibetans came closest to resolving the seeming contradictions of the psychology of Paradise with their description of the bardo realms of the soul as mentally projected, but still real. In a sense, even our experience of the physical world is self-created: two people in the same circumstance may see it in different ways. Yet we all tend to agree that there is an ultimately real, objective world "out there," with inherent rules and bounds, that is independent of our interpretations and beliefs. If the observations of the greatest sages in history are to be given any weight at all, then we must also be willing to consider the possibility that beyond the mentally projected bardos of postmortem existence there is an ultimately real inner Source of identity, meaning, and purpose that cares not a whit about our religious convictions concerning its existence or nonexistence.

Perhaps the objective world of physical form and this ultimate inner Source are separated by innumerable states of emotion and thought, conditioned by fear and desire—and perhaps in this continuum is included our "normal" waking consciousness. When the veil of illusion maintained by these states of emotion and thought thins—as in moments of extremity—we may catch a glimpse of a Being of Light, which is that ultimate inner Source. In that moment of oneness with Source there is peace, assurance, radiance, and ineffable knowing. And that is Paradise.

It may be that some little root of the sacred tree still lives. Nourish it then, that it may leaf and bloom and fill with singing birds.

BLACK ELK

CHAPTER · 12

To Get Back to the Garden

EDENIC CONSCIOUSNESS MAY BE RECOVERABLE by individuals in rare moments of spiritual insight. Perhaps nearly everyone glimpses Paradise at some instant during his or her lifetime. But is it also possible for all of us together to live in the Garden once again—to return and stay? This final chapter will offer two reasons for thinking that it *is* possible. We will see, moreover, how signs of strain and disintegration in the foundations of our present civilization, together with some intriguing developments at the growing tips of society, suggest that a new Golden Age may already be struggling to be born.

The Attainability of Paradise

The evidence of anthropology and archaeology may not prove (though it certainly does not deny) the former existence of a Golden Age—that is, of a unitary culture in which people were universally and continually telepathic, lived close to Nature, and possessed miraculous powers. But, as we saw in chapter 8, anthropological and archaeological discoveries *have* shown, almost beyond a doubt, that two of the most destructive aspects of civilization (the use and justification of violence as a means of social change, and the desire for dominance over other human beings and over Nature) were acquired only recently. The findings of archaeologists show that in the past human beings did live—*and therefore in principle are capable of living*—in peace and harmony both among themselves and with Nature.

239

Moreover, the evidence of psychology suggests not only that a subjective condition of oneness, peace, and innocence is attainable, but also that it is the *natural and healthy mode of human consciousness*. If the human body functions best in the absence of the ego-states of blame, fear, and resentment (as medical experiments show that it does), then the fact that we are living in an ego-based world, in which Paradise is the exceptional experience, must therefore be an unusual and temporary state of affairs.

If we were able to live in Paradise once, we ought to be able to do so again. And if the most natural and healthy way of life available to human beings is defined by the expression of the essential paradisal qualities of character and the subsequent experience of universal harmony, then what is natural should in principle also be attainable. In short, we may be *designed* to live in Paradise.

Why, then, do we routinely assume that Paradise is beyond our reach? Perhaps it is partly because we have an unrealistic concept of what that state is or should be. We tend to think of Paradise as a place or time in which all human desires are satisfied; since people's desires tend to conflict, we therefore assume that Paradise could never actually exist. But the Paradise of myth and vision is not a state in which conflicting personal desires are somehow all fulfilled. Rather, it is one in which all human desires and motives are completely subsumed within a larger creative purpose. If individual desires are satisfied in Paradise, this is only because it is the overwhelming desire of all individuals that the consummate accord of Nature and Cosmos be nourished and maintained.

The inhabitants of Paradise—whether in myths of the First Age or in near-death visions—are universally characterized by their expression of specific values and qualities of character. And, as Aldous Huxley (among others) has shown,[1] a comparative study of the religions of the world reveals that these values and qualities—honesty, compassion, and love—are universal and innate. Whether it was a historical reality or not, Paradise exists in the eternal present as an image expressing our deepest sense of what is right and true about ourselves.

Looked at in this way, Paradise may be seen as serving a specific function, as a *design for living* embedded in the circuitry of human consciousness. All biological organisms, including human beings, contain elements of design. We know, for example, that the pattern of the DNA molecules in our cells governs the basic design of our physical bodies. Perhaps we also contain within us a neurological or psychic program for the optimal design of social and spiritual relations between ourselves, the Cosmos, and Nature—a design of telepathic oneness and interspecies communion that represents the goal toward which our individual and collective experience would naturally tend to unfold.

Provided there are no significant interferences, the design inherent in the DNA molecules in our cells is expressed automatically and accurately in the formation of our physical bodies. Perhaps the same is potentially true of the neurological design of Paradise: provided its expression is not blocked, the pattern of oneness with the universal currents of life, as well as of miraculous abilities, should be automatically and accurately reflected in our ordinary experience.

At present, however, it is not. As we have seen, nearly all of the world's spiritual traditions agree that the innate paradisal design is being thwarted in its expression by certain now-universal patterns of attitude, thought, and behavior.

Warnings from the Collective Unconscious

When we diverge from the way we were designed to function, Nature sends warning signals. For example, when we eat foods we are unable to digest, our stomachs rebel; when we use our limbs in ways in which they were not designed to be used, our muscles and bones protest. When we do such things habitually over time, we are likely to receive not only external signals in the form of pain, accidents, or disease, but we may also receive internal signals. Such signals may take the form of nightmares and premonitions through which the body's own unconscious wisdom attempts to alert us and to influence our behavior.

If this is true for us individually, perhaps it is also true for humankind collectively—that is, if humanity is ignoring an innate paradisal design (by envisioning and working toward a world characterized by artificiality, separateness, and the suppression of Nature), then we should expect to be receiving both external and internal warnings. On the collective level, such external warning signs might take the form of war, environmental degradation, famine, or plague; internal warning signs might appear as widely occurring visions of apocalyptic events.

As Norman Cohn showed in *The Pursuit of the Millennium*, apocalyptic visions have tended to appear in profusion during historical periods of political and religious oppression, social upheaval, war, and pestilence. The Hebrew prophets lived in an age of defeat and captivity; Jesus lived at the height of the decadent and oppressive Roman Empire; and medieval millenarian movements seemed always to flourish in places and times of unusual hardship. We see the same association of apocalyptic vision with societal stress among tribal peoples: in North America, Africa, and the Pacific islands, new spiritual movements that have arisen during the last century in response to the onslaught of civilization have invariably been prophetic and millenarian in character.

There are many reasons for thinking that contemporary Western civilization is approaching a period of maximum divergence from the paradisal ideal. Instead of simplicity, innocence, and the ability to work in harmony with natural processes, industrial civilization values sophistication, abstraction, the concentration of wealth, and the complete subjugation of Nature. These values have not appeared suddenly or recently; rather, they can be traced back to the beginnings of civilization itself. But we do seem to be witnessing the culmination of their influence. And as we actualize the ultimate implications of long-term trends leading toward the centralization of social power, the technological domination of Nature, and the fragmentation of human consciousness, we find ourselves on what appears to be a collision course with a deeper reality.

We see external warning signals appearing everywhere around us. We hear, for example, of the death of thousands of lakes and forests from the effects of acid rain. As the thinning of the ozone layer creates an epidemic of skin cancer, we simultaneously discover that a greenhouse effect—created by the carbon dioxide released from the burning of fossil fuels—is altering global weather patterns. We hear of the disappearance of tens of thousands of species as the result of the clear-cutting of rain forests, and of the loss of millions of tons of irreplaceable topsoil due to modern mechanized agricultural practices. These and other warning signals portend catastrophes of truly apocalyptic dimensions, catastrophes that can be averted only if immediate steps are taken to change our fundamental relationship with the natural environment.

At the same time, we are seeing an unprecedented eruption of what could be interpreted as internal, psychic warning signals. The past two decades have seen burgeoning numbers of people turn to millenarian fundamentalism for a sense of meaning and purpose. Christian fundamentalists look toward the imminent end of the world, the destruction of unbelievers, and the restoration of an earthly Paradise characterized by all the qualities of the original Eden—peace, happiness, and, above all, the opportunity to dwell in the immediate presence of the Lord.

But while fundamentalist millenarianism draws upon apocalyptic scriptural visions from eras past, we are also surrounded by fresh and original prophetic utterances. The classic apocalyptic scenario—a final battle between the forces of good and evil, followed by the advent of a restored condition of peace and beatitude—appears, for example, in numerous science-fiction plots and in the psychic predictions of Edgar Cayce and the "channelers" of the 1980s. Moreover, near-death experiences are making their own contribution to what amounts to a contemporary explosion of apocalyptic prophecy.

While conducting his NDE studies, Kenneth Ring began to hear reports of prophetic visions (PVs) of humanity's future, and he decided to collect and compare them. Ring found that PVs seem to occur most frequently during core NDEs, and that there is an "impressive similarity" among the visions. In *Heading toward Omega*, Ring summarizes the common elements of the classic PV:

> There is, first of all, a sense of having total knowledge, but specifically one is aware of seeing the entirety of the earth's evolution and history, from the beginning to the end of time. The future scenario, however, is usually of short duration, seldom extending much beyond the beginning of the twenty-first century. The individuals report that in this decade there will be an increasing incidence of earthquakes, volcanic activity, and generally massive geophysical changes. There will be resultant

disturbances in weather patterns and food supplies. The world
economic system will collapse, and the possibility of nuclear war
or accident is very great (respondents are not agreed on *whether* a
nuclear catastrophe will occur). All of these events are transi-
tional rather than ultimate, however, and they will be followed
by a new era in human history marked by human brotherhood,
universal love, and world peace. Though many will die, the earth
will live.[2]

Ring then quotes several PV reports. The following is from a woman
whose near-death experience occurred in 1967:

The vision of the future I received during my near-death experience was one of tremendous upheaval in the world as a result of
our general ignorance of the "true" reality. I was informed that
mankind was breaking the laws of the universe and as a result of
this would suffer. This suffering was not due to the vengeance of
an indignant God but rather like the pain one might suffer as a
result of arrogantly defying the law of gravity. It was to be an
inevitable educational cleansing of the earth that would creep up
on its inhabitants, who would try to hide blindly in the institutions of law, science, and religion. Mankind, I was told, was
being consumed by the cancers of arrogance, materialism, racism,
chauvinism, and separatist thinking. I saw sense turning to non-
sense, and calamity, in the end, turning to providence.
    At the end of this general period of transition, mankind was to
be "born anew," with a new sense of [its] place in the universe.
The birth process, however, as in all the kingdoms, was exqui-
sitely painful. Mankind would emerge humbled yet educated,
peaceful, and, at last, unified.[3]

Ring attempted to find a rational explanation for the remarkably
consistent patterns of imagery in the PVs he had collected. Could
these experiences be projections of unconscious fears? Or, perhaps, do
individuals who perceive themselves as dying somehow generalize the
experience as being "the death of the world"? Ring found both of these
explanations unconvincing: Why not a greater variety of global-future
scenarios? The PVs are just too consistent to be personal projections.
Could they, then, be eruptions of unconscious Jungian archetypes?

Ring found this explanation more plausible, but he was still uncomfortable with the specificity and paranormal character of PVs. After examining all of the explanations he could devise, Ring found himself left with the interpretation the NDErs themselves insist upon: that PVs are in fact exactly what they seem to be—inspired prophecies of future events.

If this is the case, *why* is humanity propelling itself toward a cataclysmic day of reckoning? Ring invokes a sobering metaphor: he suggests that humanity is approaching—and subconsciously preparing for—a *collective* near-death experience. As we noted earlier, NDErs almost invariably undergo a sudden and radical restructuring of values. A typical comment is this: "My interest in material wealth and greed for possessions was replaced by a thirst for spiritual understanding and a passionate desire to see world conditions improve."[4]

Throughout history, moral reformers have sought to inspire humanity to change its collective values and to regain its sense of the sacred. Despite occasional and temporary successes, such exhortations have generally been ignored. We seem convinced that greed and aggression are constants, restrainable only by the force of law. But Ring's hypothesis implies that human nature, when it comes face to face with annihilation, may dissolve to reveal a deeper and more profound nature, one that has been hidden for millennia behind the veil of the human ego.

The Russians have a saying: "The peasant doesn't cross himself until he hears the thunder." That is, people tend to make basic changes in attitude and behavior only when their backs are to the wall. This observation seems as true for society as a whole as it is for individuals. Often, only a crisis will awaken us to the results of a destructive habit. In the case of late-twentieth-century humanity, the habitual behavior (and the potential awakening) is at a critical level and underlies all of our social, economic, scientific, and political realities. This crisis amounts to far more than just a serious inconvenience, or even a catastrophe on the scale of the Great Depression or the two world wars. Religious prophets and scientific futurists alike envision what amounts to the end of our entire way of life, and, conceivably—in the event of an all-out nuclear conflict or the irreversible destruction of the environment—the death of the human race itself.

We recall the prophecies of the tribal peoples concerning a Great

Purification, which will cleanse the world of human depravity but will also reunite Heaven and Earth, ushering in a new age of spirituality and light. Is this what we are all unconsciously laboring to bring about?

The New Culture

Christian fundamentalists believe that apocalypse is inevitable. Social activists and utopians, on the other hand, believe that we can avoid Armageddon by making a gradual and peaceful transition away from the attitudes and assumptions of modern industrial civilization and toward a regenerative, peaceful way of life. According to the latter view, apocalypse will come only if we refuse to work, consciously and collectively, toward the constructive reform of our present institutions.

But whether humanity is headed toward peaceful transition or apocalyptic purification, the course of action for those who are committed to a paradisal outcome is the same: to deliberately begin to plant the seeds of a new culture based on universal spiritual values. A peaceful transition may be preferable to humanly engineered cataclysm, but it can only come about as the result of changes in the attitudes and actions of individuals. However, if a period of global purification *is* somehow inevitable, the mass of humanity will require models of wholeness and stability toward which to orient as upheavals occur, if there is to be anything to build upon after the period of purification is over.

As Marilyn Ferguson, Willis Harman, and other keen observers of social trends have been telling us for the past decade, the seeds of a new culture are already appearing.[5] This new culture is not the plan of any specific human organization or agency, but rather is arising spontaneously in a thousand unpredictable ways through the efforts of people who in most instances have no idea of the interconnectedness—much less of the mythic or archetypal implications—of their actions.

One such seed is represented in widespread and increasing interest in ecology and environmentalism. While many people's concern for environmental issues may be motivated simply by self-interest—the desire to escape disaster—the contemplation of the interrelatedness of

Nature's systems seems inevitably to trigger radically new views of our proper relationship with the rest of the biosphere. As we become aware of the implications of the basic principles of ecology, inherited attitudes of exploitation tend to give way to attitudes of cooperation and stewardship. Ultimately, people who embrace environmentalism seem to be drawn back to the ancient view that the Earth is not here merely to satisfy human needs and desires; rather, that we human beings are here to nourish and steward the Earth.

Another portent of the kind of creative change that might lead to the emergence of a new paradisal culture is a burgeoning interest in native religions and comparative mythology. The word *religion* itself comes from the Latin *religare*, meaning "to bind back." Religion has always been humanity's way of seeking to recover something that has been lost. It is the expression of a universal yearning for a state of innocence and completeness—a state projected into the past, the future, or another dimension of existence, but nonetheless always felt to be real and innate, though somehow removed from our ordinary experience. The object of religion is always the recovery of the divine presence and the return of the miraculous world of Paradise.

The new spiritual revival of the past two decades seems to be directed toward the very essence of the religious experience. While drawing upon existing Native American, mystical Christian, Sufi, and Buddhist traditions (among others), its ultimate goal is a resurgence of the spirit from which *all* systems of revelation derive their meaning.

The kinds of fundamental changes in values and attitudes that we are considering tend to occur first in the details of people's lives, and are only later reflected in public policy. In their most intimate relationships, for example, many people are discovering what it is to move from a dominant/submissive mode based on need and fear toward one of partnership based on a shared sense of higher purpose. In their worldly vocations, people are finding that old values and motives centered on economic necessity and the competitive drive are stressful and unfulfilling. As the innate desire to uplift, bless, and nourish gains prominence, many people are changing careers, often trading a larger salary for a more satisfying means of contributing to the lives of others.

For some, this change of values is subtle; for others, the paradisal quest becomes an all-embracing passion. As noted in an earlier chapter, thousands of utopian communities have been founded during the last twenty years, particularly in North America. Many of these communities are virtual greenhouses for the germination of the seeds of the new culture, fostering pioneering lifestyles based on ecological awareness, new patterns of relationships, and new ways of revealing and acknowledging the sacred. Such communities provide a means of exploring change through the total commitment of the time and resources of the people involved. Ultimately, however, any individual action or social movement that furthers the values of oneness, peace, and respect for natural processes represents a seed of the new culture.

As yet, we probably cannot know in any detail what the new culture will look like when and if the transition has been made. Certainly, it will not be an exact reproduction of the original earthly Paradise. Regardless of whether our sojourn into egocentric consciousness was necessary to our evolution or merely a tragic error, we have learned a powerful lesson from the experience. We may return to innocence, but it will not be the same innocence we would have known had the Fall never occurred. Neither can we accurately predict the nature of the new culture merely by extrapolating present trends: the developments we have just considered may be leading in the direction of a renewed paradisal state, but they are as yet mere seeds. By any standard, the magnitude of the transformation required in order for humanity as a whole to return to an integrated, regenerative mode of being is immense. We have barely begun the process.

Realizing Paradise

Paradoxically, while the transition to the new culture is a project of vast proportions, it is likely to be accomplished only through changes in the attitudes and values of individual men and women—changes that may be virtually invisible to society as a whole. *How, then, can you and I actually go about making these changes in our outlooks and behavior so as to realize Paradise in our own lives here and now, and thereby contribute to the creation of the new culture?*

Civilization is built of compromises and trade-offs. Daily, we compromise integrity, intimacy, empathy, and honesty for a thousand seemingly worthwhile reasons, and we feel supported in doing so by the example and encouragement of others. We have made our lives complex and abstract. We seem to live to serve our laborsaving devices. Many of us are willing to trade a large proportion of our waking hours to work at what may be intrinsically meaningless jobs in return for economic power. At some point we must ask whether all these trade-offs are really justifiable. Returning to Paradise requires that we examine our lives honestly, and, when we find ourselves acting in ways that contradict our deepest values, that we change direction—not going backward toward some mythic past, but moving inward toward our highest vision of love and truth. We must be willing to withdraw from participation in the mechanisms of the human world as it is as we learn to simplify, sanctify, and celebrate every aspect of life.

The process of transformation need not be arduous. Indeed, in some respects it is more play than work—though not the competitive, win/lose play of civilized adults, but more the spontaneous, mutually trusting, experimental, and ecstatic play of young children and wild animals. As psychologist O. Fred Donaldson puts it, "Play is nature's way of triumphing over culture."[6] If Paradise is our natural state of being, then the deepest and most compelling force at the core of the collective unconscious is one that is always urging us toward that state of equilibrium. As we deliberately work toward a future characterized by respect and care for Nature and toward the nurturing of love, forgiveness, compassion, and celebration in ourselves and in one another, our conscious efforts resonate with the pattern at the core of our being. Heaven and Nature rush to return to a condition of balance and accord.

It is also true that as we move in the transformational process, we are working against social conditioning that continually tends to divide us both from one another and from the very ground of our own being. Hence, the need for the spiritual quest, which in all its guises is essentially a process of cutting through the crust of ego that prevents us from experiencing and revealing our own innate paradisal character.

This quest is neither new nor unprecedented. It is neither more nor less than the archetypal hero's journey, identified by Joseph Campbell as being central to every mythic tradition. Every culture remembers examplary men and women who have accomplished internal transformations, and who have left instructions by which others can do the same. While the details of the instructions may differ, all spiritual exemplars agree on the broad outline of the process. It consists, first, of a withdrawal from the world-as-it-is, and a deliberate act of purification. This is followed by a period of integration within the system of universal spiritual values. The process culminates in a final realization of unity with the ultimate Principle of all that is. While the details of the process are individual, the essential outline of the journey is always the same, as is the goal: Paradise—the realization of oneness with Heaven and Nature.

The heroic quest is fundamentally a symbolic journey, representing the progressive unfoldment of the hero's transcendent character and destiny. Jesus and the Buddha are figures who accomplished the profound inner transformation by which a door was opened between worlds, and human society was led to a partially or temporarily restored condition. Ultimately, the records of their lives are metaphors for what must occur in the experience of anyone who takes up the quest.

In every hero myth, the first stage in the journey consists simply of hearing and responding to a call. The hero or heroine must realize that the world is in need of healing, and that his or her own actions will make a difference to others. For the Buddha, the call came when he was thirty years of age and first saw sickness, old age, and death. He was so profoundly moved by the suffering he saw that he stole away from his sleeping wife and child to seek the key to liberation from the universal human condition. For Jesus, the first awareness of the call came when he was only twelve years old. He left his parents and spent three days in the temple among the doctors, discussing theology. When his worried parents finally found him, he said simply, "Wist ye not that I must be about my Father's business?"

As we lift our attention above our conditioned wants and fears long enough to become aware of the purposes of a greater Whole, we suddenly see the possibility that our lives could have significance beyond comfort and self-satisfaction. The call may be faintly sensed, or it may blare. In either case, a conscious decision must be made to either listen or shut it out. To ignore the call is to die to the purposes of life. But to listen and to accept the challenge of the quest requires a willingness to leave behind the ruts established for us by heredity and environment, and to explore unfamiliar territory. We cannot enter Paradise without leaving behind our present cultural or psychic environment.

The second stage of the quest involves coming to terms with a dragon, demon, or enemy. Seeing suffering, we seek its cause, and causes of human suffering are legion. At the beginning of this stage we may see a dragon that is external to ourselves—an immediate source of injustice and cruelty. We may decide that the dragon is embodied in a philosophy we detest, or in a person whose actions seem to cause others pain. Many people become fixed in this phase of the quest and never proceed further. Their lives are spent battling the demons of the world, which, even when apparently slain, seem to grow new heads and return to torment them again.

As long as we continue battling external demons, we are incapable of fully bringing peace to our world. Eventually, if we remain true to the call—*if we continue to listen*—we will come to understand that the real dragon is within us: all the problems of our world have been produced by tendencies present in ourselves. Until and unless our *internal* dragons can be dealt with, even the most valorous external battle cannot fully bear fruit. Some of the great heroes in religious literature seem to have realized this from the beginning. Both Jesus and the Buddha, for example, knew from the outset that the victory they sought was a triumph over their own lower natures. Gandhi, on the other hand, began his career with the belief that the dragon consisted entirely of governmentally enforced racism; only gradually did he come to see his own attitudes and behavior as the battleground for the forces of good and evil.

Once the dragon is recognized as being an internal force, a different kind of battle begins. This stage of the process, in which the hero is wrestling with his own inner demons, doesn't seem especially paradisal. It involves the exposure of one's weaknesses and the surrender of personal attachments. Paradoxically, it seems, one can only get to Paradise by being willing to go through hell. But this conflict, too, must come to an end. The resolution of the battle with the inner demon is represented in the story of Jesus' temptations in the wilderness. Before Jesus began his public ministry, and after he had fasted in the wilderness for forty days, the Devil appeared to him. The Devil first offered Jesus bread, symbolizing personal fulfillment at the physical level; then he challenged Jesus' authority; and finally he offered the kingdoms of the world, "if thou will fall down and worship me." But Jesus, refusing physical desire, the need to prove himself, and personal ambition as motives for his behavior, replied, "Get thee hence, Satan!" For him, the demon was gone.

A similar story of the Buddha says that while he was sitting under the Bodhi tree, immediately before attaining enlightenment, he was tempted by the god-demon Mara. Amid both violence and offers of pleasure and power, he simply sat and remained calm, "like a lion seated in the midst of oxen." Mara and his armies, frustrated, left in defeat.

The dragon or demon can be fully tamed only through consistent inner work over a period of years. Yet, there is an instantaneous quality to the essential transformation that eventually comes: at any time a sudden change of state may occur and Paradise will be present, if only for a moment. The hero tames the dragon not by fighting it, but by *refusing to fight it*—by facing it, courageously holding steady, and expressing the character of innocence and love. Suddenly, the hero realizes that Paradise has been there all along, unnoticed.

Even after the hero has momentarily achieved paradisal awareness, he must still learn to sustain and communicate that state. From this point on, he is certain that he has known the true and natural condition of human consciousness—the pearl of great price, for which the wise person will sell everything (Matthew 13:46).

After having developed the ability to consistently maintain paradisal consciousness, the hero returns to the mundane world with a healing balm. Having found Heaven, he must share it—which means sharing *himself*, his state of being. For the individual, the return is the culmination of the journey, but the quest is not complete until the world has been restored.

Epilogue

ID AN EARTHLY PARADISE ONCE REALLY EXIST, *or is it the product of human imagination?* Even now, at the end of our investigation, we must acknowledge that this is a problem that may never be settled by archaeologists or anthropologists. On one hand, it is impossible to prove the historical reality of a Golden Age by physical evidence alone; on the other hand, the material evidence by no means rules out the possibility, and the less tangible evidences of myth and culture simply will not allow us to dismiss it. Of course, the answer we settle on depends largely on our definition of what Paradise was, is, or should be.

The myths and traditions of the ancients do not portray Eden as the sort of technological Paradise that our present civilization tends to project into the future. If the Golden Age really existed, it must instead have been, as the Chinese describe it, an Age of Perfect Virtue—an age in which

> they were upright and correct, without knowing that to be so was righteousness; they loved one another, without knowing that to do so was benevolence; they were honest and leal-hearted without knowing that it was loyalty; they fulfilled their engagements, without knowing that to do so was good faith; in their simple movements they employed the services of one another, without thinking that they were conferring or receiving any gift. Therefore their actions left no trace, and there was no record of their affairs.[1]

Of course, there may be some trace of the First People's actions in mysterious ancient megaliths, and some record of their affairs may be preserved in myth and legend. Nevertheless, these are fragmentary and ephemeral clues. And yet the vision of Paradise—be it distorted, misunderstood, or even imaginary—has somehow insinuated itself into the vital core of every religious movement and every culture's literature and social ideals. Whatever the myth's origin—historical reality or mass delusion—it now has a life of its own in the collective unconscious.

The principal thesis presented here—which is really only a restatement in modern terms of what spiritual teachers have been saying for millennia—is that the memory of Paradise represents an innate and universal longing for a state of being that is natural and utterly fulfilling, but from which we have somehow excluded ourselves. Perhaps our most useful new clue to this lost state of being is contained in the modern study of altered states of consciousness and, in particular, of the near-death experience. The essence of Paradise is, as we have seen, equivalent to what various traditions have termed nirvana, ecstasy, divine union, and cosmic consciousness. It is the condition of the absence of the separate human ego with all its defenses, aggressions, and categories of judgment.

This interpretation may seem like an obvious one, but it has been only recently that developments in several disciplines have made it so. In the field of psychology, for example, the systematic study of alternate states of consciousness did not really begin until this century, and the greatest advances have taken place only within the last twenty years. In anthropology, it has also been only in recent decades that we have come to respect the wisdom of tribal peoples and to take seriously their beliefs about the nature of reality. The field of comparative religion—which has opened a view to the fundamental similarities of the core teachings of all spiritual traditions—has likewise only begun to come of age. All of these developments converge, enabling us to leave behind both the dogmatic religious ideas of the Middle Ages and the simplistic evolutionary assumptions of the last century. We are thus free to attain a new vision not only of the mythic past, but also of our own miraculous potentialities in the present and future.

One of my purposes in writing this book has been to bring together the principal myths of Paradise, Fall, catastrophe, and purification.

But another was to recall the texture and nuance of the spiritual worldview of ancient and tribal peoples. Their perspective, so at odds with our modern way of looking at things, may contain some of the very elements that we in postindustrial civilization need if we are to build a sustainable, regenerative culture.

We are living not in a static world that affords us endless time for leisurely academic discussion, but in one that is busily undermining its own biological viability. We have lost our sense of proportion, our sense of the fitness of things, and our sense of being contained within a greater Knowing that provides our lives with meaningful context, and to which we are responsible not only for our actions but for our motives and values as well. We have lost, in short, the sense of the sacred. The Paradise myth is the account of this loss of the sacred dimension, this loss of innocence. And if it contains clues to help us understand why we have come to this precarious juncture in history and how we may go about regaining what we have left behind, then a retelling of the story may now be a worthy undertaking.

Somehow the timing of this retelling seems to have an almost apocalyptic significance of its own. Many generations have felt that they were seeing the culmination of history, but never has any generation had better reasons for feeling this way. Perhaps we are indeed living in the time prophesied in every tradition, when the profane world of human history and the miraculous world of myth are to be somehow reunited.

We seem to have come very far indeed from the state of innocence and communion with Nature described in the Paradise myths. Depletion of the Earth's ozone layer, pollution of water and air, loss of topsoil and forest cover, the greenhouse effect, and mass extinctions of species all bespeak a way of existence tragically out of touch with the pulse of the planet on which we live. And burgeoning crime, mental illness, and drug abuse seem to signal some deep estrangement of society from the nourishing aspirations of the human spirit.

Our world is filled with complex political, economic, social, and environmental problems. Yet we cannot expect to solve these problems without first addressing the values and motives that produced them. And how are we to approach the clarification of human values and motives? Surely, we must look to the human psyche itself—that mysterious realm whose suprarational powers and dynamics find first expression in myths, dreams and visions. We are presented therefore with the apparently paradoxical likelihood that the examination of ancient and seemingly irrational stories may be one of the most practical pursuits available to us in the modern world.

Perhaps, if we are willing to become partners once again with Heaven and Nature in the realization of an already existing design that transcends self-centered human purposes, then memory and vision may converge in a realized Paradise in which the tensions that presently bedevil us—tensions between humanity and Nature, heart and mind—may be dissolved in a universal spirit of accord. If we can hear and obey a voice from the timeless source of myths and dreams, there may open before us an age not of technologically engineered comfort and prosperity, but of miraculous beginnings—a new Creation-Time. And perhaps it is only the mysterious power of Creation itself that will permit us to survive, and at last to fully live.

Notes

Foreword

1. Wilhelm Reich, *Selected Writings* (New York: Farrar Straus-Noonday Press, 1961).
2. Rupert Sheldrake, *The Presence of the Past: Morphic Resonance and the Habits of Nature* (New York: Times Books, 1988).

Introduction

1. E. F. Schumacher, *Small Is Beautiful* (New York: Harper & Row, 1973), p. 278.
2. See Robert Ornstein and David Sobel, "The Healing Brain," *Psychology Today* (March, 1987), pp. 48 ff.

CHAPTER 1: *The Mysteries of Myth*

1. Mircea Eliade, *Myths, Dreams and Mysteries* (New York: Harper & Row, 1967), pp. 59–60.
2. G. S. Kirk and J. E. Raven, trans., *The Presocratic Philosophers* (Cambridge, Mass.: Harvard University Press, 1957), p. 168.
3. C. G. Jung, *Collected Works*, vol. 9 (Princeton, N.J.: Princeton University Press, 1967), p. i.
4. C. G. Jung, "The Structure of the Psyche," in *Collected Works*, vol. 8 (Princeton, N.J.: Princeton University Press, 1968), p. 152.
5. See, for example, C. G. Jung, *Psychology and Religion: West and East*, vol. 11 of *Collected Works* (Princeton, N.J.: Princeton University Press).

6. René Guénon, "Oriental Metaphysics," in *The Sword of Gnosis*, ed. Jacob Needleman (Boston: Routledge & Kegan Paul, 1986), p. 56.
7. Mircea Eliade, *Myths, Dreams and Mysteries* (New York: Harper & Row, 1967), p. 66.
8. Quoted in Hartley Burr Alexander, "Latin-American Mythology," in *The Mythology of All Races*, vol. 11 (Boston: Marshall Jones, 1920), p. 275.
9. Marcel Griaule, *Conversations with Ogotemmeli*, quoted in Barbara Sproul, *Primal Myths* (New York: Harper & Row, 1979), p. 15.
10. Robert Johnson, *He: Understanding Masculine Psychology* (New York: Harper & Row, 1974), *She: Understanding Feminine Psychology* (New York: Harper & Row, 1976), and *We: Understanding the Psychology of Romantic Love* (New York: Harper & Row, 1983); Jean Shinoda Bolen, *Goddesses in Everywoman* (New York: Harper & Row, 1984).
11. Peggy V. Beck and Anna L. Walters, *The Sacred* (Navajo Nation: Navajo Community College Press, 1977), pp. 72–73.
12. Alastair H. Campbell, "Aboriginal Traditions and the Prehistory of Australia," *Mankind* 6 (10) (December 1967), pp. 476–481.
13. Robert H. Lowie, "Oral Tradition and History," *American Anthropologist* 17 (1915), p. 598.
14. Joseph Campbell, Foreword to Maya Deren, *Divine Horsemen: The Living Gods of Haiti* (Syracuse, N.Y: McPherson, 1968), p. 1.
15. Raymond Van Over, *Sun Songs: Creation Myths from Around the World* (New York: New American Library, 1980), p. 11.

CHAPTER 2: *In the Beginning*

1. Mircea Eliade, *Patterns in Comparative Religion* (New York: New American Library, 1974), p. 395.
2. Joseph Epes Brown, *The Spiritual Legacy of the American Indian* (New York: Crossroads, 1987), p. 76.
3. *Taitriya Brahmana* I, 5, 9, 4.
4. Mircea Eliade, *The Sacred and the Profane* (New York: Harcourt, Brace & World, 1959), p. 92.
5. Archie Bahm, trans., *Tao Teh King by Lao Tzu, Interpreted as Nature and Intelligence* (New York: Ungar, 1958), pp. 29–30.
6. James B. Pritchard, ed., *Ancient Near Eastern Texts Relating to the Old Testament* (Princeton, N.J.: Princeton University Press, 1950), p. 6.
7. Hare Hongi, "A Maori Cosmogony," *Journal of the Polynesian Society* 16 (1907), pp. 113–114.
8. Martha Beckwith, *Hawaiian Mythology* (Honolulu: University of Hawaii Press, 1970), p. 44.
9. Barbara Sproul, *Primal Myths* (New York: Harper & Row, 1979), p. 17.

10. W. G. Ashton, *Shinto, The Way of the Gods* (London, 1905).

11. G. Buhler, trans., *The Laws of Manu*, in *Sacred Books of the East*, vol. 25 (Oxford, 1886), p. 5.

12. H. H. Wilson, *The Vishnu Purana*, vol. 1 (London, 1864), p. 55.

13. Roland B. Dixon, "Maidu Myths, Part II" in *Bulletin of the American Museum of Natural History* 17 (1902–1907), pp. 39–45.

14. Ibid.

15. H. B. Alexander, *The World's Rim* (Lincoln, Neb.: University of Nebraska Press, 1953), p. 89.

16. R. T. Rundle Clark, *Myth and Symbol in Ancient Egypt* (London: Thames & Hudson, 1959), p. 142.

17. Alain Danielou, trans., *The Vishnu Purana*, in *Hindu Polytheism* (New York, 1964), pp. 367–368.

18. Sheila Savill, ed., *Pears Encyclopedia of Myths and Legends*, volume on North America (London: Pelham, 1977), p. 161.

19. Hartley Burr Alexander, "Latin-American Mythology" in *The Mythology of All Races*, vol. 11 (Boston: Marshall Jones, 1920), p. 271.

20. Fletcher and La Flesche, "The Omaha Tribe," *Twenty-Seventh Annual Report of the Bureau of American Ethnology* (Washington, D.C., 1911), pp. 570–571.

21. Joseph Epes Brown, *The Sacred Pipe* (Norman, Okla.: University of Oklahoma Press, 1953), p. 115.

22. Recorded by Mary C. Wheelwright, from Hasteen Klah, *Navajo Creation Myth* (Santa Fe, N.M.: 1942), p. 142.

23. Joseph Epes Brown, *The Spiritual Legacy of the American Indian* (New York: Crossroad, 1987), p. 92.

CHAPTER 3: *In Search of Eden*

1. See Geoffrey Bibby, *Looking for Dilmun* (New York: Knopf, 1969).

2. Albert J. Carnoy, "Iranian Mythology," in *The Mythology of All Races*, vol. 6 (Boston: Marshall Jones, 1917), p. 312.

3. Sheila Savill, ed., *Pears Encyclopedia of Myths and Legends*, volume on the Orient (London: Pelham, 1977), p. 40.

4. Vendidad, Far. II, 3–41, quoted in S. G. F. Brandon, *Creation Legends of the Ancient Near East* (London: Hodder & Stoughton, 1963), p. 48.

5. R. T. Rundle Clark, *Myth and Symbol in Ancient Egypt* (London: Thames & Hudson, 1959), p. 263.

6. Ibid., p. 264.

7. François Lenormant, *The Beginnings of History* (Paris, 1880), pp. 67, 73.

8. Quoted in S. G. F. Brandon, *Creation Legends of the Ancient Near East* (London: Hodder & Stoughton, 1963), p. 48.

9. Ibid., p. 48–49.
10. Trans. in Arthur Lovejoy and George Boas, *Primitivism and Related Ideas in Antiquity* (Baltimore: Johns Hopkins Press, 1935), p. 27.
11. Ibid., p. 32.
12. Ibid., pp. 94–95.
13. Ibid., p. 46.
14. Ibid., pp. 61–62.
15. *Mahabharata*, Santiparvan, Moksadharma, 231, 23ff., trans. in Donald A. MacKenzie, *Indian Myth and Legend* (London: Gresham, n.d.), pp. 107–108.
16. *Vaya Purana*, 8, 17ff., trans. in Lovejoy and Boas, *Primitivism and Related Ideas in Antiquity*, pp. 437–438.
17. Archie Bahm, trans., *Tao Teh King by Lao Tzu, Interpreted as Nature and Intelligence* (New York: Ungar, 1958), p. 59.
18. John C. Ferguson, "Chinese Mythology," in *The Mythology of All Races*, vol. 8 (Boston, 1932), p. 21.
19. Lao Tzu, *Tao Teh King*, p. 22.
20. Mircea Eliade, *Myths, Dreams and Mysteries* (New York: Harper & Row, 1967), p. 43.
21. Hartley Burr Alexander, "North American Mythology," in *The Mythology of All Races*, vol. 10 (Boston: Marshall Jones, 1916), p. 308.
22. Frank Waters, *Book of the Hopi* (New York: Ballantine, 1972), p. 15.
23. Hartley Burr Alexander, "Latin-American Mythology," in *The Mythology of All Races*, vol. 11 (Boston: Marshall Jones, 1920), p. 262.
24. Ibid., p. 269.
25. Jonathan Z. Smith, "The Golden Age," in Mircea Eliade, ed., *The Encyclopedia of Religion*, vol. 8 (New York: Macmillan, 1987), p. 71.
26. Mircea Eliade, *A History of Religious Ideas*, vol. 1 (Chicago: University of Chicago Press, 1978), p. 32.
27. Susan Feldman, ed., *African Myths and Tales* (New York: Dell, 1963), p. 37.
28. Paul Schebesta, *Bambuti-Pygmaen vom Ituri*, iii, (Brussels, 1950), p. 165, trans. in Wilhelm Koppers, *Primitive Man and His World Picture* (London: Sheed & Ward, 1952), pp. 43–44.
29. Herman Baumann, *Schöpfung und Urzeit des Menschen im Mythus der afrikanischen Völker* (Creation and the Primal Era of Mankind in the Mythology of African Peoples), (Berlin, 1936), pp. 267ff. Quoted in Mario Jacoby, *Longing for Paradise* (Boston: Sigo, 1985), p. 18.
30. Ibid., p. 45.

CHAPTER 4: *Images of Paradise: Common Themes*

1. J. G. Frazer, *Folklore in the Old Testament* (New York, 1923), pp. 4, 83.
2. Wilhelm Koppers, *Primitive Man and His World Picture* (London: Sheed &

Ward, 1952), p. 42.

3. Hartley Burr Alexander, "North American Mythology," in *The Mythology of All Races*, Vol. 10 (Boston: Marshall Jones, 1916), p. 159.

4. W. F. Warren, *Paradise Found* (Boston: Houghton Mifflin, 1885), p. 129. See also David Talbott, *The Saturn Myth* (New York: Doubleday, 1980), pp. 120ff.

5. *Yasna*, x, 10.

6. *Bundahisn*, xxvii, 5.

7. Samuel Noah Kramer, *Sumerian Mythology* (New York, 1972), p. 81.

8. W. F. Warren, *Paradise Found*, p. 147.

9. See Mircea Eliade, *Cosmos and History: The Myth of the Eternal Return* (New York: Harper & Row, 1959), p. 125.

10. Frank Waters, *Book of the Hopi* (New York: Ballantine, 1972), p. 8.

11. Vine Deloria, Jr., *God Is Red* (New York: Dell, 1973), p. 116.

12. Louis Ginzberg, *The Legends of the Jews*, vol. 1 (Philadelphia: The Jewish Publication Society of America, n.d.), p. 64.

13. Amarna tablets, I, 1–6, quoted and trans. in Philo Mills, *The Asiatic Arcadia* (Washington, D.C.: The Bengalese Press, 1931), p. 15.

14. Hartley Burr Alexander, "Latin-American Mythology," in *The Mythology of All Races*, vol. 11 (Boston: Marshall Jones, 1920), pp. 165–166.

15. Ibid.

16. Frank Waters, *Book of the Hopi*, p. 15.

17. Louis Ginzberg, *The Legends of the Jews*, vol. 1 (Philadelphia: The Jewish Publication Society of America, n.d.), p. 71.

18. Quoted and trans. in Arthur Lovejoy and Goerge Boas, *Primitivism and Related Ideas in Antiquity* (Baltimore: Johns Hopkins Press, 1935), p. 50.

19. Ibid.

20. Paul G. Zolbrod, *Diné bahane': The Navajo Creation Story* (Albuquerque, N.M.: University of New Mexico Press, 1984), p. 36.

21. Julien Ries, "The Fall," in Mircea Eliade, ed., *The Encyclopedia of Religion*, vol. 7 (New York: Macmillan, 1987), pp. 256–257.

22. Quoted in Lovejoy and Boas, *Primitivism and Related Ideas in Antiquity*, p. 437.

23. Rutherford Platt, Jr., ed., *The Forgotten Books of Eden* (New York: Bell, 1980), pp. 6–7.

24. Lovejoy and Boas, *Primitivism and Related Ideas in Antiquity*, p. 437.

25. Ibid., p. 97.

26. Burton Watson, trans., *Chuang Tzu* (New York: Columbia University Press, 1964), pp. 73–74.

27. A. M. Hocart, *Kingship* (Oxford: Oxford University Press, 1927); *Kings and Councillors* (Chicago: The University of Chicago Press, 1970).

28. *Mahabharata*, Santiparvan, Moksadharma. Quoted and trans. in Lovejoy and Boas, *Primitivism and Related Ideas in Antiquity*, p. 436.

29. Alice Werner, "African Mythology," in *The Mythology of All Races*, vol. 7 (Boston: Marshall Jones, 1925), p. 173.
30. See Mircea Eliade, *The Two and the One* (Chicago: The University of Chicago Press, 1979), p. 104, and references there.
31. Johannes C. Andersen, *Myths and Legends of the Polynesians* (Tokyo, 1969), p. 420.
32. Mircea Eliade, *Shamanism* (Princeton, N.J.: Princeton University Press, 1972), p. 134.
33. Mircea Eliade, *The Two and the One*, p. 166.
34. *Critias*, 120e, 121a. Trans. in Lovejoy and Boas, *Primitivism and Related Ideas in Antiquity*, p. 161.
35. Peter Tompkins, *Mysteries of the Mexican Pyramids* (New York: Harper & Row, 1976), p. 347.

CHAPTER 5: *The Saddest Story*

1. Susan Feldman, ed., *African Myths and Tales* (New York: Dell, 1963), pp. 36–37.
2. Alice Werner, "African Mythology," in *The Mythology of All Races*, vol. 7 (Boston: Marshall Jones, 1925), p. 125.
3. Maria Leach, *The Beginning* (New York: Funk & Wagnalls, 1956), pp. 143–144.
4. Thomas Buckley, "World Renewal," in *Parabola* 13 (2) (May 1988), p. 83.
5. Frank Waters, *Book of the Hopi* (New York: Ballantine, 1969), pp. 15–16.
6. MacKenzie, *Myths of India* (London: Gresham, n.d.), p. 108.
7. Hesiod, *Works and Days*, lines 126–179. Trans. by Hugh G. Evelyn-White in *The Homeric Hymns and Homerica* (Cambridge, Mass.: Harvard University Press, 1914).
8. Arthur Lovejoy and George Boas, *Primitivism and Related Ideas in Antiquity* (Baltimore: Johns Hopkins Press, 1935), pp. 148–149.
9. Sheila Savill, ed., *Pears Encyclopedia of Myths and Legends*, volume on Oceania (London: Pelham, 1977), pp. 64–65.
10. Paul Schebesta, *Bambuti-Pygmaen vom Ituri*, iii (Brussels, 1950), p. 165. Quoted and trans. in Wilhelm Koppers, *Primitive Man and His World Picture* (London: Sheed & Ward, 1952), p. 44.
11. Ibid.
12. Sir James George Scott, "Indo-Chinese Mythology," in *The Mythology of All Races*, vol. 12 (Boston: Marshall Jones, 1913), p. 265.
13. *Bhagavad Gita*, trans. by Sir Edwin Arnold, with revisions by Uranda (Loveland, Colo.: EDL, n.d.), p. 9.
14. Elena Marsella, *The Quest for Eden* (New York: Philosophical Library, 1963), p. 45.

15. Hans Jonas, *The Gnostic Religion*, 2nd ed. (Boston: Beacon, 1963), pp. 148–153.
16. Wesley W. Isenberg, trans., in *The Nag Hammadi Library*, ed. James M. Robinson (New York: Harper & Row, 1981), p. 132.
17. Chuang Tzu, in Wm. Theodore de Bary et al., eds., *Sources of Chinese Tradition* (New York: Columbia University Press, 1960), p. 70.
18. *Lankavatara Sutra*, in *A Buddhist Bible*, ed. Dwight Goddard (Boston: Beacon, 1966), pp. 292, 299, 309.
19. *Bhagavad Gita*, p. 11.
20. H. Leisegang, *La Gnose* (Paris, 1951), pp. 247–248, quoted and trans. in Mircea Eliade, *Myth and Reality* (New York: Harper & Row, 1963), p. 127.
21. Henry Corbin, quoted in Mircea Eliade, *Myth and Reality*, p. 128, on the beliefs of the Harranites.
22. Hans Jonas, *The Gnostic Religion*, 2nd ed. (Boston: Beacon, 1963), p. 83.
23. Ibid.
24. Paul Schebesta, *Bambuti-Pygmaen vom Ituri*, iii (Brussels, 1950), quoted and trans. in Wilhelm Koppers, *Primitive Man and His World Picture* (London: Sheed & Ward, 1952), p. 165.
25. Mircea Eliade, *The Sacred and the Profane* (New York: Harcourt, Brace & World, 1959), p. 92.
26. Rutherford Platt, Jr., ed., *The Forgotten Books of Eden* (New York: Bell, 1980), pp. 6–7.
27. *Popul Vuh*, trans. in Hartley Burr Alexander, "Latin-American Mythology," in *The Mythology of All Races*, vol. 11 (Boston: Marshall Jones, 1920), pp. 165–166.
28. Rutherford Platt, Jr., ed., *The Forgotten Books of Eden*, p. 9.
29. Ibid., p. 12.
30. Ibid., p. 11.
31. *Metamorphoses*, Book I, quoted and trans. in Lovejoy and Boas, *Primitivism and Related Ideas in Antiquity*, p. 47.
32. Thomas Buckley, "World Renewal," p. 83.
33. Genesis 7:2, 3, 12, 21; 8:22.
34. *The Gilgamesh Epic*, trans. Alexander Heidel, quoted in Alfred Rehwinkel, *The Flood* (St. Louis: Concordia, 1951), pp. 158–159.
35. Ovid, *The Metamorphoses*, Book II, trans. Horace Gregory (New York, 1960), p. 38.
36. Julius Africanus in A. Roberts and J. Donaldson, eds., *The Ante-Nicene Fathers* (1896), VI, p. 132. Quoted in Immanuel Velikovsky, *Worlds in Collision* (New York: Doubleday, 1950), p. 148.
37. Suryakanta Shastri, *The Flood Legend in Sanskrit Literature* (Delhi: S. Chand & Co., 1950), p. v.
38. Alfred M. Rehwinkel, *The Flood* (St. Louis: Concordia, 1951), pp. 140–141.
39. Cyril Havecker, *Understanding Aboriginal Culture* (Sydney: Cosmos, 1987),

pp. 1–2.

40. Hartley Burr Alexander, "North American Mythology," in *The Mythology of All Races*, vol. 10 (Boston: Marshall Jones, 1916), pp. 299–300.

41. Lowell Thomas, *Hungry Waters, the Story of the Great Flood* (Philadelphia, 1937), pp. 188–189.

42. Martha Beckwith, *Hawaiian Mythology* (Honolulu: University of Hawaii Press, 1970), p. 314.

43. Hesiod, *Theogony*, trans. by H.G. Evelyn-White (Cambridge, Mass.: Harvard University Press, 1914), pp. 693ff.

44. F. M. Cornford, *Plato's Cosmology* (New York, 1937), pp. 15–16.

45. Quoted in Velikovsky, *Worlds in Collision*, pp. 31–32.

46. Hartley Burr Alexander, "Latin-American Mythology," in *The Mythology of All Races*, vol. 11 (Boston: Marshall Jones, 1920), p. 273.

47. Quoted in ibid., p. 311.

48. Frank Waters, *Book of the Hopi* (New York: Ballantine, 1972), pp. 16–17.

49. Ibid., p. 20.

50. F. M. Cornford, *Plato's Cosmology*, p. 15.

51. Giorgio de Santillana and Hertha von Dechend, *Hamlet's Mill* (Boston: Godine, 1969), p. 5.

52. Thomas Buckley, "World Renewal," p. 83.

53. Quoted in Alfred de Grazia et al., eds., *The Velikovsky Affair*, (New York: University Books, 1967), p. 121.

54. Immanuel Velikovsky, *Mankind in Amnesia* (New York: Doubleday, 1982), p. 95.

CHAPTER 6: *Prophecy: The Once and Future Paradise*

1. Quoted in Mircea Eliade, *Cosmos and History, The Myth of the Eternal Return* (New York: Harper & Row, 1959), p. 128.

2. *Yast*, XIX, 14, 89. After James Darmesteter's trans. in *Le Zend-Avesta* (Paris, 1892), quoted in Mircea Eliade, *Cosmos and History, The Myth of the Eternal Return*, p. 124.

3. Quoted in Arthur Lovejoy and George Boas, *Primitivism and Related Ideas in Antiquity* (Boston: Johns Hopkins Press, 1935), p. 84.

4. Ibid., p. 88.

5. Ibid., p. 89.

6. E. O. G. Turville-Petre, trans., *Myth and Religion of the North* (London: Weidenfeld and Nicolson, 1964), p. 42.

7. *Koran*, LXIX, LVI; trans. by A. J. Arberry, quoted in Mircea Eliade, *From Primitives to Zen* (New York: Harper & Row, 1967), pp. 397–398.

8. Ibid.

9. *Mahabharata*, Vanaparvan, 190. Quoted in Lovejoy and Boas, *Primitivism and Related Ideas in Antiquity*, pp. 442–443.
10. Masaharu Anesaki, *Nichiren, the Buddhist Prophet* (Cambridge, Mass.: Harvard University Press, 1916), p. 110.
11. See Edwin Bernbaum, *The Way to Shambhala* (Los Angeles: Tarcher, 1989).
12. Hartley Burr Alexander, "North American Mythology," in *The Mythology of All Races*, vol. 10 (Boston: Marshall Jones, 1916), p. 116.
13. James Mooney in *The Fourteenth Annual Report of the Bureau of American Ethnology* (1896). Quoted in Mircea Eliade, *From Primitives to Zen*, pp. 403–404.
14. Dan Katchongva, *From the Beginning of Life to the Day of Purification*, trans. Danaqyumptewa (Los Angeles: Committee for Traditional Indian Land & Life, 1977), pp. 30–33.

CHAPTER 7: *Paradise as a Force in Human Culture*

1. See Howard R. Patch, *The Other World According to Descriptions in Medieval Literature* (Cambridge, Mass.: Harvard University Press, 1950); R. W. B. Lewis, *The American Adam* (Chicago: University of Chicago Press, 1955); A. Bartlett Giamatti, *The Earthly Paradise and the Renaissance Epic* (Princeton, N.J.: Princeton University Press, 1966); Harry Levin, *The Myth of the Golden Age in the Renaissance* (Bloomington, Ind.: University of Indiana Press, 1969); and John Armstrong, *The Paradise Myth* (London: Oxford University Press, 1969).
2. Doris Lessing, *Shikasta* (New York: Vintage, 1981), p. 35.
3. Ibid., p. 38.
4. Chogyam Trungpa, *Shambhala, The Sacred Path of the Warrior* (Boulder, Colo.: Shambhala, 1984), pp. 25–27.
5. Quoted in Mircea Eliade, *The Quest* (Chicago: University of Chicago Press, 1969), p. 91.
6. Increase Mather, *Discourse on Prayer*, quoted in Charles L. Sanford, *The Quest for Paradise* (Urbana, Ill.: University of Illinois Press, 1961), pp. 82–83.
7. Thomas More, *Utopia*, trans. by Paul Turner (Middlesex, England: Penguin, 1965), p. 131.
8. P. L. Nasaru, *The Essence of Buddhism* (Madras, India, 1907).

CHAPTER 8: *Paradise as History*

1. William F. Albright, *The Archaeology of Palestine* (Baltimore: Johns Hopkins Press, 1965), p. 123.

2. Dora Jane Hamblin, "Has the Garden of Eden Been Located at Last?", *Smithsonian* 18 (2) (May 1987), pp. 127–135.

3. Ibid., p. 131.

4. Jared Diamond, "The Worst Mistake in the History of the Human Race," *Discover* (May 1987).

5. Max Charlesworth, "Introduction," in Max Charlesworth, ed., *Religion in Aboriginal Australia* (Queensland, Australia: University of Queensland Press, 1984), p. 5.

6. Elman R. Service, *Primitive Worlds: People Lost in Time* (New York: National Geographic Society, 1973), p. 13.

7. Stanley Diamond, *In Search of the Primitive* (New Brunswick, N.J.: Transaction Books, 1974), p. 156.

8. Lewis Mumford, *The Myth of the Machine* (New York: Harcourt, Brace & World, 1967), p. 216.

9. W. J. Perry, *Children of the Sun* (New York: E. P. Dutton, 1923), quoted in Henry Bailey Stevens, *The Recovery of Culture* (New York: Harper & Bros., 1949), p. 99.

10. Laurens Van der Post, "Wilderness: A Way of Truth," in Vance Martin and Mary Inglis, eds., *Wilderness: The Way Ahead* (Findhorn, Scotland: Findhorn Press, 1985).

11. Stevens, *The Recovery of Culture*, p. 101.

12. Ibid., p. 120.

13. Riane Eisler, *The Chalice and the Blade* (New York: Harper & Row, 1987), p. 11.

14. Ibid. pp. xv–xvi.

15. Chester Carlton McCown, *The Ladder of Progress in Palestine* (New York: Harper & Bros., 1943), p. 57.

16. Eisler, *The Chalice and the Blade*, p. 18.

17. Ibid., p. 31.

18. Ibid., p. 36.

19. Ibid., p. 45.

20. Ibid., p. xx.

21. Stanley Diamond, *In Search of the Primitive*, p. 126.

22. P. S. Martin and H. E. Wright, eds., *Pleistocene Extinctions: The Search for a Cause* (New Haven, Conn.: Yale University Press, 1967), p. vi. See also Bruce Bower, "Extinctions on Ice," *Science News* 132 (October 31, 1987), pp. 284–285 .

23. Quoted by Peter Tompkins in *Mysteries of the Mexican Pyramids* (New York: Harper & Row, 1978), p. 373.

24. Ibid.

25. Ralph Franklin Walworth, *Subdue the Earth* (New York: Delta, 1977), p. 101.

26. J. B. Birdsell, quoted in William Fix, *The Bone Peddlers* (New York: Macmillan, 1984), p. 107.

27. Björn Kurtén, quoted in William Fix, *The Bone Peddlers*, p. 105.

28. See, for example, the discussion in *Science Frontiers*, no. 57 (May-June, 1988), and Warwick Bray, "The Paleoindian Debate," in *Nature* 332 (107) (1988).

29. For an extensive survey of these and similar anomalies, see William R. Corliss, *Ancient Man: A Handbook of Puzzling Artifacts* (Glen Arm, Md.: Sourcebook Project, 1978).

30. For example, Charles Fort, Ivan T. Sanderson, and William R. Corliss. William Corliss publishes a semimonthly digest of scientific anomalies from the current literature, entitled *Science Frontiers*.

31. See John Anthony West, *Serpent in the Sky* (New York: Julian Press, 1987).

32. John Michell, *City of Revelation* (London: Sphere, 1973), p. 12.

33. John Michell, *The New View over Atlantis* (San Francisco: Harper & Row, 1983), p. 83.

34. Patrick Pender-Cudlip, "Oral Traditions and Anthropological Analysis: Some Contemporary Myths," *Azania* 7 (1972), pp. 3–24.

35. Humphrey Case, "Illusion and Meaning," in *The Explanation of Culture Change: Models in Prehistory*, ed. Colin Renfrew (London: Gerald Duckworth & Co., 1973), pp. 35–46.

36. Alice B. Kehoe, "Revisionist Anthropology: Aboriginal North America," in *Current Anthropology* 22 (5) (October 1981), pp. 503–517.

CHAPTER 9: *Paradise as Metaphor*

1. W. E. H. Stanner, "Religion, Totemism and Symbolism," in *Religion in Aboriginal Australia*, ed. Max Charlesworth (Queensland, Australia: University of Queensland Press, 1984), p. 137.

2. Jamake Highwater, *The Primal Mind* (New York: New American Library, 1981), p. 118.

3. Owen Barfield, *The Rediscovery of Meaning and Other Essays* (Middletown, Conn.: Wesleyan University Press, 1977), p. 15.

4. Mario Jacoby, *Longing for Paradise* (Boston: Sigo, 1985), p. 5.

5. Augustine, *The Confessions; The City of God; On Christian Doctrine* (Chicago: University of Chicago Press, 1952), p. 371.

6. Jerome, *Adversus Jovinianum*, I,6; I,10,20; quoted in Elaine Pagels, *Adam, Eve and the Serpent* (New York: Random House, 1988), p. 94.

7. Quoted in Frank E. Manuel and Fritzie P. Manuel, *Utopian Thought in the Western World* (Cambridge, Mass.: Harvard University Press, 1979), p. 44.

8. *The Ante-Nicene Fathers*, vol. 4 (Grand Rapids, Mich., 1956), p. 14; "On the Apparel of Women," Book I, Chapter 1.

9. The evolution of attitudes toward sexuality and nature in the early Church is explored by Elaine Pagels in *Adam, Eve and the Serpent*.

10. John Donne, seventeenth *Elegy*.
11. Howard N. Wallace, *The Eden Narrative* (Cambridge, Mass.: Harvard University Press, 1985), pp. 128–129.
12. Sigmund Freud, "Construction in Analysis," in *Works*, vol. 23, ed. and trans. James Strachey (New York: Norton, 1976), p. 269.
13. Theodor Reik, *Myth and Guilt* (New York: Grosset & Dunlap, 1957), p. 142.
14. Geza Róheim, "Women and Life in Central Australia," in *Religion in Aboriginal Australia*, ed. Max Charlesworth (Queensland, Australia: University of Queensland Press, 1984), p. 344.
15. Stanner, in *Religion in Aboriginal Australia*, p. 166.
16. Quoted in Manuel and Manuel, *Utopian Thought in the Western World*, p. 43.
17. F. Schiller, *Thalia* (1790). Quoted in Mario Jacoby, *Longing for Paradise*, p. 215.
18. F. Schiller, *Werke*, vol. 16. Quoted in Jacoby, *Longing for Paradise*, p. 215.
19. Ernst Cassirer, *The Philosophy of Symbolic Forms*, 3 vols. (New Haven: Yale University Press, 1953–7); Nicholas Berdyaev, *The Destiny of Man* (New York: Harper & Bros., 1960); Jean Gebser, *The Ever-Present Origin* (Athens, Ohio: Ohio University Press, 1986); Erich Neumann, *The Origins and History of Consciousness* (Princeton, N.J.: Princeton University Press, 1973); Carl Sagan, *The Dragons of Eden* (New York: Random House, 1977); Ken Wilber, *Up from Eden* (New York: Doubleday, 1981).
20. Ken Wilber, *Up from Eden* (New York: Doubleday, 1981), p. 27.
21. Erich Neumann, *The Origins and History of Consciousness*, quoted in Wilber, *Up from Eden*, pp. 27–28.
22. Mircea Eliade, *The Sacred and the Profane* (New York: Harcourt, Brace & World, 1959), p. 166.
23. Ibid., p. 93.
24. Ibid., pp. 211–212.
25. Ibid., p. 211.
26. Ibid., p. 212.
27. Mircea Eliade, *Myths, Dreams and Mysteries* (New York: Harper & Row, 1967), p. 110.
28. Mircea Eliade, *Patterns in Comparative Religion* (New York: New American Library, 1974), p. 193.
29. Joseph Campbell, with Bill Moyers, *The Power of Myth* (New York: Doubleday, 1988), p. 107.
30. Ibid.

CHAPTER 10: *Unfolding Images: The Mirror of Myth*

1. See, for example, Charles T. Tart, ed., *Altered States of Consciousness* (New York: Wiley, 1969) and *States of Consciousness* (San Rafael, Calif.: Psycho-

logical Processes Inc., 1983); and John White, ed., *Frontiers of Consciousness* (New York: Avon, 1974).

2. R. M. Bucke, *Cosmic Consciousness* (New York: Dutton, 1969), pp. 1–3.
3. William James, *The Varieties of Religious Experience* (New York: Mentor, 1958), pp. 292–294.
4. Stanley Dean, "Metapsychiatry: The Confluence of Psychiatry and Mysticism," in S. Dean, ed., *Psychiatry and Mysticism* (Chicago: Nelson-Hall, 1975), pp. 3–18.
5. Roger Wescott, *The Divine Animal* (New York: Funk & Wagnalls, 1969).
6. Roger Wescott, "Aster and Disaster: The Golden Age (Part II)," *Kronos* 10 (2) (1985), p. 78.
7. Robert Ornstein and David Sobel, "The Healing Brain," in *Psychology Today* (March 1987).
8. Alan Watts, *Psychotherapy East and West* (New York: Ballantine, 1969), pp. 127–128.
9. See A. P. Elkin, *Aboriginal Men of High Degree*, 2nd ed. (Queensland, Australia: University of Queensland Press, 1977).
10. Mircea Eliade, *Myths, Dreams and Mysteries* (New York: Harper & Row, 1967), p. 87.
11. Åke Hultkrantz, *The Religions of the American Indians* (Berkeley, Calif.: University of California Press, 1979), pp. 71–73.
12. Elkin, *Aboriginal Men of High Degree*, p. 127.
13. Mircea Eliade, *Shamanism* (Princeton, N.J.: Princeton University Press, 1964), p. 99.
14. John Lilly, M.D., *Communication between Man and Dolphin* (New York: Julian Press, 1978); Jim Nollman, *Animal Dreaming* (New York: Bantam, 1987).
15. Toni Eatts, "Nimbin Spirits," Sydney *Sunday Telegraph* (July 1987).
16. Quoted in Mircea Eliade, *Shamanism*, p. 482.
17. Knud Rasmussen, *Intellectual Culture of the Iglulik Eskimos* (Copenhagen, 1930), quoted in Mircea Eliade, *The Two and the One* (Chicago: University of Chicago Press, 1979), p. 23.
18. Quoted in Eliade, *The Two and the One*, p. 61.
19. Ibid., pp. 97–98.
20. Ibid., p. 97.

CHAPTER 11: *Paradise Now: Between Heaven and Earth*

1. Raymond Moody, *Reflections on Life after Life* (New York: Bantam, 1977), pp. 9–10.
2. Patrick Gallagher, "Over Easy: A Cultural Anthropologist's Near-Death Experience," *Anabiosis* 2 (2) (1982), pp. 140–149.

3. George Gallup, Jr., *Adventures in Immortality* (New York: McGraw-Hill, 1982).
4. Kenneth Ring, *Heading toward Omega* (New York: Morrow, 1985), p. 141.
5. Wilder Penfield, *The Mystery of the Mind* (Princeton, N.J.: Princeton University Press, 1975).
6. Michael Sabom, *Recollections of Death* (London: Corgi, 1982), pp. 160–161.
7. Ibid., p. 251.
8. Ibid., p. 252.
9. W. Y. Evans-Wentz, *The Tibetan Book of the Dead* (Oxford: Oxford University Press, 1927), pp. 102ff.
10. Kenneth Ring, *Heading toward Omega*, pp. 226–227.
11. Hartley Burr Alexander, "North American Mythology" in *The Mythology of All Races*, vol. 10 (Boston: Marshall Jones, 1916), p. 10.
12. Arnold Toynbee and Arthur Koestler, eds., *Life after Death* (London: Weidenfeld and Nicolson, 1976), pp. 238–239.

CHAPTER 12: *To Get Back to the Garden*

1. Aldous Huxley, *The Perennial Philosophy* (New York: Harper & Row, 1970).
2. Kenneth Ring, *Heading toward Omega* (New York: Morrow, 1985), p. 197.
3. Ibid., p. 198.
4. Quoted in ibid., p. 133.
5. Marilyn Ferguson, *The Aquarian Conspiracy*, 2nd ed. (Los Angeles: Tarcher, 1988; Willis Harman, *Global Mind Change: The Promise of the Last Years of the Twentieth Century* (Indianapolis: Knowledge Systems, 1988).
6. O. Fred Donaldson, "Play to Win and Every Victory Is a Funeral," *Somatics* (Spring/Summer 1984), p. 29.

Epilogue

1. Donald A. MacKenzie, *Myths of China and Japan* (London: Gresham, n.d.), p. 276.

Index

Photo and Illustration Credits

The line drawings on pages 22 and 66 are by Janet Barocco. All others are by the author.

For information regarding courses and seminars based
on the material in this book, please write:

DISCOVERING PARADISE
4817 North County Road 29
Loveland, CO 80538